M000305065

# Jockeys

## and

# Jewels

## Bev Pettersen

# DEDICATION

To Mom and Dad who scrimped and saved to buy my first horse.

# ACKNOWLEDGMENTS

Early readers: Jan Pettersen, Becky Mason, Elaine Bremner, Barb Snarby and Anne MacFarlane. Your faith and support inspired at a critical time.

Farrier Leon Hebb who knows all about feet and helped plot the best place to hide stones.

Former RCMP officers Martina Thornton and Archie Mason who gave invaluable expertise and patiently answered all questions about guns and procedures. Any mistakes are mine.

Ron Carlyon who taught me to love racing, back when a two-thousand dollar claimer was a pretty fast horse.

Authors Julianne MacLean, Judith James, and Pamela Callow who give so generously of their time and knowledge, even when immersed in their own deadlines.

Dr. Homer Noble for assigning numerous five-thousand-word essays at Liverpool Regional High School; he made writing fun.

My son, Hans, who was content with frozen dinners when I was too busy to cook.

Fabulous editors Pat Thomas and Rhonda Stapleton for their insights and suggestions. They made this book much better.

Romance Writers of Atlantic Canada, Pixie Chicks and the Ruby Slippered Sisterhood; your encouragement and camaraderie is priceless.

And lastly to my daughter, Brenna who was beside me every inch of the way and knows a good horse when she sees one. Thanks for everything, honey. Those early mornings at the track are cherished.

# CHAPTER ONE

The track looked safe—no holes, no ruts, no reason for a horse to break a leg—but Kurt's sense of foreboding grew. He yanked up the collar of his oilskin, hoping the raw weather accounted for his unusual edginess. A red-coated man with jowly cheeks trudged through the mud, blasted on his bugle, and the post parade began.

Most fans sought refuge in the clubhouse, yet ten feet away two women in stylish raincoats also braved the drizzle. Their heads swiveled as they analyzed each prancing horse, and the gusting wind carried their words more effectively than any loudspeaker.

"That guy next to us is Kurt MacKinnon," the shorter one said. "Might be worth putting money on his horse. He trains the good-looking gray."

"They're both lookers," the second lady said. "But ugly tries harder. Besides that gray doesn't want to get wet. Don't know if he'll run well."

Kurt kept his head averted, indifferent to their opinions, although the second lady was absolutely correct. He didn't know if Lazer Cat would run well either. The horse had performed poorly in four starts on a sunny day, but maybe he'd like the shitty weather. Lazer really couldn't run much worse. Kurt hated to give up on the colt, but he had to show some ability. And soon.

The line of horses moved closer. Kurt's optimism plunged when he noticed the antics of his contrary horse. Lazer humped his back and flattened his ears as he tried to sidestep the rain and retreat to the barn. Only a stoic escort pony kept him in line.

It was obvious the horse hated the weather, hated the track, hated to race.

The phone in Kurt's pocket vibrated. He pivoted from the rail, giving the two ladies a polite nod as he passed. Ignoring their self-conscious giggles, he scanned the display. *Unknown caller.* What fool would call just before a race?

"MacKinnon." Concern roughened his words as he climbed the grandstand steps. Not many people had his private number, and his racing assistant was extremely competent. It had to be a mistake. Or an emergency.

"Hello, Kurt," a familiar voice said. "It's Archer."

Kurt sucked in a breath. Archer wasn't the type to press wrong numbers. "Hello...boss," he said, then paused for a second. "How're things at headquarters?"

"The usual. How about you? Heard you're a full-time trainer now, making bags of money."

"Everything's good. Got a race about to start." Kurt's mouth tightened as the horses approached the starting gate and Lazer shied from a swooping bird, almost dumping his jockey. The colt wheeled and rammed a member of the gate crew, but two men with squared shoulders and a no-nonsense attitude rushed forward, locked their arms behind Lazer's tail and shoved the reluctant horse into his slot. Good job, guys, Kurt thought, marginally relaxed now that Lazer was in the gate.

"It's been a while since you requested the leave of absence," Archer said. "Bet you miss police work." Kurt jerked to a stop and for a moment forgot about the race. Eleven months ago, drained by his undercover job, the lies, the deception, he'd handed Archer his resignation from the Royal Canadian Mounted Police. Archer had convinced Kurt to accept a leave instead. They both knew he didn't miss police work.

He shook off the raw memories, tucked the phone between his ear and shoulder, turned and re-focused on the horses clustering around the gate.

The race would start soon, just three left to load. Lazer was the only gray in the race so he would be easy to spot, especially easy since his habit was to gallop at the back of the pack, sightseeing.

"We need to talk." Archer's voice pricked like a stubborn mosquito.

Kurt regretted answering the call. He liked and respected Archer, but it seemed a lifetime since he'd reported to him. He made a sound deep in his throat that he hoped passed for agreement but kept his attention on the gate.

All the horses were in. Lazer stood straight, ears forward, well balanced. Despite the colt's flightiness, this might be the day he lived up to his pedigree. A knot coiled in Kurt's stomach as he waited for the gate to spring. He hated having no control, but it was up to the jockey and horse now. Any second—

"We need you on a case."

"Sorry," Kurt said, watching Lazer's forehead and willing the horse to break clean. The white bridle gleamed through the bars of the starting gate, a beacon even on this drab April day. "I'm through with police work," he added. "Go ahead and process my resignation."

"But it's just a few weeks," Archer said. "We need you to race in Calgary. I know it's a hick track, and you're a big-time trainer, but this is critical."

Despite the rain, Kurt's mouth felt dry. Long seconds passed in taut silence. Archer's breathing sounded frayed. Kurt squeezed the phone, his fingers as tight as his voice. "What's wrong?"

"We need an inside man we can position fast." Archer's words escaped in a rush. "Someone who knows racing but has undercover experience. You're the only qualified officer available."

"But I'm not available."

Archer cleared his throat with an ominous growl, a sound Kurt had heard too many times before. He wanted to close the phone. Shut out bad news.

"This isn't a routine drug buy." Obvious regret thickened Archer's voice. "Connor O'Neil died working it."

Kurt jerked back, gut punched. Squeezed his eyes shut, struggling to breathe even as the starting gate clanged open. He'd partnered with Connor on a nine-month job in Halifax where they'd infiltrated a biker gang and stopped millions of dollars of crack from hitting the streets. It had also forged a sincere friendship between the two men.

"I'm sorry," Archer added.

Kurt forced his questions past the brick of pain clogging his throat. "How? Where—" But grief split his words and he stopped, hating the emotion weakening his voice.

"Connor was posted in southern Alberta," Archer said. "Kept an eye on drug flow between Calgary and the U.S. border. Yesterday was his day off, but somehow a horse trailer caught his attention. He gave roadside assistance then ran the plate and followed the vehicle. Our last fix was at the Calgary track, where he spoke with a jockey named Julie West. Ten hours later he was found in his vehicle, north of the city. Shot with a twenty-two. Two bullets to the chest, one to the head.

"You'll report directly to me," Archer went on. "We'll give unlimited support. Just poke around a bit. Check out this Julie person. Leave your best horses home though, so you don't draw attention."

Kurt stared across the infield, numb to Archer's relentless voice and the crowd's cheers. Grief churned with rage as he fought to regain his composure. Any return to the bleak undercover world filled him with distaste, but it was obvious he'd accept this assignment. Some ass-wipe had murdered Connor.

And as Lazer straggled across the finish line, last in an undistinguished field, Kurt's mouth twisted in a humorless smile. At least he had the perfect horse to ship to Calgary.

# CHAPTER TWO

Crisp air nipped Julie West's face as she balanced in the saddle and concentrated on holding her horse to a steady gallop. Hooves pounded behind them. Another rider charged past, spraying dust and dirt. Julie's horse flattened his ears and shoved at the bit.

"Not yet, Skippy," she murmured, conscious of the trainer's instructions. She checked over her shoulder for other runners before dropping the gelding in on the rail. On the backside, in front of the neat row of barns, she finally loosened her grip and crouched further over his neck.

The horse rocketed forward, his powerful burst filling her with adrenaline. The rail knifed past as they hugged the turn and charged down the lane. Thirty feet past the grandstand, she rose in the stirrups, letting her weight fall onto the reins. Skippy slowed to a canter then down to a bouncy trot.

Perfect. She stroked his sweaty neck, grinning her approval. The old horse felt great. He was such a pro too, never wasting energy but not holding anything back. She let him relax by the gap in the rail before turning and walking off the track.

Ed Harrison, Skippy's trainer, stepped forward, and her hope soared when she spotted the rare smile cutting his craggy face. Maybe today would be a breakthrough. For five weeks she'd exercised his horse. If Harrison let her ride in a race, it would be a major step toward acceptance as a jockey. The veteran trainer was well respected and if she picked up a mount from him, other trainers would surely follow.

Harrison dragged a thoughtful hand over his moustache before attaching a leather line to the bridle, every movement methodical. She sensed he was coming to a decision, but nothing ever hurried the cautious trainer. Skippy galloped better for her than anyone else, but would Harrison think she was good enough to ride in a race?

She scratched the horse on his damp neck, trying to steady her rapid breathing, waiting for the decision that might launch her career.

"Not bad." Harrison's slow nod was almost grudging. "At first the old guy seemed to be asleep, but he found another gear when you brought him in on the rail. Guess I'll name you as his jockey this Friday."

She clamped her mouth, knew she should look cool, but her emotions pushed through and she vaulted from the saddle, a huge grin on her face. Even Harrison acknowledged the occasion with a rusty smile before leading Skippy away, careful to avoid an approaching rider.

"That's right! Keep your distance," the rider bellowed. Sandra's thick ponytail, the same color as the chestnut filly she led, swung jauntily beneath her dented helmet. "This horse of Chandler's is a menace."

Julie adjusted her protective vest as she studied the next horse on her gallop schedule. The young filly was wide-eyed and skittish, and it was reassuring that her friend was ponying. Sandra was one of the most experienced escort riders at the track, and she and her Quarter Horse, Okie, could calm the most unruly animal.

Sandra heaved a martyr's sigh as she stopped the horses beside Julie. "Ponying for Bill Chandler isn't worth the measly pay. That man is a pain in the ass." She snapped the lead just in time to keep the high-strung filly from nipping her thigh. "So is his horse," she muttered.

Julie tightened her helmet, her euphoric glow untarnished by Sandra's complaints. It didn't matter what kind of horses she rode the rest of the morning because it was finally happening. She was going to ride a nice horse in a real race. Nothing could mar this day. She was still smiling, even when the filly shied from the bellowing trainer behind them, and she was forced to scramble away from the horse's swinging hindquarters.

"My horse is sensitive," Bill Chandler called. He seemed unaware his strident voice and quick movements had frightened his own horse. "You girls are always yakking. You need to shut up."

Julie turned her head and shot Sandra a silent plea for patience. Sandra was outspoken, with little tolerance for fools. Yet Bill had promised Julie she'd be the jockey for his young filly, so it was important to humor the eccentric trainer.

"Young fillies are moody," Bill said as he began another of his monotonous lectures. "I want you girls to carry peppermints. The white ones, not the pink." He frowned as though considering an ingredient label. "Pink have more sugar, I think."

He waggled a long finger in front of Julie's nose. "Jog Princess half a mile. Then gallop around twice. Stay together. I'm paying Sandra to escort, and I want my money's worth."

"Sure thing, Bill." Julie forced an agreeable nod as he boosted her into the saddle and continued preaching about the parallels between horse and dog training.

Sandra rolled her eyes as she led Julie's horse onto the track. "I can't believe he has a trainer's license. This filly, Precious Princess, is so spoiled, she's dangerous."

"Guess that's why pony girls get the big bucks," Julie said, keeping a solemn face. Sandra was always broke but would never quit her job for a horseless career.

Sandra snorted. "I make more money than you. And speaking of big bucks, did you see what moved into our barn?"

"Big buck, as in big horse?"

"Nope." Sandra's grin was slightly lascivious. "As in big shoulders, long legs and narrow hips."

"Narrow hips?" Julie pretended to frown. "That's not good. You always said racehorses need hips for power."

Sandra sighed in exasperation. "All you think about are horses. But this new guy has a gorgeous horse with a huge hind end. Best of all, he's looking for a rider. I gave him your name. Said you're a good exercise rider."

"Thanks. But you're supposed to say good jockey. Or at least, good apprentice jockey."

"If he watches you gallop, he'll know you can handle them in a race." Sandra paused a beat, then her voice turned serious. "It's tough to break into the jock ranks. Your mom did but remember the hours. She was so tired..." Sandra broke off, her voice thick with regret.

Julie averted her head, trying to control her rush of guilt. She still didn't like to think about it.

"I only mean other things are important," Sandra said, swiveling in the saddle. "It would be better if you were ugly. Better still, if you were a guy. Trainers can't see your toughness. But I know how much you want to be a jockey, so don't quit."

Julie squared her shoulders. She had no intention of quitting. This was her best week yet, and a trainer, a normal trainer, was giving her a horse to ride. She adjusted her reins, eager to share her news about Skippy but giving Sandra another minute to finish her rant.

Sandra was an old family friend but rather opinionated and believed in sharing those opinions. However, she'd watched out for Julie ever since that scary day six weeks earlier when Julie had walked into G barn with only her saddle and her dreams.

Sandra continued her complaint about trainers and their God-like status but seemed to be winding down, and she glanced at Julie as though making sure she was listening. "Just make sure you charge the new guy. Exercising horses for free is piss-poor business."

"If I show up for morning gallops there's a better chance the trainer will let me ride in a race." It was impossible to remain silent any longer, and Julie's words came in a rush. "Harrison is putting me up on Skipper Jack this Friday."

"Woohoo!" Sandra jabbed her fist in the air but seconds later turned in the saddle, her forehead creased with concern. "You can't expect too much from Skippy. He's long in the tooth. Definitely pushing retirement."

"He felt pretty good today," Julie said. "And he's a smart horse. He knows how to save energy."

"Maybe." But doubt filled Sandra's face. "Anyway you'll have this young filly of Bill's. And if you gallop his horse, he'll use you as a jockey. That makes assholes easier to take."

Julie's gaze held Sandra's for a poignant moment. Difficult trainers were the ones most willing to take a chance with a green jockey, and Bill Chandler was a prince compared to Otto Laing. Otto was downright creepy. However, five years of part-time university had limited Julie's riding to the tiny bush circuit, and few successful trainers even knew her name. She had to ride, had to be seen, and if it meant biting her tongue, she'd do it.

Unfortunately time was running out and soon her age would work against her. She forced away the sobering thought and focused on her good news. Friday's race.

Sandra loosened the lead. The filly bucked as they increased their speed, but Julie barely noticed. She was too busy analyzing Skippy's competition.

The speedy sprinter from Seattle was entered and of course, any horse Gary Bixton rode would be the favorite. Rightly so. Bixton was the best jockey around. Still, the race would be great exposure for her as long as Skippy ran well.

It wouldn't earn her any mounts if they finished last.

She shook her head. Negative thoughts wouldn't help. It was always best to think positive. So she imagined Skippy powering down the stretch with the crowd cheering as they crossed the wire, alone and in front.

By the time they reached the backstretch she'd ridden Friday's race twice in her mind, winning both times, and had to force herself back to reality. The filly was moving surprisingly well, perhaps inspired by Julie's daydreams, and didn't resist when pulled down to a trot.

Sandra frowned at Princess, making no effort to hide her disappointment. "That filly was no fun today. I like watching them try to buck you off. Ah shit, look." Her face darkened as she gestured at Okie's front bandage. The fluorescent purple wrap was torn, split by the filly's errant hooves, and one end dragged on the ground, ripped and caked with mud.

Sandra pulled off her lead line and freed Princess.

"Wait." Julie stiffened. "Bill told us to stay together."

"Yeah, but I'm not wrecking Okie's wraps, not for Bill and his measly ten bucks." Sandra dismounted once they passed through the gap in the rail. "What can happen anyway? Bill's over there by the rail."

"All right," Julie said, aware Sandra was paid per horse and had more important trainers waiting. Sandra probably wouldn't even pony for Chandler if Julie hadn't been the rider.

She lifted a rein and turned toward Bill, but the filly balked, flattening her ears, reluctant to leave the company of Sandra's horse.

Julie clucked and pushed the filly forward, her thoughts drifting back to Friday's race. She hoped Skippy would draw a good post position. It would be disastrous to be stuck with an outside post, but the rail was bad too. The three or four hole would probably be best considering the forecast. A little rain...

"I told you not to ride Princess alone!" Bill scuttled toward them, yelling and waving his spidery arms. The filly's fragile courage caved. She lunged to the left, smashing Julie's knee into the rail.

Pain seared. The impact jerked Julie's leg from the stirrup, followed by a numbing burn that left her unable to feel the saddle. She yanked on the left rein but the horse was now shying from Bill's wife, who'd popped out from a knot of onlookers. The woman's high-pitched shriek filled the air, and her bulky purse smacked against her hip with each awkward step.

The filly stared, immobilized with fear. *Thump, thump.* Julie could feel the panicked beat of the horse's heart, the trembles of her sleek body. Heard Bill's nylon jacket crackle as he lunged for the reins, his hand a mere inch away...

Behind them, a shrill whistle sliced the air as a horse thundered an imperious challenge.

It was too much commotion for the pampered filly. In an acrobatic fishtail, she tossed Julie sideways and bolted for the safety of the barns. Julie gritted her teeth but managed to grab a chunk of mane. Images blurred like a broken movie: Bill's horrified eyes, the unyielding ground, horsehair slick with sweat. And when the filly leaped over the tip of the sprawling manure pile, Julie tumbled off, amid a tangle of arms, legs and horse dung.

She heard Bill curse, his wife's grating squeal, then pounding feet. Julie lay unmoving, consumed with shame. The manure was fresh, and a warm wetness seeped through her clothes.

"You okay?" The deep voice above her sounded choked, as though the man struggled to hold back laughter.

She propped herself up with an elbow and peered through his long legs, watching as Princess galloped along the row of barns, stirrups flapping, tail streaming like a victory banner. Bill lurched after his filly, trailed by his caterwauling wife. Sandra followed more sedately, waving her purple wrap and yelling something that sounded suspiciously like 'Tally Ho!'

"You okay?" the voice above her repeated.

Julie squeezed her eyes shut, unable to answer the man's simple question. Was she okay? No, not really. She'd spent a hard month working with that filly, an unpaid month, now wasted. Bill would never hire her as a jockey. Even worse, his comments could affect the other trainers. Harrison might even change his mind about letting her ride Skippy.

Tightness clawed her throat. She glanced at the stranger towering over her. Damn him, he thought it was funny! Wasn't even trying to hide his grin. Even the haughty horse he led looked amused.

She averted her head, hit with the horrible feeling she might cry, and that sure wouldn't raise her status at the track. If only the man and his horse would keep walking. It was quite apparent she wasn't hurt.

But he just waited, an unwelcome witness to her humiliation.

"I'm fine, thanks," she managed, swiping at a piece of straw stuck on her chin and sneaking a quick rub to the corners of her eyes.

"At least you found a soft landing." His voice was deep and low and assured, a beautiful voice really, except for the amusement. "Manure is always good for that." He chuckled.

Great, a joker. She shot to her knees. Winced at the stab of pain but unsnapped her helmet with a resentful click. From her vantage point, it was clear his horse was a stallion. Sandra had always said people shouldn't walk horses close to the gap, especially unruly ones.

"This was partly your fault, you know." She glanced at the man and sucked in a quick breath. He looked rather... intimidating. Probably why he thought he could get away with laughing.

11

"Maybe a little my fault but not much." He spoke with irritating assurance. "You weren't paying enough attention to your horse. Come on, kid, let's get you out of there."

He offered a big hand along with a crooked smile, and her resentment spiked. How did he know her attention had wandered? Much of it had been pure bad luck: Bill flailing around, his wife's cracking purse, the aggressive horse so close to the gap. And she was damn tired of being called babe and kid.

"Was it your colt who called to my filly?" She spoke through gritted teeth.

"Yeah, this is Lazer." The man's voice rippled with lazy affection as he shrugged and gestured at his horse. "He always has quite an effect on the ladies."

She pulled her gaze off the man's chiseled jaw, didn't want to admit he'd also produced a similar effect. The track was already overflowing with spit and swagger. As though a smile and a shrug could fix this. The manure pile. By noon, everybody on the grounds would be snickering. Her fingers curled so tightly her nails bit into her palms.

"I don't need any help." She ignored his hand and rose to her feet, regal as she could be with straw on her cheek. "But there are some good trainers around who might help *you* with that horse's manners."

The stranger's arm lowered. His smile remained, but there was no humor left in his cool gray eyes. And no wonder. She had deliberately insulted his training ability.

She had a fleeting impression of a mask dropping and something not so handsome, something dangerous. He gave her no time to analyze, just politely inclined his head and walked away.

Regret swept her. She squeezed her eyes shut, wishing it were possible to pluck back her hasty words. Frustration with trainers like Bill Chandler and Otto Laing was no excuse. Besides, the man was absolutely right—she hadn't been paying attention to the filly. Even Bill had warned her about staying with the escort pony. Now she had blown her chance with Bill, as well as insulted the only person who'd tried to help.

Heavy with shame, she limped after him, determined to apologize. Her knee throbbed, but she forced herself to speed up. The stranger had a very fast walk. So did his horse.

And what a nice horse. She stopped composing her apology, distracted by a horse-lover's appreciation for a good-looking animal. The gray was magnificent, straight-legged and well muscled, striding out with huge swinging hips.

Oh, shit. Despair dragged her to a stop, and her shoulders slumped, as deflated as her jockey prospects. This must be the new guy Sandra had been excited about—the trainer with two nice horses, the trainer who needed a rider, the trainer she'd just criticized.

Her apology fizzled to a groan. She'd lost much more than Bill's filly. She'd just blown any shot of riding one of the nicest-looking horses she'd ever seen. And the gray's flinty-eyed trainer didn't look the type to give second chances.

# CHAPTER THREE

Dust clogged Kurt's nose as he bedded down the last stall. The itch grew until he sneezed three times, a staccato of noise that made his spotted horse turn and stare. He tossed a flake of straw against the back wall and retreated to his tack room. His tiny tack room.

He hung his pitchfork on two crude nails and blew out a resigned sigh. This backwater track was definitely a change from his usual setup. No air purifier, no desk, no coffee. Barely enough space to cram in some tack and a cot. At least his stay here would be brief—two weeks, three at the most. If he solved this case, it would happen quickly.

Archer had given him a license plate and two names—Julie West and Otto Laing. And the trailer Connor had called in, only hours before his murder, was still parked on the lot. Kurt had noted Otto's plate when he took Lazer on an exploratory walk.

Tonight, when the grounds were quiet, he'd take a closer look. Maybe the trailer had a false floor. Something had aroused Connor's suspicions, enough that he'd run the license plate and followed Otto to the track.

A horse clopped down the concrete alley, the sound resonating through the thin door of Kurt's tack room. "Come on, Okie," a female voice said.

He recognized the voice of the friendly pony rider he'd met earlier, so he opened the door and stepped into the aisle. "Hi, Sandra," he said. "How's that loose horse I saw you chasing?"

"Fine. Quite a commotion though. The trainer was hysterical." She shrugged with the nonchalance of someone who'd seen everything. "How you settling in? Find everything you need?"

"So far. But I have to rent a trailer while mine has some bodywork. Would the owner of the blue Sundowner consider renting?"

"No way." Her scowl was so fierce, her eyebrows almost touched. "That belongs to Otto Laing. You don't want that wreck anyway." She brightened. "But Julie West—that's the rider I was telling you about—her dad, Adam, has a nice three-horse trailer he sometimes rents."

Kurt nodded, filing away every bit of information. Sandra had worked at the track for almost twenty years and would be a useful source. It was already clear she loved to talk.

"I also need an exercise rider," he said. "This Julie you recommend, is she dependable?"

"Sure. Shows up early every morning, ready to ride." Sandra slapped her stirrup over the horn and tugged at her cinch. "She's good too. Not scared of much."

"Where can I find her?"

Sandra jabbed her head in the direction of the end door. "That's her coming now."

He turned to study the approaching figure. Sunlight streamed through the end door, shadowing Julie's face, but her body was clearly outlined. Petite with a tiny waist and good shoulders, the perfect riding silhouette.

"Sorry I left you alone," Sandra called to Julie, blasting the words much too close to Kurt's ears. "Bill Chandler wasn't happy. Says he's going to quit and go back to training dogs."

Kurt edged away from Sandra's hollers but kept his attention on Julie, the last person reported to have seen Connor alive. She was only five stalls away when recognition struck, and he smoothed his flare of distaste.

This was the same kid who'd been dumped in the manure pile. The startling green eyes were unmistakable. Not a kid though. The vest and helmet were gone, freeing shoulder-length blond hair and high cheekbones, a face startling beautiful without the dirt.

Damn curvy too. He gave a hard gulp. She didn't look much like a murderer, and his distaste was joined with a more irritating reaction. He yanked his gaze back to her face, afraid he'd been ogling. Besides, looks were irrelevant. It was already clear she had a quick temper and way too much pride.

Not a coward though. She walked right up to him. Didn't avoid eye contact, didn't slow her step, didn't hide her regret. He heard her soft intake of breath as she squared her shoulders, seemingly resigned to letting him choose the tone of their next encounter.

And his tone was set. She was to be his new best friend, unpleasant though her company would surely be.

"Hello, Julie," he said. "I'm Kurt MacKinnon. I believe we met earlier."

"Yes, we did." She gave a cautious smile, as though surprised by his civility. "I'm very sorry about what I said earlier. Thank you for trying to rescue me from the...mud."

Her diction was precise, almost formal, but her smile carried a hint of dimples, a whisper of mischief. He almost smiled back but stopped himself, preferring to keep her on edge and observe a little longer. He crossed his arms and used his deadpan expression that always made people twitch.

She waited, not fidgeting, not speaking, just looking at him with a guilelessness that surprised him. Such beautiful eyes, darkened now with a myriad of emotions. Regret, shame, hope— she was young, open, and a cinch to read.

Excellent. Relief softened him, and he finally nodded and smiled back. There'd be no trouble learning what she knew about Connor's death. It might even be possible to wind the case up by week's end and return to his real race business.

A stall door banged shut. "Come see his horses!" Sandra called.

"I already saw the gray," Julie said to Sandra. "He looked huge but I was flat on the ground." She turned back to Kurt, and dimples fluttered in her cheeks. "You were right about not paying attention. I was thinking of something else."

"What was on your mind?" He was careful to display only polite interest.

"Another horse," she said so ruefully, he grinned. A bit of a surprise since he wasn't a spontaneous man. Control was a quality he'd learned to value.

"Come on, Julie." Impatience edged Sandra's voice and she pointed over the stall door. "That's Cisco, his track pony."

The Appaloosa remained at the back of his stall, uninterested in the attention of strangers. He rested a hind leg, and the hair on his fetlocks was so long it curled in the straw. Only his ears moved, flicking back and forth as he appraised his visitors.

Sandra chuckled. "You can always hire me if that lazy horse can't keep up."

"Cisco knows his job," Kurt said, remaining behind them, amused at how quickly Sandra dismissed his Appaloosa. Everyone always underestimated the scruffy gelding. Neither he nor Cisco cared.

Julie gave Cisco a polite appraisal then followed Sandra to the adjoining stall.

"This is your two-year-old, right?" Sandra asked, glancing back at Kurt. "Mature-looking guy. You want a maiden race for him?"

Kurt nodded. "Yeah, that's Ace. Hope to get his first start in the next couple of weeks once he's gate approved."

But Sandra had already turned and was tugging on Julie's arm. "This last guy is Lazer Cat, the horse I told you about. You gotta see him." Her voice rose as she dragged Julie to the third stall. "He's out of a Storm Cat mare."

"Wow." Julie spoke in a reverent whisper.

"That's the colt you saw earlier," Kurt said, studying Julie and wondering how he'd ever mistaken her for a kid. Of course she'd worn a helmet and vest, and her face had been covered with straw. "Guess you heard him too," he said, feeling a twinge of regret for leading the colt so close to the gap. Perhaps his horse had played a part in the filly's meltdown. He hadn't been thinking, had been too intent on scoping out the track and locating Otto's trailer.

"Yup, we heard him," Sandra said. "Even if Bill Chandler stays, he won't ask me to pony again. Or Julie to ride again." She shot Julie a sideways glance. "Sorry. I shouldn't have left you alone."

"No big deal," Julie said. "It's just one horse."

But her voice had thickened, and Kurt guessed it was a bigger deal than she pretended. Obviously she didn't have much business which suited him perfectly. He'd already planned to use her for Lazer's morning gallops. It would be a quick way to gain her trust, and she'd be more accessible if she rode for him.

He turned to her, keeping his voice casual as though the idea had just occurred, as though he hadn't been planning his strategy over the last two days. "Do you want another gallop job? Lazer needs an exercise rider, and he could replace the filly you lost. We can see how you get along tomorrow."

"Yes. Yes, of course." But she tilted her head and stepped back, studying him with those candid green eyes. "You're new here," she added, "so it's only fair to admit I haven't been riding here long. And your horse isn't my usual type."

His mouth twitched, and he hid his amusement with a quick cough. Her honesty surprised him, although it was irrelevant. Archer had already summarized her background, and Kurt knew she was inexperienced. Soon he'd know much more about her.

He gave a dismissive shrug. "Lazer's just an expensive loser. He's had five races, all clunkers. This is his last chance to prove he belongs at a track." Plus, Lazer was his slowest horse and the only animal he could race in Calgary that wouldn't be a standout. But he couldn't admit that.

Julie's head tilted as though absorbing his offer, but hope brightened her eyes. She was almost hooked, he guessed. She'd obviously had a shower since her fall. Her hair was pulled back in a ponytail, but he could smell a hint of shampoo. He edged a step closer, not sure if it was flowers or something peachy.

"Where did he run?" she asked, staring over the stall door at Lazer.

Kurt jerked his attention off her hair and back to his horse. "Woodbine," he said. "But that's a synthetic surface. I shipped here hoping he'd like a dirt track and some easier competition. He's agile and should be able to handle the tight turns. His mind is a problem, though." Kurt glanced back at Julie. "It won't be an easy job," he went on, gauging her expression, aware jockeys were intensely competitive. "I need an exercise rider who can turn him into a racehorse. Someone dependable. Someone who isn't afraid of his immaturity."

The challenge drew her in exactly as he anticipated.

"I'm not afraid," she said quickly. "I'd love to work with Lazer. And you."

She smiled with such gratitude, he grinned back like a fool then clamped his mouth shut, annoyed by his reaction. He was too experienced to be softened by an attractive woman. He'd learned that lesson long ago. Besides, she was one of Archer's murder suspects, a person of interest. At the very least, she could be a link to the murderer.

And much as he hated the role he'd been thrust into, Machiavellian behavior had always been his strength. If charming Julie was required, that's exactly what he'd do. And God help her if she had anything to do with Connor's murder.

## CHAPTER FOUR

A keyboard clicked, the only sound in the dingy motel room, as Kurt updated his case journal. Contact had been made with the woman on Archer's list, and tonight he'd have a chance to inspect Otto's trailer.

Satisfied, he closed the laptop and jammed it back in his metal briefcase, next to his gun and holster. No need to carry the Sig. He hadn't provoked anyone, not yet. He spun the combination lock and placed the case in his room safe.

A few flexes didn't help the kinks in his shoulders, so he tossed the truck keys back on the desk. The barns were close, and a brisk walk might loosen some tension.

The motel was a dive but conveniently located. He reached the track's public entrance in seven minutes flat; however, the doors were locked, the clubhouse deserted. He was forced to circle to the side where a squat guardhouse blocked his way.

He paused by the grilled window and flipped open his trainer's license. The narrow-eyed guard wore a crisp khaki uniform and was so polite Kurt guessed he was new. He scrutinized Kurt's training credentials, carefully matching photo to face before gesturing him through the horsemen's gate.

Kurt followed the row of dimly lit buildings to G barn and paused outside the door. It was library quiet, devoid of humans, so he walked down the aisle to Cisco's stall. The horse blinked and charged the door, ever hopeful for food.

"Not breakfast time yet," Kurt murmured as he scratched the base of Cisco's shaggy ears. He'd known a lot of horses, but Cisco was his all-time favorite.

*Crack!*

The abrupt noise made them both jump. Across the aisle a horse kicked with such force the wall boards quivered. Curious, Kurt approached the stall, but mismatched planks had been nailed over the wire mesh, blocking any view of the stall's unruly occupant.

Something moved above his head—a dark muzzle snuffling between the top board and ceiling. Nostrils flared, revealing a healthy pink lining.

"Don't hurt yourself," Kurt said, reassured the agitated horse was okay.

The muzzle disappeared and hooves cracked the planks again, so Kurt eased away. Obviously his presence didn't improve that animal's disposition.

He continued his sweep of the barn, noting the absence of security cams, then slipped out the end door and onto the graveled lot.

Exterior barn lights cast only a feeble glow, and trailers of assorted shapes and sizes loomed in a murky row. He counted as he walked, five rigs over, one row back. And there it was—the slant load with Montana plates that Connor had described in his last call to dispatch.

Otto Laing's trailer.

He gave the side door a shake but it was warped and welded shut. He circled to the back, eased two bolts out and lowered the ramp. *Creak.* The grating metal made him cringe and he paused, but the area remained still, silent except for peeping frogs and the rumble of traffic beyond the river.

He edged up the ramp, groping in his pocket for gloves, bag and flashlight.

The beam of his light revealed worn and jagged interior walls. Something fluttered. He jerked back, his heart racing until he saw it was merely a clump of tail hair caught on a wooden sliver. He tugged the hair loose and dropped it in his bag.

The floor mat was heavy and awkward, but he pulled the rubber aside, breathing through his mouth, ignoring the acrid smell of urine. Ants scurried to escape and, within seconds, vanished into a crevice. He propped the flashlight between his knees and scraped at the exposed crack. Insect eggs gleamed as rotten wood crumbled in his hand. Not much of a hiding place, only a home for ants.

He replaced the mat, careful to press it down in the corners before stepping outside.

There wasn't much clearance under the trailer, but he dropped to the gravel and squeezed beneath the floorboards. Gravel pricked his back, along with a growing sense of urgency. Still, he checked every inch.

Found nothing.

He sprawled on the cold ground, heavy with frustration, stymied by the unremarkable floor. He'd assumed drugs were involved. That was Connor's specialty, his motive for joining the RCMP, but Kurt simply couldn't see what had prompted him to follow this particular trailer.

Gravel crunched, and the smell of chewing tobacco wafted on the breeze. Damn. He pocketed the bag and gloves, rolling to his feet just as a hulking figure charged from the shadows.

"What the fuck you doing with my trailer?" the man snarled.

"You must be Adam West." Kurt grabbed a name Sandra had mentioned, keeping his voice relaxed. "Heard you rent your trailer. My horse is tall, and I need to make sure he'll fit."

"I ain't West. His trailer's over there somewhere." The man had close-cropped hair, a thick neck and a head like a Rottweiler. He jerked his arm to the left but kept his suspicious gaze locked on Kurt. "Kind of dark to be looking at a trailer, ain't it?"

"Only time I had." Kurt extended his hand. "I'm Kurt MacKinnon. Sorry for the mix-up, Mr.?"

"Otto." The man ignored Kurt's hand. "Now get away from there."

Something throbbed behind Kurt's right eye, but he forced his voice to remain mild as he trailed Otto back toward the lights of the barn. "Guess I'll have to check Adam's trailer tomorrow. Can you recommend an exercise rider?"

Otto was silent for so long it seemed he wasn't going to answer. Finally. "I use Adam West's girl. Nice tits."

Kurt rubbed hard at his forehead. "Well, I guess that's important. But can she ride?"

"She don't fall off."

"But can she ride?" And now Kurt didn't try quite so hard to keep his voice mild.

"Do I look like a fucking information center?"

"Not a bit." Kurt's hands fisted. He forced them open then deliberately let them fist again. He'd never had much patience with assholes. "Real sorry if the question's too tough for you," he added.

Otto took one menacing step then twisted his mouth and spat a stream of tobacco, just missing the toe of Kurt's boot. "Fuck off," he said, before stomping into the barn.

A hunter's awareness swept Kurt, an exhilaration he hadn't felt since turning in his badge. Otto was the type of suspect he liked working with, the type of man he didn't mind lying to. Obviously though, his people skills had eroded. Archer had asked that he ingratiate himself with the locals, yet somehow he'd managed to rile both Otto and Julie on the very first meet.

Smiling, he stepped over the gob of tobacco and headed toward his motel. The wind had pushed holes in the cloud cover, and stars glinted through the gaps. It was a relaxing walk, quiet and serene. Serene until the kick of a horse echoed from the barn Otto had just entered. The sound jarred the night with its protest and made him wonder why even the animals didn't like Otto.

# CHAPTER FIVE

The sun nudged over the eastern ridge with a promise to ease the morning chill. Kurt parked his truck beside the barn. He yawned as he entered, then gathered feed from his tack room and dumped it into his animals' stalls.

Happy horses gobbling grain always left him content, and he strolled down the aisle, enjoying the sounds. Bleary-eyed grooms carried buckets and pushed wheelbarrows, but there was no sign of Otto or Julie—only grooms immersed in their chores.

A stable hand would be useful, would free up more time for investigative work, and no doubt Sandra could recommend someone. But at this hour his priority was coffee.

The distinct smell of frying bacon drew him to a weather-beaten building close to the oval. A bulletin board by the entrance was crammed with faded race notices, sale announcements and a sign-up sheet for a ping pong tournament.

He pushed open the door and entered a room pulsing with energy, conversation, and kitchen smells. A harried cook wearing a stained apron sold him a coffee, and he snagged a chair at the last vacant table.

The mug warmed his hand, and he took a moment to inhale the steam. Hot and strong. The smell alone prodded him awake. He settled back, content. Undercover work was largely a matter of patience: watching, asking questions and, if needed, prodding. He stretched his legs and observed.

The track community churned around him—exercise riders grabbing breakfast, anxious-eyed trainers planning their horses' schedules and owners chatting in their impractical Italian loafers.

It was easy to spot the most successful trainers. They were the ones swarmed with deferential nods, phone calls and clients.

"Okay if we sit here?"

Kurt looked up, nodding at the two middle-aged men standing beside him. The shorter man pulled off his Stetson, exposing a tanned forehead rimmed with white. He dropped into the chair beside Kurt, shoved aside a sticky container of pancake syrup and laid his hat, crown down, on the vinyl table. There was hardly a break in their conversation, a vigorous discussion that centered on Friday's race card.

"So damn wet this spring, that inside post is the kiss of death. I'm betting Bixton's horse will bounce. Going with Julie." Stetson Man slammed his mug on the table, emphasizing his opinion.

"Nah, best to go with Bixton," the second man said. "Jock's hot. If the horse has four legs and a heart beat, the post won't matter."

Kurt focused on Stetson Man. Faded jeans, denim shirt, oversized belt buckle. Probably a rancher. "I met a Julie yesterday," Kurt said, leaning forward. "Julie West. She's galloping for me today. Good rider, is she?"

"The best." Stetson Man spoke emphatically but chuckled when his companion elbowed him in the ribs. "Actually, Julie's my daughter," he added, "so some folks might think I'm biased. Which I'm not." His smile faded but his eyes twinkled. "You new here?"

"Yeah. Kurt MacKinnon."

"Adam West."

Kurt shook Adam's hand. Clearly Julie's mother was the looker. All Julie seemed to have inherited from her father were the man's astute green eyes, although Adam's were much shrewder, even cynical.

Best to be careful around this man.

Adam seemed sincere when he spoke. "Julie can ride anything. She has a good feel for horses, especially young ones. Learned a lot on the bush. Lots of Quarter Horses, lots of speed." His eyes narrowed as he studied Kurt's arms, still tanned from racing in Florida. "You don't live around here?"

"Not yet, but I plan to buy a place in the foothills," Kurt lied easily. "I want to take a ride up there and get a feel for the land, but my trailer needs work. Sandra mentioned you might rent yours?"

"Maybe," Adam said, his penetrating eyes searching Kurt's face.

But Kurt had perfected the silent stare and held his gaze.

Twenty seconds later Adam nodded, and the image of an affable rancher returned. "Yeah, I suppose you can rent my trailer," he said. "Julie might help if you need a guide. She knows the area from tagging along on all our hunting trips."

Perfect. Kurt picked up his coffee, hiding his satisfaction as he drained the mug. Adam and Otto might not be friends—the men seemed polar opposites—but at least if they talked, Kurt's excuse for poking around Otto's trailer would hold.

"What's the track like?" He slid his empty mug to the center of the table.

"A bit hard, except for the rail. Supposed to be nice for the next half hour. If you don't like the weather, just wait ten minutes."

Kurt smiled and glanced out the window, checking the blue patch of sky. The weather was fickle, affected by the nearby mountains. It had been hailing when he woke but now it was sunny and warm, a perfect spring day.

Adam turned to his companion, and their conversation bottomed to a tractor and the astronomical price of hay. Nothing more to be gained here. Kurt scraped back his chair and left.

The walkway skirted the rail, and he relished the surrounding sounds—the primal thud of hooves, the friendly shouts of riders—activities so familiar, so benign, he had to remind himself he was here on police business. Nasty business.

Kurt slowed before entering the barn, letting his vision adjust to the interior lights. He grabbed Lazer's grooming kit and tied the horse to a ring in his stall. The horse seemed relaxed, standing quietly to be brushed. Hopefully he'd behave for Julie. Lazer had earned a reputation as tricky to ride. Not mean, just energetic and easily distracted.

It would be safer if he escorted her with Cisco, at least for her first attempt. Sandra considered Julie a competent rider. So did Adam. But only yesterday, Kurt had seen her sprawled on the ground, and he didn't want her hurt. He didn't like to stick his horse with a poor rider, but the case took precedence and unfortunately Lazer was the sacrifice.

He finished grooming Lazer and stepped into Cisco's stall. The Appaloosa flattened his ears, aware brushes meant work, and Kurt gave him an affectionate slap. Cisco was a confirmed asshole, but Kurt empathized with his cranky personality. He'd never owned a more useful horse.

The grooming ritual was a rare chance to spend time with his horses and he enjoyed it. His vigorous strokes left a shine on Cisco's coat. Back east, his network of runners was stabled at three different tracks and staff looked after the daily chores, overseen by his racing assistants. Here it was just him and three horses. A nice break, almost a vacation...

Otto's gravelly voice shattered the serenity. "My horse ain't lame, and I want you to ride her."

Kurt edged behind Cisco, trying to remain unseen. Footsteps thumped closer.

"She might need time off, Otto. She doesn't feel right. The vet could scratch her."

Julie's voice. Kurt remained hidden in the stall, shamelessly eavesdropping as he plucked white tail hairs from his brush.

"Doc's an idiot. That man don't know nothing."

"Maybe she hurt herself when she kicked the wall," Julie said. "No horse likes to be locked up. Perhaps if you took the boards down. Let her see out."

Kurt's hand stilled over the brush. So it was Otto's horse in the boarded-up stall. Archer had arranged for Kurt to be in the same barn as Otto, but it was sheer luck the man's stall was directly across the aisle. Strange the horse in solitary was a mare. He'd assumed it was a stallion, a bad actor that needed isolation.

"Whip the bitch and you'll see how hurt she is. Listen, girl. We both know you ain't got many offers. If you want to race my horse Friday, you best climb on her today." Otto's voice thickened. "You'd get more business if you weren't so stuck up. You oughta try being nicer to men. Nicer to me."

Kurt's disgust flared, along with his relief. Julie and Otto didn't sound like happy partners. He shoved open Cisco's door and stepped into the aisle.

Otto loomed over Julie, standing much too close, using his size to intimidate. But Julie's hands were balled, her shoulders squared and clearly she was too stubborn to step back.

Kurt forced a benign smile. "Good morning, Julie," he said. "Good morning, Otto."

She turned and walked toward him, not rushing but not dawdling either. The relief on her face was so apparent he instinctively moved closer. Otto watched her go, making no effort to hide his blatant appraisal.

A pulse ticked on the side of Kurt's jaw. The man was not only rude but a bully. Kurt had known people like that, had even worked with some of them. Never had liked it. Yet Otto was key to the investigation, and he had to make some attempt to get along.

"Your horse did kick this morning," he said mildly, resisting his urge to step forward and block Otto's view.

"So what?" Otto's gaze swung from Julie to Kurt. "Ain't no one's business but mine."

"Sure," Kurt said, "but at some point she'll hurt herself. Must be hard to keep shoes on her too."

Otto's eyes slitted. "You better worry about your own horses." He stared at Kurt for a moment before stomping from the barn.

Kurt glanced at Julie. "Touchy fellow. Know him well?"

"No." She clasped her arms, rubbing them as though chilled. "But he's probably not someone you want as an enemy."

"Is that a warning?"

"Yes, I guess it is." She raised her head, her eyes troubled. "Most people avoid him. I was surprised to see him so early. Usually I ride for him in the last set, nine-thirty, when more people are around."

"You don't like him, yet you gallop for him?"

"It's the horse I'm with, not Otto. And I'm helping his animals, even if it's only in a small way. Besides, I don't just gallop for him. I ride races too." She crossed her arms, her voice turning wistful. "Unfortunately I can't afford to turn down rides. Someday maybe, but not yet."

"Racing is a cut-throat business," Kurt said. "We'd all like to pick and choose who we work for…who we get involved with."

She nodded but determination blazed in her face, emphasizing those killer cheekbones, and it was clear she was thinking of nothing but riding. Probably she had no involvement in Connor's murder. She seemed exactly who she appeared, an apprentice jockey desperate to earn mounts.

It'd be damn tough. She'd picked a hard and bruising career yet was utterly feminine. Her weight appeared perfect in spite of her generous curves…

Jesus. He needed a kick, wasn't usually this distracted. He corralled his thoughts, turning away from her as he pointed at Otto's horse. "What's her story? I've never seen a horse locked up so tight."

"Otto likes his privacy," Julie said. "That mare arrived last week and is entered for Friday. I've galloped her four times, but she feels sore. Otto doesn't want to hear about it though."

Kurt made an encouraging sound designed to keep her talking and walked to Otto's stall. There was a knothole near the bottom of the middle board. He crouched, pressing his eye to the opening, as he strained to see the horse behind the wall. Julie scuffed her leather boot on the concrete, and he could feel her edginess, radiating like a wave.

Maybe she was linked with this after all? "What's wrong?" he asked.

"Otto," she said simply. "He'll be really pissed if he sees you checking his horse. And sometimes his reactions are extreme."

Kurt relaxed, pressing his eye back against the hole. "I just wonder why the mare kicks so much. She might hurt herself, although she seems quiet now."

The horse had definitely settled, had even edged toward his voice. Her neck stretched as she sniffed at the hole, and the long hairs on her muzzle tickled his eyebrow. She looked normal but thin. Her front legs were nice and straight. Good bone. No obvious injury.

He ran a hand over his jaw and straightened. Noticed Julie had moved to shelter him from anyone entering the barn even though he was twice her size. She obviously believed he was interested in nothing but the welfare of the horse.

Of course she had no reason to distrust him. Not yet. His smile slipped a notch.

"All Otto's horses get upset when he's around," she said. "They're not much to look at either. Not like your big gray." She glanced toward Lazer's stall, clearly eager to ride.

Kurt turned to his tack room. "I'd rather have an ugly horse that can run than a pretty one that can't. Want to use your saddle or mine? I'm tacking up Cisco so I can escort you."

Disappointment swept her face, and he had the odd urge to sugarcoat his words, to see her smile again. Usually he didn't give a damn what anyone thought. But there was something about her, a hint of vulnerability in those beautiful eyes that tugged at him.

"This track is new to me," he added, downplaying that he doubted her ability, "and I want to check the ground."

"Of course you do," she said. Her dimples flashed, and he was glad he'd added the blatant lie.

# CHAPTER SIX

Julie felt like a queen, surveying her realm over Lazer's arched neck. The horse's power was inspiring. He was built to cover ground, and the idea of galloping over hills and fields and valleys was wonderfully enticing.

She blew out a sigh and peeked at Kurt who trotted beside her on his ugly Appaloosa. Clearly he'd been worried about her ability. But now, after a lap around the track, he seemed reassured. His grip on Lazer's lead had loosened, and a relaxed smile softened his handsome face.

Handsome indeed. She averted her gaze, afraid he might feel her scrutiny and somehow suspect her thoughts. Besides, she never mixed business with pleasure, especially when that business involved an influential trainer from Woodbine. It was totally normal to want to look at him though—totally normal.

Last night she'd searched the Internet and discovered he'd managed a family breeding operation for eight years. There wasn't much information, but over the past year he'd switched to training and successfully parachuted to the top levels, with stables at Gulfstream, Belmont and Woodbine. He must come from money.

She took another peek at his rugged profile. It really wasn't fair—good looking, successful, rich. But he was actually here, a top-tier trainer. And she was riding his horse.

This was a rare opportunity, and she wasn't going to let anything screw it up. Lazer's caliber was unmistakable. He felt like a Cadillac and so far, they'd only trotted. She loved galloping at the track: the sounds, the camaraderie, even the smells, but it was definitely more enjoyable when she was on a good horse.

She couldn't resist another glance at Kurt. She liked his voice, smooth, confident, even amused, and she was glad now Chandler's filly had dumped her. She blew out a sigh then realized Kurt was looking at her.

"This horse sure is smooth," she said quickly. "Feels like we're floating."

"He's smooth, but the quick acceleration makes him hard to control. You seem comfortable though. Want to try him on your own?"

She nodded, her hands tightening around the reins. Kurt was obviously decisive and wanted to see if she could handle the colt. It was a big opportunity...and a bigger risk. Lazer was strong, bursting with energy after being cooped up in a trailer. She'd never been entrusted with such a pricey horse, and no matter how hard she tried to block the fear, it edged in, knotting her gut and making her feel inept.

Kurt reached over and removed the lead. "Keep him to an easy gallop. I don't want him doing much today."

He trotted Cisco to the outside rail. Suddenly she was alone. On Lazer. She gulped—her thoughts ping ponging. The colt was expensive, impeccably bred, probably ridden by famous exercise riders, famous jocks, people she'd only read about or watched on TV.

What if she fell off? He might get loose, like the filly yesterday. Might hurt himself. Just last week a horse had slipped on concrete and broken a leg. Aching regret filled her as she pictured the animal, a lovely chestnut mare, thrashing on the ground then valiantly hopping into the trailer. Then—

*Stop. Don't think of it.* Her damp hands clutched the reins. She always daydreamed at the wrong times. Lazer bucked, questioning her control, and she straightened her thoughts, softened her grip. He immediately steadied, and his stride lengthened into a smooth gallop.

Damn. He was magnificent, with an effortless reach. His sheer ability blew away her fears. He cruised around the track, thrilling her with a promise of untapped speed. But when they rounded the backstretch turn he abruptly threw his head and grabbed the bit, almost hauling her from the saddle.

She played with the reins, asking him to relax, desperate to avoid a battle of strength he was sure to win. However, the wind shoved her soothing words back in her face. The grandstand was a blur as she called on all her skill to rate the colt, frantically trying to remember everything her mother had ever said.

Lazer blasted by a horse on the rail. With ears flattened but galloping at less than full throttle, they stormed into the clubhouse turn. She braced her feet in the irons, her ragged breathing blending with his churning hooves.

Shit. She knew this was a test, her only chance. If she couldn't control the colt, Kurt wouldn't let her gallop Lazer again.

The colt pinned his ears and shoved at the bit, his muscled neck stiff with resistance. For a second, she was in trouble. But in sudden submission he softened his jaw and relaxed, and by the middle of the backside she'd coaxed him down to a floating trot.

It hadn't been easy. Her breathing escaped in painful gasps, and her arms and legs throbbed. She definitely needed to lift more weights, starting that very afternoon. Maybe jog an extra mile.

A horse and rider pounded alongside them. Kurt reached over and snagged Lazer. "Good job," he said with a nod of approval.

"Thanks." The word burst out in a throaty gasp as she struggled to catch her breath. She sensed his appraising gaze and straightened, wishing she were better at hiding her feelings, hoping he wouldn't spot her fatigue.

"You handled him well. Good job," Kurt repeated. "Horse seems to like the track too. Can you breeze him tomorrow?"

Joy skidded through her, warmed her chest and slipped out the corners of her mouth. She'd passed the first test. "Yes! Oh, yes. I'd love to ride him again. Whenever you want."

She closed her mouth, not wanting to appear too eager…but what a day, what a horse. A major turnaround from yesterday's disaster. And this was the big track. She was no longer riding on the bush circuit. The trainer too! Kurt MacKinnon for Bill Chandler. She'd take that trade any day.

It was tempting to give her arm a quick pinch, but instead she gave Lazer an enthusiastic pat. The horse hadn't pulled any nasty tricks and had, in fact, made her look good. She was grateful.

Kurt hid his surprise as they walked toward the barn. Julie was a much better rider than he'd anticipated and that eased any qualms about letting her gallop Lazer. Plus the colt was the perfect lure. She'd be more malleable if she were trying to earn the jockey ride. And he needed to get close to her. Needed to extract every word Connor had said during his fateful visit to G barn on what had turned out to be the last night of his life.

She was clearly winded so he waited for her breathing to steady. Dirt dotted her left cheek, and he had the odd urge to wipe it off but jerked his eyes away.

"Are you galloping Otto's mare this morning?" he finally asked, his voice huskier than usual.

"A light gallop. Otto entered her for tomorrow."

"Purse money is tempting." He carefully picked his words and glanced back at her, trying to spot her dimple beneath the dirt.

She laughed, a melodious sound that brightened the morning, and even Cisco flicked a curious ear. "Otto doesn't win much," she said. "He hauls around, mainly between Alberta and Montana. Runs cheap horses, claimers."

"I see." Kurt slowed Cisco, surprised they had almost reached the barn. "How many times does he ship?"

But Otto stepped from the doorway, and Kurt quit talking. Damn poor timing. Julie was relaxed and chatty after the gallop, and he liked her smile. He really liked that smile. However, they were only twenty feet from Otto, well within earshot, and further questions would have to wait.

He stepped off Cisco and held Lazer while she unbuckled the ancient saddle she'd insisted on using.

"I've been waiting for you to ride my mare," Otto said, folding his arms over his barrel chest and shooting Kurt a scowl.

A pissy kind of guy, or merely annoyed she was busy with another trainer? Get used to sharing her, buddy, Kurt thought as Julie walked toward Otto, cradling her worn saddle as though it were priceless.

He led Cisco and Lazer into the cool barn. Left Cisco in his stall contentedly munching hay, and guided Lazer to the wash rack. The sun was warm, the sky unmarked by a single cloud. A horse played on a hot walker, kicking with abandon as he circled beneath the mechanical arm. Lazer bucked once in a show of solidarity then stood still while Kurt hosed water over his sweaty chest and legs.

The colt dripped a trail of water when Kurt led him from the wash rack to where he could nibble on the sweet spring grass. Lazer chewed greedily until a ruckus sounded behind them. He snorted, head high, grass forgotten. Kurt tightened his grip on the lead before checking out the commotion.

Two horses appeared on the walkway. The first, a bay mare, bounced like a pogo stick, churning up clouds of dust. Otto lumbered beside her, big fist clenched around the chain that circled her nose. A rider perched precariously on the mare's back, head and shoulders set with concentration, and he spotted one curving cheekbone, a strand of blond hair. *Julie.*

He squeezed his eyes shut in dismay. This wasn't good. He needed both Otto and Julie at the track. Needed them both healthy and accessible, not out of reach in some damn hospital.

Sandra detached herself from the melee and trotted her gelding toward Kurt, stopping a cautious distance from Lazer. She jerked a thumb over her shoulder, her face sparkling with anticipation. "Rodeo time. Come watch. Otto's gallops are always the highlight of our day."

Kurt's gaze swung back to the tiny rider perched on the furious horse. "Why the hell does she risk her neck like that?"

Sandra shrugged. "She has to prove herself. It's the fastest way." She wheeled Okie but called over her shoulder. "It's okay. She doesn't usually come off."

Doesn't usually come off. The words nipped at Kurt as he hurried Lazer back to his stall. It was dangerous enough to gallop sane horses. Otto's mare didn't seem to belong in that category.

Besides, he needed Julie, at least until he found out what she knew about Connor. He blew out a sigh and joined the people rubber-necking by the rail.

Julie, still in the saddle, seemed unfazed by the mare's contortions. It was hard for the horse to drop her head and buck while Otto manhandled her, but Julie would be alone on the track. Otto hadn't even hired a stable pony. He should have stayed on Cisco, Kurt thought grimly. He would have been willing to pony the mare.

Otto reached the gap, whipped off the chain and leaped back. The mare wheeled, lashing out with murderous hooves that sliced the air only inches from his head. Free from his stranglehold, she dropped her head and ripped out a series of jolting bucks.

Kurt squeezed the rail in a sympathy grip, watching Julie lean back, brace her feet and pull the horse in a circle. She'd lengthened her stirrups since riding Lazer. Now she looked like a bronc rider. A damn good one.

The mare hesitated. Julie picked up the opposite rein, calmly asking her to turn, and amazingly enough the mare listened. The pair trotted off along the outside rail, the horse suddenly a picture of obedience. The onlookers drifted away amid a chorus of jeers and cheers. It seemed the show was over.

Kurt's grip on the rail loosened but he lingered, puzzled by the change in the horse's attitude. Now she acted like any other animal on the track although, as Julie had said, she wasn't quite sound. She stepped evenly in the front but there was a slight hitch in the back. Not a hip problem—it appeared lower, and she didn't track up with either hind leg.

He glanced at Otto, only fifteen feet away, holding the lead shank and hunched over the rail. Sweat drenched the man's t-shirt, and dark stains looped beneath his armpits. It was hard work leading an animal who didn't want to cooperate.

"Do you have more than one horse, Otto?" Kurt struggled for a friendly tone.

Otto grunted.

"Pardon," Kurt said, hoping the man only had one horse. No rider should have to tolerate dangerous behavior like the mare's.

Julie galloped for Kurt too, so of course he had an interest in her well being. Only natural.

But Otto ignored him, and Kurt's jaw tightened in frustration. At this rate, they wouldn't be on speaking terms for another two months. They didn't have time for this shit. The case was turning cold.

"I just wondered if you have another horse." Impatience edged Kurt's voice but Otto only grunted again, and the sound blasted Kurt out of his civility zone. "One grunt yes, two grunts no?" he asked.

"Fuck off," Otto said.

Ah, finally. As usual, poking stirred a reaction and that seemed the best way to pull any response from Otto. Kurt had never liked placatory pretending anyway. He preferred to whip up emotions, any emotions, so long as they weren't his own. Connor was the pacifist. One of the reasons why they worked well together.

*Had* worked well together.

He braced against the rail, staggered by an abrupt sense of loss, then dug his heels in the dirt and wheeled back toward Otto. "Sure hope you have some other runners. Looks like your mare only has two wheels." Remembering Otto's reaction to Julie's vet suggestion, he added, "Maybe I should call the doc over? Get your mare some attention?"

Otto's face mottled and a thick vein bulged in his neck. "Mind your own damn business, Mr. Hotshot. No one touches my horses but me."

Kurt could no longer look at the man who was quite possibly Connor's killer, and the angry throbbing in his head had to be controlled. Deep breaths, they'd taught him. But Otto was glowering, swinging the chain on the lead line in an obvious challenge, and the urge to get close and personal was almost overwhelming.

Clenching his jaw, Kurt turned and walked away. It took a few moments to steady his breathing, to relax his fists, but all in all, it wasn't a bad day.

At least he'd learned one very important thing—Otto was even more protective of his horse than the trailer—which made Kurt very keen to examine the man's volatile mare.

# CHAPTER SEVEN

Back in the privacy of his motel room, Kurt entered his password and tapped some keys, waiting as the laptop downloaded a glut of information. Archer's office had forwarded a summary of the cases Connor had been involved with, including call history and a timeline of his activities.

Kurt scrolled down, choosing two pages for scrutiny—persons of interest in Connor O'Neil's murder. The list was short, only two, and one he now considered as more of a witness.

WEST, JULIE A.: Female Caucasian, Age 23, Green Eyes, Blond Hair, Weight 48.9 kg/108 lb, Height 1.5 meters/5 ft 2 in. Occupations: university student. Distinguishing Features: none. Prior Convictions: none.

He skimmed her history. No siblings, mother deceased. Plain vanilla. He wished for more. Was rather curious about Julie. He'd request a more comprehensive report in the morning, more pictures too. This one was rather blurry. She wasn't smiling and it didn't do her justice, not one bit.

He flipped the page over and turned his attention to Otto. Ah, now this page wasn't as pretty, but it was definitely more interesting:

LAING, OTTO P.: Male Caucasian, Age 36, Brown Eyes, Brown Hair, Weight 109.7 kg/242 lb, Height 1.8 meters/5 ft 11 in. Occupations: trucker, metalworker. Dual U.S./Canadian citizenship. Distinguishing Features: scar on right shoulder. Prior Convictions: assault and battery. Prior Charges: robbery, drunk driving, resisting arrest, spousal abuse, rape. (See Report B0T-1826-1)

Kurt reached into the bar fridge and pulled out a can of beer before tackling Report B0T-1826-1. He snapped open the can and turned to the glowing screen.

Otto's adult record had begun in Montana. Convictions included drunk driving and assaulting a police officer. He'd spent time in jail for various misdemeanors, but a rape charge had been dismissed when the alleged victim disappeared.

The man's history was extensive, although one omission was gaping. It didn't include drugs.

Kurt tilted in the wooden chair, propping his feet on the bed as he tried to draw a link between Connor and Otto Laing. The room was an ideal thinking spot, silent except for the drone of the laptop and the occasional ticking of a pipe. However, he couldn't find anything to connect the two men. Couldn't imagine what Connor had seen on the highway.

Dispatch records showed he'd stopped to help Laing with a flat tire. A racehorse had been reloaded; everything appeared routine. But something had triggered Connor's suspicions, enough that he'd run the man's license plates and followed him to the track. It had to be something noticeable, something other than Otto's abrasive personality.

The trailer had been unremarkable. Had to be the animal.

There were no races tonight. In a few hours the backside would be empty, the perfect time to poke around the barn. Kurt tilted the beer can and took a speculative swig as he wondered what he'd find on Otto's horse.

"Good evening, sir," the guard said. "You keep long hours."

The same young guard watched the horsemen's gate, but now he was lonely and slightly more talkative. Short hair emphasized his skinny neck, and a lumpy Adam's apple rippled when he spoke.

Kurt flipped open his trainer's license. "One of my horses is prone to colic. Have to make regular checks. Many people around?"

"Just a few guys." The guard scanned his credentials and returned them with solemn authority. "Should be quiet the rest of the night."

Excellent. Kurt slid his license back in his pocket and followed the dark path to G barn.

He eased into the barn and paused, stopped by insolent eyes. A black cat with a sagging belly sprawled in the aisle, a squeaking mouse pinned beneath its claws. The cat picked up the mouse, glaring at Kurt as it chewed. The squeaking stopped as the mouse disappeared, tail last, but the cat lingered in the aisle, licking its paws.

Kurt eyed the far wall, wondering which path the cat had taken. He wasn't keen to invite any bad luck, but he also didn't want to inconvenience himself over a silly superstition. Always a quandary.

"Scat." He waved his arm. The cat ran to the left, leaving clear passage along the right side of the aisle. Cisco leaned over the stall door, ears pricked, as though amused by Kurt's maneuvering. That horse was too damn smart.

Kurt avoided Cisco's gaze and walked directly to Otto's stall. He crouched down and peered through the knothole then jumped, startled by the big brown eye staring back. Obviously the mare had discovered the peekhole and now kept close watch on barn traffic.

He slid the latch back and opened the door. She rushed back, pressing against the far wall, tail clamped, her trembles visible even in the gloom.

"Easy, sweetie." He stepped into the dank stall, concerned by her reaction. Examining her would take much longer than anticipated.

He left the door slightly ajar. From the outside, no one could see it was unlatched. But if the mare went berserk—and that seemed a distinct possibility—he could escape. He waited, fighting the urge to rush, trying to show he wasn't a threat. And finally, she turned. She still hugged the far wall but at least faced him, nostrils flaring as she sucked in his scent. He edged forward, pausing each time she considered wheeling until finally she was close enough to touch.

"Easy, sweetheart. I'm just going to check you over." He kept his voice calm, unhurried, even though every instinct screamed to rush. Gradually her trembles subsided as he stroked her smooth, silky shoulder. Then—not so smooth after all—his fingers stilled over a large welt.

He pulled out his flashlight and ran the light over her coat. Abrasions marred her back and chest, and several welts were thick and crusted. A rope? Or some type of hobble? They seemed recent, the scabs a week to ten days old. He skimmed the light over the rest of her body but found no incisions to mark a hiding place.

One more spot to check. A sensitive one. He slid his hand down her rump toward the top of her tail. She humped in protest and he paused, uneasy, afraid the ruckus was too loud in the quiet barn.

He changed tactics, smoothing his hands over her hindquarters then down her legs, gentling her again to his touch. At this rate it would take some time to check her cervix. Her trust in humans had clearly been shattered.

He touched her left leg, noting how her ears pinned. Obvious pain and heat. Reached over and gently felt her other leg. Both hind legs were swollen, the puffiness extending along the tendons from the hocks to the fetlocks. He leaned forward and shoved the straw away from her hooves.

Disbelief rocked him back on his heels.

He'd never seen such a mess. Nail holes riddled her hoof walls. So many holes—

The mare's sudden leap knocked him off balance, and she flung herself against the side of the stall, smashing at the boards with lethal hooves. What the hell? Then he heard what she already knew. Voices. And very close.

He sprinted across the aisle, thankful the mare's noise muffled the latching of her door. Vaulted over the top of Cisco's stall and rolled under the startled gelding's belly.

The speakers entered the barn. Two voices. One was Otto's but the second had a harsh accent. German or Scandinavian maybe?

The mare's kicking increased as they moved closer and her angry hooves pounded the wall, blocking pieces of their conversation.

"Be suitable to ship next week. Get one race in before the trip to Idaho…take her next week while I'm away," the accented voice said.

"Okay, we'll race…leave on Monday. When do I get my money?" Otto's voice was different, oddly meek.

Kurt considered rising from the straw and meeting Otto's companion. But two night visits within twenty-four hours? Even Otto might question that. And the skin on the back of his neck prickled, always a barometer of danger.

So he remained flat in the straw, curbing his sneeze while hiding behind a stoic Cisco. The muffled voices shifted to the far entrance, lingered for an endless moment, then faded. Kurt's breathing steadied. He allowed himself a muffled sneeze but waited a full fifteen minutes before leaving the sanctuary of the stall.

He gave Cisco an affectionate pat before crossing the aisle and peering through the hole. The mare was calm again, staring with a soulful eye. She was priceless too, better than a watchdog when it involved Otto, and he whispered his thanks.

But when he eased outside into the friendly darkness, his hands fisted. He still had no idea what had sparked Connor's interest in the mare. Tomorrow he'd have to pump Julie for information. Pump her hard.

Sexual images nudged into his thoughts, thoughts he muscled into line. He hadn't come here to socialize. Had never been reluctant to play hardball. As always, he'd do what was necessary to make sure she cooperated, and feelings had nothing to do with it. Absolutely nothing.

## CHAPTER EIGHT

Dawn's colorless light seeped through the motel curtain. Kurt turned on his back and rolled to the middle of the bed. He liked mulling over a case when he was half asleep, when ideas drifted and took shape. But foreign sounds kept intruding: the hum of the clock radio, the slam of a car door, water swooshing through pipes.

Sighing, he propped his head on the lumpy pillow and stared at the ceiling. Wide awake now, he had no need to rush. His horses had been fed, his stalls cleaned. Sandra had found a teenager who was eager to earn money working as a stable hand. And the luxury of extra time this morning was appreciated. He felt sluggish, his sleep disrupted by confusing pictures of Connor and Otto…and Julie.

Why was Otto hauling the horse back to the States so quickly? Julie said he was determined to race the mare tonight. But based on the conversation Kurt had overheard in the barn, there had been no concern about the horse's health or about her readiness to run. They'd only discussed her suitability to ship. Race results seemed irrelevant.

It was possible the horse was used for smuggling, although he hadn't found any signs. A vet check might show how they hid the contraband, and he also wanted a farrier to look at her, but it would be impossible to confiscate the animal without exposing the investigation. And it was premature to do that. Shaking his head, he flung back the sheet and rose.

His frustration lingered after his shower. It was ironic both he and Connor had transferred from the undercover street team, frazzled but still functioning. Kurt had left police work and immersed himself in the race world. Connor, older but less emotionally scathed, had stayed with the RCMP but retreated to a relatively undemanding job in southern Alberta.

It had been nine months since Kurt last talked to him, nine months since Kurt had jotted down his phone number and promptly tucked it away. Regret seared him. He should have talked longer. Should have asked more questions. Should have made more effort.

At least Connor had sounded content. He'd even joked about his boring job. A boring job that had resulted in his murder. Kurt winced.

He yanked on his boots, consumed with the need to discover what had drawn Connor to Otto's mare. Connor's report stated he'd encountered an emergency traffic hazard so had assisted with a flat tire and helped reload a horse. In that twenty-minute period, he must have spotted something illegal.

Edgy with purpose, Kurt slammed the motel door and slid into his truck. When Connor had signed in at the track gate, he'd asked directions to Otto Laing's barn but had said little else. Julie was the last person to speak with Connor, the last known person to see him alive. Kurt had to get her talking. She might remember something Connor had said, some small detail that would expose a motive for murder.

He detoured for coffee and a bagel. By the time he rolled onto the track parking lot, the backside bustled. A sleepy-eyed attendant sold him a race program. Kurt flicked through it while balancing two coffee cups in his right hand.

Otto's horse was listed on page sixteen. She was entered in the seventh race tonight: a ten-thousand-dollar claiming race for fillies and mares. Her registered name was Country Girl. Julie West was the jockey. Otto Laing was listed as both owner and trainer.

Kurt scanned the horse's past performance. Her previous races were in Idaho and Montana. All were claiming races, a low-level race where any horse could be claimed for the stated amount. Her best finish was a second at the seventy-five-hundred dollar level.

The steep jump in class was noticeable. Otto didn't want to risk losing the mare so he'd bumped her from seventy-five hundred to ten thousand. It was doubtful anyone would claim her for ten when she couldn't win at the lower price tag. Her breeding was unremarkable; even with the dollar exchange the mare would be a poor bargain. A bad claim.

Kurt's stride quickened, spurred by a simple idea. The horse was a bad claim for racing but not for the police. If he claimed Otto's horse tonight, she could be inspected at leisure—they'd be able to run any test they wanted. Hot coffee splashed his hand but didn't dampen his enthusiasm.

He entered the barn and saw Julie waiting by Lazer's stall, saddle and helmet at her feet. She looked perky at seven in the morning and obviously was keen to get back on his horse.

"Good morning," she said. "I wasn't sure what time you wanted to work this guy?"

"This is good. But the tractors are harrowing now so we have time for coffee."

She accepted the cup with a grateful smile but jerked back when his fingers deliberately brushed hers. *Interesting.* Brave enough to take on Otto, but she jumped from his touch. She edged back another foot, ostensibly to drop the tab of her lid in the garbage can, but it was clear she was shutting him down.

Or trying to.

"Milk? Sugar?" he asked, not surprised when she shook her head at the packets. Riders learned to shave calories whenever they could. She didn't look like she had problems—he indulged in another discreet perusal—but for most riders, battling weight was a way of life.

She remained about five feet away. It was clear she was more comfortable with that distance. Preferred some space. Maybe she'd experienced a few hassles from some other trainers. The idea annoyed him, although he wasn't sure why. Clearly she could take care of herself; she hadn't been reluctant to send him packing that first day.

She didn't rush to speak, but her gaze over the rim of the cup remained steady and assured. Good. He liked silence with his first cup of the day. She was an easy lady to be around.

46

Of course, he couldn't stand around all day, drinking coffee and watching Julie. Time to get to work.

"I saw you on Otto's mare yesterday," he said. "Horse didn't seem happy."

"All his horses react to him," she said. "They usually behave fine when he isn't around."

"Odd, don't you think?"

"Not odd at all. He doesn't treat them very well. Sandra complained to the office a few times, but nothing changed." Her expression turned mischievous. "I've made some direct suggestions too, but trainers never seem grateful when I tell them what to do."

He shook his head in exaggerated dismay. "Trainers always think they know best." He didn't intend to let her turn the conversation, but it was impossible not to joke when she flashed those dimples. "So you're not buddies with Otto?" he added.

Her nose wrinkled with distaste. Obviously she and Otto weren't partners or even friends, and he could tell Archer to cross her off the list. All that remained was to chat her up. Find out what she and Connor had discussed. The police report stated she'd given Connor directions, but hopefully she knew something more revealing.

He adjusted the lid of his cup, padding his words with just the right amount of friendly interest. "I imagine Otto's mare will be full of fight tonight?"

"Yes. It'll be rough in the paddock, but once we're on the track she'll listen. She wants to please. Maybe she'll even finish in the top three." Julie shrugged. "I'm just not sure of her soundness."

Jesus. He abruptly snapped the plastic tab from his lid, stiffening at her casual comment. She seemed more concerned about the finish of the race than the consequences of a horse breaking down. Often young riders didn't think accidents could happen, not to them. Even if they did, riders couldn't afford to turn down mounts.

A muscle ticked above his right eye. He knew there was something wrong with the mare's hind end, but there was little he could do about it. Besides, he couldn't worry about Julie. The mare had to start in the race for him to make a claim.

He took a hasty gulp of coffee. The mare would be fine. Julie would be fine. It was more important to steer this conversation around to Connor, and quickly, before they were interrupted.

"Is Otto the sole owner of the mare?" he asked. "He never seems to have any visitors." He took another sip, pretending more interest in his coffee than her answer, hiding the tension in his shoulders as he waited for her to mention Connor. Or even the accented visitor from last night.

"I think so, but who knows. Otto keeps to himself, even shoes his own horses." She dumped her cup in the garbage and glanced at her watch. "I have other horses to gallop but I can come back if you prefer."

Damn. "No, that's fine. I'll get Lazer." But his mouth tightened as he turned toward Lazer's stall. It might be necessary to draw her away from the track in order to develop any meaningful type of conversation. She was always in a hurry, always businesslike, at least with him.

The realization irked him more than it should, but he shrugged it off. He'd find a way to work her. He always did.

He tacked up Lazer and led the colt down the aisle. Slipped his hands under Julie's leg and boosted her into the saddle. He had a fleeting impression of strength and balance and heat and kept his hand on her leg a shade longer than necessary.

She looked down, those green eyes wary.

"What's your weight?" he asked quickly, already knowing the answer but cursing his odd impulsiveness. The last thing he needed was to scare her, and that wariness in her face was not a good sign.

"One hundred and eight pounds," she said, her eyes turning hopeful. "But the bug gives me a five-pound weight allowance. Less weight would help Lazer in a race."

He shrugged but kept his expression noncommittal, as though he were really thinking about riding weight and jockey assignments. At least she looked hopeful now. He wanted her to stay that way. Everyone talked more when they were positive and upbeat, but he was damn sure not committing to Julie when he'd never even seen her race.

The weight allowance that apprentices, or bug boys, received meant little if she didn't have the talent. Morning gallops and race riding weren't the same. Exercise riders didn't always make good jockeys, and many good jockeys didn't have the intuitive feel that the best exercise riders had.

But she was looking at him with those beautiful eyes, not imploring but yeah…they were imploring, and it was hard to admit he'd originally had no intention of letting her ride Lazer in a race. Hell, he hadn't even intended to race the colt in Calgary. He grabbed the lead shank and turned Lazer toward the track.

"I don't think weight is this colt's problem," he said. "He gets distracted and starts to loaf. Blinkers haven't helped."

"But an apprentice's weight concession can't hurt."

"No, it can't." He glanced back, liking her determination as well as her work ethic. She lacked experience, but so far her riding was fine. And it wouldn't hurt to enter Lazer in a race. The horse was fit and ready to run, and it would cement his cover story. Which meant he now needed a jockey.

He dragged his left hand over his jaw. He didn't often use apprentices, didn't feel the weight concession was worth the rider's inexperience. But he liked Julie. Didn't see how it could damage the case if he helped her out at the same time.

"No promises," he said, "but I'll watch you race tonight. We'll see how it goes. Then we'll talk about jockeys."

"I appreciate that, Kurt," she said softly, eyes shining.

Something kicked in his chest and he turned away. No matter how her voice wrapped around his name or how pretty her smile, he'd do whatever was best for his horse. It would be interesting to see how she handled Lazer at speed though. She looked in sync with the colt, and Lazer did like her. The horse was unusually composed, as though eager to please his rider, and that in itself was baffling.

Frustration tightened his jaw, the way it always did around Lazer. The colt had enough talent to run at the top-tier tracks but just didn't seem to want to race. At least, he was proving to be a valuable prop for police work.

"Take him around twice easy," Kurt said when they neared the gap. "At the three-eighth pole, breeze him home. He'll be more aggressive now that the road trip is behind him. You handled him perfectly yesterday, so I left Cisco in the barn."

She nodded like an eager student as he released Lazer. The colt gave an exuberant buck that she seemed to relish, and he caught a gleeful dimple as he stepped back to watch from the rail.

She definitely had finesse, persuading Lazer to settle into a trot without any huge arguments. Not an easy thing to do with a strong-opinioned horse. The realization surprised him. The Calgary track was several tiers below Woodbine or Gulfstream, yet Julie managed Lazer as well as any of his previous riders. Maybe a race here wasn't such a bad idea.

"Is that the three-year-old from Woodbine?"

Kurt turned toward the deep drawling voice. The man behind him was lithe with a confident smile and crisp white shirt. Only a few inches taller than Julie. Probably a jockey. His dark head reached Kurt's chest.

"Yeah," Kurt said. "Horse shipped in a few days ago."

"I'm Gary Bixton. I like your horse. Julie's doing a good job out there. Nice to see her on a quality animal."

"What does she usually ride?"

Bixton snorted. "Stuff nobody else will touch. She's a good rider though. Gutsy, and a fast learner."

Kurt glanced back at the track to watch Julie guide Lazer around the oval. The colt cruised into the clubhouse turn, his stride quickening as he powered down the backstretch.

"Nice turn of foot," Bixton said. "Big change from Otto Laing's runners."

"Otto's? A change in what way?"

"No legs, no brains," Bixton said. "I've warned her. She shouldn't even sit on Otto's horses. No one should."

Kurt propped his hip against the rail, assuming a nonchalant pose while he studied Bixton, the jockey everyone talked about with such respect. The man radiated the confidence most top athletes possessed. Designer sunglasses hid his eyes but laugh lines crinkled around the edges, and his mouth permanently tilted as though he was well pleased with life.

"Are Laing's horses that bad?" Kurt asked, glancing at a dainty filly trotting on the outside rail.

"The four I remember were cripples," Bixton said. "So mean they'd put you on the moon if they had a chance to kick."

"All mares?"

Bixton shook his head. "Nope. Geldings. But cheap claimers, every one."

Geldings, damn. There went his theory. Drugs couldn't have been hidden in the boys. Kurt crossed his arms and turned his attention to Lazer. The colt had reached the three-eighth pole. Julie crouched over his neck asking for more speed and the big horse gave it to her. He scorched around the track, so fast even Bixton stopped talking.

Kurt stared across the infield, his gaze locked on the gray colt. He'd never seen Lazer run with such enthusiasm.

"I'd be glad to ride your horse," Gary drawled. "Any time."

Julie galloped midway down the backstretch before she was able to turn Lazer and head back toward the gap. Though exhausted, a grin curved her lips. This horse was magnificent. He'd worked beautifully too, except for a second when he was alongside another horse and had, very briefly, lost his focus. Not long. Only a second. She doubted Kurt had even noticed, not from his position on the backside.

Her excitement fizzled when she spotted Gary, and she wished Kurt hadn't met the accomplished jockey quite so soon. Gary only rode the best, and it was now obvious Lazer belonged in that select group. It was also obvious she couldn't compete against Gary.

"Morning, Jules," Gary called, a wicked grin creasing his face. "Looks like that hoss has some run. Think you can handle something that goes so fast?"

Julie shot him a withering look but felt Kurt's assessing gaze and knew it was important to remain poised. Gary's grin widened, as though he fully expected her temper to blow. She knew it wasn't anything personal. Trash talking was part of the game, and Gary was King of Cool. He hadn't become top jock by letting others needle him. And neither would she.

She tilted her head, pretending sympathy as she looked down from her elevated position on Lazer's back. "Actually this was my slowest ride today," she said sweetly. "But maybe you couldn't see. We all heard about your failed eye test. Gosh, it's going to be tough for you to get rides."

She shot Kurt a glance, hoping he didn't mind that she'd dissed his horse, but he winked, seemingly with approval, and something clenched low in her stomach. For a second she forgot Gary and stared into Kurt's dark eyes. Moistening her lips, she jerked her head away. Maybe he didn't realize Gary was top dog.

Very good. If she could keep Kurt to herself for another day or two, it would give her more time to earn the mount. Gary wouldn't be a good fit for Lazer anyway. The colt needed someone to gallop him every morning, not an established jockey who only climbed aboard for the race. The colt's focus issues had to be understood—understood and addressed. Kurt should know Gary wouldn't be around to gallop in the morning.

She gave Lazer's neck a possessive pat. "I'm surprised you're even here right now, Gary. Why are you out of bed so early?"

"Maybe because you're not there with me, darling." Gary's voice hardened as though he knew exactly what she was trying to do. "The fact is I sometimes show up for morning gallops if the horse is good enough. But we can discuss my sleep habits tonight if you'd like."

Kurt abruptly stepped in front of Gary, blocking her view as he reached up and hooked his lead on Lazer. His face was impassive, but she had the distinct impression he didn't enjoy their banter.

"See you around, Gary," Kurt said, his voice clipped.

She was so shocked she almost fell from the saddle. Kurt had just dismissed Gary Bixton. She'd heard it. Everyone in Calgary begged for Gary's time, his attention, his advice. Not Kurt. Maybe he didn't know who Gary was.

But no way would she introduce them. It was in her best interest to remain silent, exactly what any jockey would do. She tightened her mouth, but her guilt magnified into full-blown discomfort—Gary deserved more.

She swallowed. "Kurt, this is Gary Bixton," she heard herself say. "He's a good friend, a good rider, and the leading jockey here…and in Edmonton…" Her voice trailed off, miserable with the knowledge she'd just gift wrapped Lazer.

But Kurt only nodded politely and led Julie and Lazer away. She stared between the horse's ears, too stunned to speak. He'd said he'd watch her race before committing to a jockey, and he meant it. He was actually giving her a chance.

Gratitude warmed her chest and her head felt light, but she realized Kurt was talking and tried to focus on his words.

"Lazer definitely liked the track," Kurt said. "We'll see what the clockers say. Did you feel anything when he passed that horse in front of the grandstand?"

She blinked, surprised Kurt had noticed Lazer's attention swing. The man was very astute, and she hesitated. Some trainers only wanted to hear good things about their runners. However, Kurt was so honest he wouldn't want the truth varnished, and he was asking her opinion as though it mattered.

"Lazer's very talented." She chose her words carefully. "Best horse I've ever ridden. But for a second his attention slipped. I tried chirping, shaking the reins, even waved the stick but nothing worked. It wasn't long, just a few strides."

"But a few strides can make a difference in a race," Kurt said. "That attention lapse has always been the problem. He starts gawking and forgets his job. Some kind of horse ADD, maybe. You analyzed it well." His gaze drifted past her and his mouth tightened.

She glanced over her shoulder, following his gaze. Gary still lazed against the rail, his white shirt and smile dazzling beneath the bright sun. He wouldn't be alone long. Already three people were bee-lining to his side.

"Is Bixton waiting for you?" Kurt asked, his voice clipped. "Or do you have time to ride my two-year-old?"

"I have time," she said, trying to hide her surprise. He hadn't mentioned his second horse before; she hadn't dared dream she'd be able to gallop both his horses.

"Ace is scheduled for gate work. You can have the job if you want it." He glanced back with such a deep smile, her breath caught.

"Of course I want the job," she managed. But her voice sounded breathless. It was lucky he didn't smile like that very often, the type of smile that connected to his eyes and made her chest tighten in a most annoying way.

She reached forward and straightened Lazer's already perfect mane, determined to keep Kurt in the business side of her brain. His casual questions helped her relax, and she soon slipped into an easy conversation. He was a good listener and seemed especially interested in G barn, and she was surprised when they reached the barn so quickly.

She dismounted. A lanky teenager appeared with a red cooling sheet draped over his wiry arm.

"This is Martin," Kurt said as he unbuckled her saddle. "He's working mornings and evenings for me."

She nodded, remembering Martin and what Sandra had confided. The teenager was a loner, a non-achiever at school, and worked his spare hours at the track. Julie had glimpsed him hot walking horses, but Martin was shy and rarely spoke.

"Hi, Martin," she said. "Glad to meet you. Sandra says you're a good hand with a horse."

"Thanks." A flush stained his cheeks and he studied the floor. "I saw you ride at Lethbridge once." He scuffed the toe of his worn boot, peering at her from beneath too-long hair. "You're the toughest rider I've ever seen." He gave a bashful smile.

She grinned. Martin had an endearing smile and a cowboy's sweet manners. Once he had more confidence, he'd have plenty of girls chasing him. "It's not hard to stay on," she said. "The real job is teaching horses to run straight. If you want, Sandra and I can give you some riding tips."

His eyes sparkled but he said nothing more. Only an emphatic nod revealed his interest.

"Walk Lazer around until he's cool, Martin," Kurt said, his tone mild. "I'll wrap his legs later."

Martin nodded again, and another clump of brown hair escaped from beneath his ball cap. Julie watched as he expertly turned Lazer and guided the colt along the walkway. Sandra was right. Martin was assertive enough with horses, just uncertain with people. Her gaze met Kurt's, and she realized he'd been watching her. She dipped her head and adjusted the zipper of her vest.

"Let's see how you and Ace get along," Kurt said, his voice husky as he turned and walked down the aisle. It was a relief his attention had switched to his horse. He'd seemed to be scanning her face, looking for something, and despite the cool morning, his appraisal made her feel oddly warm.

# CHAPTER NINE

Julie watched as Kurt tied his two-year-old to a ring in the stall. The brass tag on the leather halter read 'Ace of Spades.' Ace stood quietly for the saddle and even lowered his head to be bridled. She doubted many horses argued long with Kurt. He had a fearlessness that animals probably sensed; she certainly sensed it, although that first day she'd mistaken it for arrogance.

He wasn't arrogant, just...bold. She wiped her warm forehead and tucked a lock of hair behind her ear. Gave a quick swipe to her cheeks, hoping her face wasn't dirty then reminded herself that her appearance didn't matter.

It was more important she ride well tonight. He'd promised to watch the races, and if he liked what he saw, she'd earn the mount on Lazer. Simple. No sucking up or feeding peppermints or smiling at stupid jokes. And he was letting her work Ace from the gate, so she might have a chance to earn that mount too. Finally her business was picking up. She let out a sigh of contentment, a sigh so tiny she was surprised when he turned and arched an eyebrow.

"You okay with this?" he asked. "Working a green horse from the gate?"

"Of course," she said, embarrassed he'd heard her sigh but even more mortified he'd attributed it to nerves. "I was just wondering why you gelded Ace before he ever raced?" she asked quickly.

"He's a little knock-kneed, and his breeding isn't fashionable. I picked him up cheap as a yearling." Kurt gave a reassuring smile, but his eyes probed her face. "He's been popped from the gate before, so there shouldn't be any problem."

His lingering gaze made her uneasy, although the feeling could also be attributed to the upcoming gate work. There was an element of danger when a horse was confined to a tiny stall, and it always provided an adrenaline rush. She'd been squashed between a flipping horse and steel bars before, but helping with a young horse did earn extra points with the trainer.

Besides, Ace didn't look like he'd be much trouble. His eye was calm and steady, and he stood rock still as Kurt turned and adjusted his bridle, lowering the snaffle several buckle holes. She stepped closer. "Isn't that snaffle a bit low? I mean...it looks low."

He glanced over his shoulder, his expression unreadable. "Are you a trainer too?" he asked.

He probably wasn't used to being questioned but at least he wasn't frowning, and she edged a step closer. It was risky when equipment malfunctioned, and she'd learned to check the tack. "If the bit's too low, it's useless," she said.

"Remember what you said earlier?" His lean fingers moved deftly over the buckles. "When you said trainers don't appreciate advice from their riders?"

It might have been a warning, but she guessed he was much too confident to be thin skinned. "But I'm the one on Ace's back," she said stubbornly, "so it's important his steering works."

He raised his head and looked at her, and his eyes seemed to darken. "I'm not going to let you get hurt," he said. And then he slanted her a deep smile, the kind that made her insides soften, although that probably wasn't a good thing to happen when she was about to gallop a thousand-pound horse. "Let's go." He surprised her with a gentle rap of his knuckles on the side of her helmet and led Ace from the stall.

She followed, disarmed by his gesture. But she still wasn't certain about the bit. Sandra considered all trainers idiots until they proved otherwise, although Kurt certainly was no idiot.

He was also damn attractive. His broad shoulders and lean hips looked good from the back, and it was obvious he worked out by the way his shirt tightened over his arms. It had been a long time since she'd really looked at a man, other than how they rode or trained. Since her mother's death, she hadn't dated;

Sandra thought it was because of the accident, but she didn't understand.

Still, there was no reason not to check out Kurt's tight butt, the way he walked, with a slight hint of a swagger. Everything on him looked hard. She had the crazy impulse to slide her hand along his jeans and find out for herself—

She jammed her hands in her pockets and yanked her gaze to Ace, to the sweep of his silky tail and the way it swished over his hocks. Not nearly as stimulating, but definitely safer.

Besides, Kurt received enough attention. Girls were always ogling him. One of the grooms from Harrison's barn had even asked for his motel number, and Julie refused to join the gaggle of admirers.

Kurt stopped Ace in the center of the aisle. "Don't scowl," he said, looking back at her. "The bit's okay. No wrinkles because I don't want pressure on his mouth, not unless you put it there. You have a nice touch, and I want to take advantage of it."

"The bit?" She swallowed. "Oh, yes, of course."

"Come on. Mount up." He splayed a firm hand over the small of her back, guiding her closer to the saddle. His fingers felt oddly intimate as they slid along her hip to her boot, his touch so warm the leather over her ankle seemed paper thin.

She perched in the saddle, staring straight ahead, dismayed at her reaction. She wasn't going to be much of a jockey if she turned all fuzzy every time a good-looking trainer boosted her into the saddle. Of course, it wasn't just any trainer; it was Kurt.

She adjusted her toes in the stirrups, suddenly impatient. She was just relieved Kurt had a relaxed side. It made him easier to work with. When they'd first met, his watchful smile never touched his eyes, but now he was different, more open. He was kind too; she'd noticed his easy way with Martin. She might have been interested in him, if they'd met outside the track. If she actually dated.

She flipped her reins to the other side of Ace's neck, switching her thoughts to more important things. Like racing this evening. It would be a big night, although she wasn't going to agonize about weather and post positions and the competition. No more mental lapses like she had with the filly. The manure pile incident and subsequent teasing were too fresh, and her reputation couldn't take another hit.

At least Kurt was giving her a chance, especially generous considering the way she'd lost her temper, and for that she was grateful.

They walked in companionable silence to the gap where he removed Ace's lead. "You have about twenty minutes before the starter calls you. Give him a sightseeing tour, then warm him up with a slow lap. Slow," he repeated.

She nodded and walked Ace onto the track, letting him check out his surroundings before moving into a jog and then a canter.

Fifty feet past the grandstand, the wind tossed a vagrant cowboy hat and the gelding's ears pinned forward, tracking the straw hat as it stalled and flipped. He didn't spook or try to bolt, and she murmured her approval. Some horses would have gone bonkers, Bill Chandler's Princess for one. But Julie was riding quality horses now, horses trained by an expert. She no longer had Bill's business, but her riding prospects had definitely improved.

She heard a shout, garbled by the wind, and glanced at the chute. The starter, a figure of absolute authority, gestured at the horses scheduled for gate approvals.

"Bring him in," an outrider relayed.

She trotted Ace toward the starting gate, joining two other horses that circled behind the gate. A score of people lingered by the rail, Otto included. He often watched gate work, although she suspected he really wanted to see an accident. She jerked her head away from his insolent eyes.

A wide-eyed chestnut was called first. The assistant starter reached up to guide the filly in, but she planted her feet. Undaunted, the loading crew turned her in three circles until she was inches from the opening. Two men stepped behind her, hooked their arms together and pushed her in the slot.

Ace was called next. He sidled up, ears flat, attention pinned on the looming gate. Too nervous, he rushed in, clipping the assistant's heels. The man cursed and jumped on the tiny ledge. His gnarly fingers wrapped around the bridle as he cranked Ace's head to the left.

*Clang!* The door slammed shut, the noise vibrating through the entire gate. Ace charged forward but there was no place to go. He waited, trembling, and pressed against the grill. Julie stroked his sweaty neck, trying to calm him, but the shivers didn't stop.

*Thud.* A man hollered and she peered over her shoulder. The last horse to load, a chestnut colt, was full of fight, and soapy lather coated his neck. He whirled, knocking his handler down, flecking the air with specks of white. The colt plunged away, but his rider—she knew him only as Joe—pulled him around before he could bolt.

Furious, the horse bucked high and hard, hurling the rider over his shoulder. Joe landed catlike on his feet and managed to keep a grip on a rein.

Julie straightened, determined to ignore the ruckus. She adjusted her goggles, wrapped her hands around a thick clump of Ace's mane and waited. When the gates opened she needed to be ready for an explosion of speed. Or risk the ignominy of being left behind, sitting in the dirt.

Beneath her, Ace trembled, claustrophobic and resenting the enclosure. His earlier poise had crumbled, and his inexperience showed. He scrambled against the closed door, striking it with a hoof, unnerving them both with the loud clang.

She shot another glance over her shoulder, willing them to hurry. Ace felt like a time bomb, and the filly next to them was beginning to fret too.

The gate crew conferred, opting to load the resisting horse without his rider. They produced a blindfold, confused the animal with a few circles then guided him into the slot. Joe swung over the bars, placed his toes in the irons and an assistant whipped off the blindfold.

"Not yet!" Joe yelled as the horse jackknifed. The handler straightened the horse and pointed his nose in the vee of the gate.

Julie caught herself watching and cursed. *Concentrate on your own horse.* She stared through the grill, trying to re-focus her thoughts. A split second of calm. Then the starter pushed the button, cutting the electric current to the plates that held the doors shut.

Ace reared as the door cracked open. His feet found the ground but his legs crossed and he stumbled, furrowing the dirt with his nose. Legs tangled, he struggled to keep his balance.

She was flung onto his neck. Her hands crisscrossed his mane and she tightened her grip, knowing Joe's horse was behind her. Staying on Ace's back was the only way to avoid lethal hooves.

Time suspended as Ace fought to regain his balance. Sounds sharpened—gasps, yells, Otto's gleeful chortle.

What an ass. Anger gave her strength. She willed Ace to be determined enough, athletic enough, to stay on his feet. He seemed to absorb her message and gave a last desperate lurch then straightened and started running.

She began breathing again, using his long mane to regain her seat and find a rhythm with his lengthening strides, and they charged down the lane after the galloping filly.

Ace caught the horse just past the finish line. Julie rose in the stirrups and gradually slowed him to a trot. The filly was on her right but the third horse was missing, and she checked over her shoulder in concern.

"Joe's horse is stubborn as a mule," the filly's rider said, trotting beside her on the way back to the chute. "Damn horse didn't want to go in. Now he won't leave. Trainer should have done more work with him." He shook his head at the blazed chestnut still propped in the gate.

The young horse had obviously refused to run when the doors opened and still stood rooted in the gate, with Joe vainly trying to urge him out.

The filly's rider gestured with his stick. "Look at that nut. He must have a death wish walking by an open gate."

Julie stiffened as Otto lumbered in front of the frightened colt, waving his arms and hollering. She could see the whites of the horse's eyes, how his head raised in panic as Otto loomed closer.

The colt abruptly catapulted from the gate, smashing Otto with his shoulder and driving him into the dirt.

Julie pulled Ace to a halt, staring in horror. A bird trilled from the infield, its cheery song discordant with a man prone on the ground. A loud fly buzzed around her ear. No one spoke.

Otto raised his head and her breath escaped in a whoosh. His arm moved, then both legs. He slowly picked himself out of the dirt. A communal sigh of relief was replaced by a groundswell of mutters.

"Teach him not to stand in front of a loaded gate," someone said.

Two men at the rail nodded, followed by more grumbles.

The starter gestured with his thumb. Julie had never seen the stony official show so much emotion, his expression a mixture of relief and anger.

"Leave the area now," he snapped. "I won't tolerate interference like that!" He turned toward the horses. "Riders! Bring them back in."

She couldn't tell if Otto was disoriented or merely stubborn, but he ignored the starter's command and glared at Joe, who had trotted back on the reluctant chestnut.

"Man, I'm sorry," Joe said, his voice squeaky with relief. "No way to avoid you. My horse was scared when you cornered him and busted out on his own. Nothing I could do."

Otto's hands fisted, and Julie's breath hitched. Surely he wouldn't be stupid enough to drag Joe off his horse, not in front of the officials. Otto stalked closer, his eyes narrowed on Joe.

*He's going to be kicked off the track.* Julie's relief was tempered with dismay. Otto gave her the creeps, but he was also one of the few trainers she jockeyed for. His mare was scheduled to race that evening, and if he was kicked out now, the mare wouldn't be allowed to run. What bad timing.

"Excuse me, sir." Kurt's calm voice sounded from behind the rail. "I'd like to check my horse before he goes back in the gate. He might have cut himself when he stumbled."

The starter turned his attention to Kurt. "Make it quick," he said, still edgy after the incident.

Otto seemed to regain control. He shot Joe a dark glower, shoved his hands in his pockets and stalked away.

Julie pulled her gaze from Joe and Otto. Ace seemed to be fine, but it was fortunate Kurt's request had distracted the starter and given Otto a chance to cool down. She leaned over Ace's shoulder as Kurt approached. "We had a sloppy break," she said, scanning his face for signs of displeasure. "I'm sorry. The next one will be better."

"Not your fault. You did a good job keeping him on his feet." He crouched down and ran a hand over Ace's legs.

"Ace won't be so tight next time," she said, forestalling any lecture. "There was a lot of excitement. I'm glad Otto's okay. Thought he'd finally be banned."

"Not banned yet." Kurt rose, his hooded gaze following Otto, and she blew out a relieved sigh as it truly seemed he wasn't obsessing about the break. Chandler would have lectured endlessly.

She followed Kurt's gaze, watching as Otto trudged along the walkway. A hoof print marked the back of his shirt, but he walked evenly and showed no other sign he'd just been trampled by a horse.

"He's tough as an oak tree," Kurt said, so quietly it seemed he was talking to himself.

"Come on. Let's get those horses in." The starter gestured impatiently at Julie. "You first."

"Keep his head up," Kurt said softly. "You did fine." He wiped some dirt off Ace's muzzle then squeezed her boot. Turned and stepped back over the rail.

She tightened her lips, listening as the trainer of Joe's horse shouted loud instructions about using the whip to make the colt listen. She was glad she was riding for Kurt.

"I want your horses coming out together or we'll be doing this another day. We're already pushing the regs," the starter warned as a handler grabbed Ace and led him into the gate. The two other runners entered the slots. Julie grabbed a chunk of mane, steadied her breathing and waited.

The gate rattled. Someone cursed. But she stared through Ace's flattened ears, determined not to let her distractions filter down to Ace. Her mother had been a big fan of visualization, and Julie pictured Ace coming out straight and fast.

*Crack!* The doors opened and the three horses broke as one—running hard, running straight.

Two straining heads bobbed on her right, and whoops and whistles cut the air. She was vaguely conscious of her own yells as she urged Ace down the lane. He galloped strongly, even passing the other two horses. She rose in the stirrups, pumped with excitement as she eased him up before the turn.

Gate work was an important step in a young horse's career. Races could be won or lost at the start, and fear of the gate often launched many bad habits. She stroked his neck, absorbing the new bounce in his trot. The two horses beside her also seemed more confident as they headed back to their waiting trainers. Even the chestnut pranced, strutting now that he'd overcome the scary gate.

Kurt snagged Ace's reins and led him through the gap, where Julie dismounted.

"Good job," he said, nodding with approval. "Starter said he's ready to race."

"Ace is a nice horse," she said. Her voice bubbled with adrenaline. "He gallops straight, businesslike. And the bit worked perfectly too. I've never seen a snaffle so low."

"Me neither," Kurt said. "Surprised it worked."

She jerked back, shocked by his admission. She'd trusted him; yet, he'd put her out on a green two-year-old, not knowing if she'd have any control? The side of his mouth twitched, and she realized he was teasing.

She punched his arm, then dropped her hand, appalled. Good grief. What was she doing? Hitting trainers now? She turned and unbuckled her mother's old saddle, her fingers fumbling at the buckle.

"Good thing you didn't fall off." Kurt didn't seem to notice her embarrassment. His deep voice rippled with amusement. "You might have been banged up. And I'm sure you wouldn't forgive me if you missed tonight's race."

She nodded, grateful for the diversion. She hadn't been thinking. Had been way too comfortable. She wouldn't do that again. Besides, his arm had felt like bedrock. She suppressed a wimpy urge to rub her knuckles.

"I actually have two races tonight," she said, pulling off her saddle and edging back a step. "Otto's mare and a classy old sprinter." It was the first time she'd ever had two rides in one night, so she definitely wouldn't have welcomed a training spill. Not today, not when she was so close. Just the thought of a fall made her throat tighten.

His eyes narrowed. "Why aren't you riding Ace back to the barn?"

"If you don't mind, I have some horses to gallop at this end." She paused, hoping he was still considering her as a jockey, even though Ace's first break from the gate had been far from stellar. "You'll watch me tonight?" She moistened her lips. "Watch me ride?"

"Definitely." His eyes darkened. "We can meet after the races. Go for a drink."

Her palms felt moist as she gripped her saddle like a shield. Part of her wanted to see him, but it could cause all sorts of complications. And though she liked being around him, knew she could learn a lot, she felt much safer when she was mounted. He jumbled her emotions, and she didn't like it. Didn't like it one bit.

"We'll talk about Lazer," he added, his face expressionless.

She swallowed. Then nodded slowly. "All right." She forced her most businesslike tone, the one she always used when trainers turned too familiar. "We'll meet...have a meeting, later."

But her formal attempt only seemed to amuse him because his mouth twitched, and the glint in his eyes didn't look at all businesslike.

# CHAPTER TEN

Kurt rubbed his jaw and stared absently through the motel window, imagining Archer's reaction to his succinct e-mail. A recommendation to claim a racehorse was certain to raise objections; plus, he also wanted a border alert placed on Otto.

Experience had taught him to make requests in pairs, one as a throwaway so there was room to negotiate what he really wanted. But he needed both these things, and he needed them now.

His attention drifted over the stained curtain—three cigarette burns and another mark that resembled blood—and he dragged his chair sideways, suddenly resentful of the grungy room. It would be a relief when this sordid chapter of his life was over. One last job. A few more lies.

Halfway houses and cheap motel rooms had been tolerable with a partner—a partner kept you sane and helped preserve your honest side. Connor had been one of the best, a guy who would go to the wall for you. Kurt had never worried when Connor was behind him.

*Connor.*

He slammed his fist on the desk, uncoiling with such force the chair shot back and cracked against the wall. He pinched the bridge of his nose, using the pressure to steady his anger. Usually he had no trouble keeping his emotions blanketed, and his unexpected weakness surprised him.

It never helped to brood. Connor was dead.

The only thing left was to catch his killer. Claiming Otto's mare was a key step but authorization for her purchase required diplomatic wrangling, and Kurt didn't have much wiggle room. The mare had to be claimed tonight.

He clicked his laptop shut with a streak of defiance. Sometimes it was easier to ask forgiveness than permission, and this was one of those times. He'd finish the report in his tack room and send it to Archer at the end of the night. After he owned Otto's horse.

When Kurt strode into the barn, Sandra had commandeered a large section of the aisle and scrubbed at her saddle with a mangled toothbrush. Her purple shirt and silver belt were festive, but her dark scowl dampened the effect.

He couldn't resist teasing. "A cowgirl happily cleaning tack," he said. "Such a rare sight."

"It's cleaned every year, whether it needs it or not." She gestured at the extra sponges. "A nice guy would help me out."

"Then I hope you can find one."

She gave a rueful shrug. "It was worth a try. I'm a bit lonely."

He glanced down the aisle. The barn was deserted, and he did need to talk to Sandra, preferably in private. He hooked a bale of hay and straddled it beside her. "Maybe I'll help this once but don't confuse me with a nice guy."

"I don't think I'd ever do that," she said.

He checked her expression but she was busy scrubbing a soapy lather on the saddle; he couldn't see her eyes. "You working all the races tonight?" he asked, picking up a round sponge.

"Most of them."

"You ponying Otto's mare in the seventh?"

"Nope. Otto's too cheap to pay even though his horses are loco. That's why none of the regular jocks will ride for him. They're exhausted before they even reach the gate."

"Sounds like Julie will need help," he said. "Will you pick the mare up at the barn and take her back after the race? Since she's extra work, I'll pay double."

He pulled a fifty-dollar bill from his pocket and anchored it with the shiny tin of saddle soap.

Sandra didn't touch the money, just stared at him with narrowed eyes. "You do know Julie is focused on her career?"

"Yeah. I noticed that." He jabbed far too much soap on the sponge.

"What I mean is," Sandra tossed him a stained rag, "she doesn't date. All the guys try, of course, but they're wasting their time. She has her reasons."

He leaned forward, unable to resist a little probing. "Which are?"

"None of your business."

"And it's not really any of your business," he said, "why I want a pony for the seventh. Can you do it? Or should I find someone else?"

"No problem. I'm always glad to make extra money." She scooped up the bill, fingering it as though checking for counterfeit.

He was disappointed she wasn't going to talk about Julie, but it was more important to swing the conversation around to Otto. He worked up a white lather on the breastplate, scrubbing the leather as though it were the most important thing on his mind.

It was rather enjoyable. The mindless rubbing and the smell of soapy leather reminded him of a more innocent time in his father's tack room. His dad had always believed in working one's way up, and Kurt had spent long hours doing menial chores.

"This looks brand new." He trailed a finger across the glistening leather but watched Sandra's face while he spoke. "Maybe we should hire out. Otto's tack look filthy."

She made a disgusted sound and shook her head. "I hate cleaning leather. And most of Otto's stuff is so old it belongs in a museum. All that hobble shit. Nobody uses that any more."

"Does he use it much?"

"Hard to say what he does with it, the way his stall is boarded up. But one night, Julie and I were late. He was fighting with a horse in there. Lots of scuffling."

"Did he put the boards on that stall or were they already there?"

"Dunno." Sandra's forehead wrinkled. "Can't remember."

Light steps sounded, steps he immediately recognized. He glanced up, watching as Julie walked gracefully down the aisle. "I don't believe this." Her eyes widened. "Sandra? Cleaning tack? Kurt, you're sweet to help."

Sweet. He almost choked. He'd never heard that before, although he'd been called many other names, usually by someone being hauled away in cuffs. But it didn't hurt for her to think he was sweet; in fact, he kind of liked it.

"I'm a full-service trainer," he said lightly. "You ready to ride tonight?"

"Definitely," Julie said. "But Dad shipped in a horse about an hour ago and wanted me to check on her."

"Where is she?" Kurt rose from the bale, ignoring Sandra's knowing smile.

"Stall twenty-four." Julie gestured and walked further down the aisle. Kurt followed until she stopped in front of a pretty bay with inquisitive eyes and a splash of white on her forehead.

"Are you galloping her tomorrow?" he asked.

"No, she ripped a shoe off in the trailer. We can't take her out until the farrier comes by."

"Maybe Otto would nail it on for you. You said he shoes his own horses?"

Her eyes flared with horror. "I wouldn't ask him. He'd probably cripple her in the process."

"You've noticed something…about his horses' feet?" Kurt edged closer, watching her face. Her cheeks were flushed, and her nose wrinkled with distaste.

"Hey, guys!" Sandra called. "I'm off to lay my bets. What are Skippy's chances in the third, Julie?"

Kurt swallowed his frustration, as Julie turned and gave Sandra a confident thumbs up. "Don't leave Skippy out of your exotics. There's a chance Country Girl will be in the money too."

"Okay. I'll wheel them with the favorites. What a payout that would be!" Sandra's eyes gleamed as she dug in her back pocket and rushed from the barn, waving her crumpled bills.

"You believe you can get Otto's mare up for a piece?" He turned to Julie, surprised she'd encourage Sandra to waste her precious cash.

"Of course," she said simply. "I wouldn't have told Sandra to bet on Country Girl if I didn't."

"No," he said, "I guess you wouldn't." Her honesty was refreshing but somewhat disconcerting. He was used to a life of subterfuge. Julie said exactly what she thought, what she felt. Even when she'd introduced him to Bixton, it was clear she'd been reluctant; however, her sense of fair play had prevailed.

Not that it had even mattered. Bixton's agent had already approached him, and Kurt had told the agent the same thing he'd told Julie—he hadn't decided on Lazer's jockey yet.

His gaze drifted to Otto's reinforced stall. In a few hours, the mare would be his, and he needed a place where a vet could examine her, far away from Otto's prying eyes. He looked back at Julie. "Is there room at your ranch to board a horse for a couple weeks?"

She blinked with dismay. "You want to move Lazer? Or Ace?"

"No, a mare."

"Oh," she said, clearly relieved Ace and Lazer were staying at the track. Understandable, since she was trying hard to earn the jockey mounts on both his horses.

"This filly's paddock is empty now." She gestured over her shoulder at her father's horse. "We could put your mare in her spot. It has a run-in with some grass. Where's she now?"

"Grass would be nice," he said, avoiding Julie's question. "I'll talk to your dad, and if it's okay with him, haul her out tomorrow. Want to grab something to eat?"

"No, thanks." She checked her watch and edged toward the door. "I never eat before a race. Besides, it's time to report in, and I still need to study the program."

Of course. Naturally she wouldn't want to eat. Even if she met her riding weight, there was too much risk of an accident, and surgery required an empty stomach. He was rather impulsive where she was concerned. But there was a good chance she knew something about Connor's visit, and she certainly knew a lot about Otto. It was important to get her talking.

She waved as she slipped out the door, but it was clear her focus had already switched to the upcoming race card. It was also clear she intended to avoid being alone with him. Sandra had been correct.

He blew out a reluctant sigh, knowing he was going to have to push. He needed time with her, time for a private conversation that lasted a little longer than two minutes.

Of course, he'd enjoy more than conversation.

The admission stuck in his mind, refusing to leave. Not that it wasn't justifiable. He hadn't been able to coax her into talking about Connor through normal channels, so a different approach was certainly warranted. Effective immediately.

A rush of anticipation charged through him, a heated buzz not entirely related to hunting down a killer.

# CHAPTER ELEVEN

Horses for the first race circled in the paddock, waiting to be saddled. Kurt flipped open his program and scanned the conditions: four-thousand-dollar claimers going a mile. If the track favored speed, the three horse should win, gate to wire.

He shoved his program back in his hip pocket. The speed horse was the heavy favorite, so the race probably wasn't worth betting. Besides, it was more important he prepare his claim on Otto's mare. His gaze prowled the crowd as he angled toward the claim box.

Otto had no reason to think anyone would drop a claim on his overpriced mare. There were better horses in the race that could be bought for the same tag. Still, Kurt felt uneasy, as though someone watched.

He signed the form and wryly checked it over. Claiming races were a simple way to keep the competition fair. If you raced a good horse too cheaply, you might win the race but risked losing your horse. He'd claimed many horses before, the first when he was eighteen; from a racing viewpoint, however, this was the worst claim he'd ever made.

"Buying something tonight?"

Adam West's voice. He tucked the slip in his pocket before turning to face Julie's father. "Yeah, an interesting mare. I spoke to Julie about boarding her at your place for a few weeks. If that's okay, I'd like to trailer her out tomorrow."

"Sure, we have some room." But Adam frowned and raised a bushy eyebrow. "Earlier you said you wanted to rent my trailer. Is yours fixed already?"

"Yeah, repairs went faster than expected," Kurt said but gave himself a silent reprimand for the mistake. Little lies often caused more problems than the big ones. "I'll get some directions from Julie," he added, "and bring the mare out in the morning."

"All right," Adam said. "It's supposed to be nice weather. While you're out our way, you should ask her to take you for a trail ride. Be a good chance to check out the area you're looking at buying."

Kurt nodded, leery of Adam's watchful eyes. This man was sharp and had a troublesome memory. However, the story about buying land did have its advantages since it would be child's play to grill Julie on a trail ride. "That's a good idea," he said.

"Hey, Nick!" Adam abruptly hollered, and a barrel-chested man detached himself from the crowd, approaching with a bowlegged walk and an amiable grin. A zippered scar notched his jawbone, and he moved with a slight limp. "Nick," Adam repeated. "Can you shoe my filly tomorrow? She's at the track now, G barn."

"Sorry." Nick shook his head. "Been busy as hell, and I'm roping tomorrow. Can't fit her in until next week."

"At least do her front," Adam said. "She lost a shoe so Julie can't get her out to gallop." He jabbed his thumb as though in afterthought. "This is Kurt MacKinnon. In from Woodbine. He's got some horses in G barn too."

Kurt shook Nick's callused hand. Half the farrier's index finger was missing, but it didn't weaken the man's grip.

"Good to meet you," Kurt said. "I've heard your name."

"Really. What'cha hear?" Nick's voice rumbled with confident curiosity.

"That you're the best farrier around," Kurt said. "Better than a vet at figuring out leg problems."

"Hell." Nick chuckled. "Folks just say that because they like free advice. And advice is something I love to dish out. Here's something you boys can tuck in your wallet." His voice lowered to a conspiratorial whisper. "This race is easy money if you throw out the three horse. He was sore as hell from a stone bruise when I shod him yesterday."

"The three horse, you say?" Adam flipped open his *Racing Form.*

Nick nodded, pressed a big finger to his lips then turned and resumed his jaunt to the betting windows.

"Well, that makes it easier," Adam said as he studied the page. "Maybe I'll bet the trifecta. Think the number one horse can get up for third?"

"Not a chance," Kurt said, scanning the past performances and noting the slow times. "That horse would need the race of his life just to keep the others in sight. His speed figures are way too low."

Adam shrugged with genial disagreement. "Time only matters in jail. I think the one horse will do fine. And if I can throw out the three horse, I'm smelling money."

Kurt chuckled, watching as Adam jotted down his bets. The man had a stubborn set to his jaw that reminded him of Julie. Probably had her temper too. He wasn't surprised that he liked the man. People streamed around them, rushing to the wickets, but Kurt remained beside Adam for the post parade, enjoying his company and local insight.

Sandra was in the parade of horses and ponied the favorite, number three, a flashy bay going off at odds of two to one. The horse Nick said had a stone bruise.

"Number three's a lunch bucket horse," Adam said. "Doesn't know the word quit. On a normal day he'd be five lengths ahead of this bunch. But if Nick is right and he's sore, number six will win, eight will be second, and the one horse will come third. In spite of his slow times." He smiled a good-natured challenge, hiked up his jeans and headed to the betting window.

Kurt leaned on the rail as the three horse trotted off. The limp was slight, barely noticeable, but the horse did favor his left front. With the favorite hurting, the race would be wide open, and a savvy better could make some money.

Unable to resist the farrier's inside tip, he placed a twenty-dollar win bet then wandered through the mezzanine. It was a motley crowd—ranchers with big hats and dusty boots, downtown oilmen in fancy suits and women sporting bulky purses and hopeful eyes. He tried to pick up the accent of Otto's late-night visitor in the hubbub but had no luck.

With two minutes to post, he returned to the rail with a cold beer in each hand. Adam was studying the tote board, watching as the changing odds flashed red.

"I can't believe the two horse is the second favorite. But if he gets an easy lead, he might wire it. Shit, I should have boxed him." Adam looked distraught at his betting oversight then accepted the beer with a rueful sigh. "Thanks," he said. "Racing is the only sport I know where being a spectator is such hard work. But damn, it's great therapy for whatever ails you."

Kurt nodded in total accord. He swigged his frothy beer, savoring the magic of the track, and hoped Otto wouldn't appear any time soon. Life didn't get better than this.

A bell clanged. The horses charged from the gate.

Adam pleaded and hollered, his yells deepening as the runners surged across the finish line. The crowd groaned as the favorite finished fourth and out of the money.

"I think six got it. Then two. Shit, I missed the exactor." Adam scowled at his betting stub. "But I got the win, thanks to Nick. Where did the slow horse finish?" he asked with a pointed grin.

"Third," Kurt said. "You were right. It didn't matter about his times. That horse just ran the race of his life." He crumpled his ticket. Horseracing was always perplexing, one of the great mysteries of life, and he didn't expect to figure it out anytime soon. Only recently he'd accepted he liked training better than police work, but both involved a lot of intuition. And luck.

"Are you betting on Julie tonight?" Kurt asked, subtly checking the price on Adam's stub. Not a big gambler—ten dollars was the man's total bet.

"Yeah," Adam said, "but purely on emotion. She's riding long shots."

"Has she had a win yet?"

"Not at this track. She doesn't get the good horses."

Kurt nodded, wondering if he could risk squeezing in another question. Julie was a beautiful girl. Falls, breaks and much worse were a reality of racing. She'd told him about some of her previous injuries—broken wrist, broken collarbone, broken leg. But in the supplementary files he'd requested, he'd also discovered she'd fractured her tailbone. She hadn't even mentioned that one, although clearly she'd been damn lucky. It had to be hard on her father.

"Do you get nervous when she rides?" Kurt asked.

Adam snorted. "I have to go for a piss every time she steps in the gate. It's not so bad when she's on steady horses, but the stuff that Otto fellow gives her..." He scowled and shook his head. "If I had the money, I'd buy better animals. But she's like her mother, too proud and committed to ever turn down a horse. Bad as some can be."

Kurt nodded and lobbed his cup into the garbage bin. Stiffened when he saw Otto barge past, only twenty feet away.

"I'm going to place my bets for the second race," he said and followed Otto into the building.

Caution wasn't necessary. Otto was engrossed with his *Racing Form*, head bent as he shouldered a path to the windows. Kurt positioned himself in the next line, where he was able to hear the man's impatient growl.

"Two hundred to win number six, fifty dollar exactor six and one, twenty dollar triactor six, one, seven."

Kurt scribbled the numbers on his program, hastily placed a two-dollar bet and followed Otto back to the rail.

The man was edgy, his interest split between the fluctuating tote board and *The Form*. He ground his tobacco between tight jaws, shifted his weight from boot to boot.

Had Connor stumbled on a betting scheme? Kurt checked the odds of the three horses Otto had backed. They were short, probably too short to be worth the risk, and Otto hadn't made contact with anyone. None of the jockeys had even looked at him.

*Clang!* The horses charged from the gate. Otto leaned over the rail, urging on the six horse as the field thundered around the final turn. But his hollers turned ugly when the number one horse poked his nose in front.

"Fucking dog!" Otto dropped his clump of tickets and barreled back to the pari-mutuel window where Kurt heard him place another hefty bet.

In the next race, Otto was close, but again couldn't pick the winner. He tossed his fluttering stubs in the air and stomped toward the barns.

Kurt blew out a breath when Otto left, and the tightness in his shoulders eased. At least Otto's absence would let him enjoy Julie's race. It was clear the man was a big bettor, but where Otto—a struggling trainer by any definition—found that kind of cash was a key question.

Now though, Kurt wanted to concentrate on Julie and her jockeying skills, or lack thereof.

He staked out a spot at the paddock and studied Skipper Jack as the gelding ambled around the walking ring. The bay was rangier than most sprinters and wore a breast collar. He had a Roman nose and probably was a fighter—the horse did have a stubborn look—but his performance had tanked over the last few years.

Color flashed, and riders filed from the jockeys' room, vibrant in the owners' racing silks. Kurt had seen a few jockeys at morning gallops but most were unfamiliar, and he used his program to match names with faces. Julie was one of the last riders to appear, distinctly feminine in fitted nylon pants and green silks.

A chestnut stopped for a tack adjustment, blocking his view. He edged sideways, trying to see Julie receive her riding instructions. She looked tense. So did the bay's trainer. The solemn man stroked the tips of his moustache, unable to keep his hands still. Only Skippy seemed relaxed. The horse ambled around the walking ring, his nose so low it almost dragged in the dirt.

Kurt checked the board. At sixteen to one, Skippy and Julie weren't getting much respect, and the crowd had made Bixton's horse the overwhelming favorite.

"Riders up!" the paddock judge called.

Kurt turned and climbed the grandstand, high enough that he could see over the infield. So far tonight, he liked the way

Bixton rode as well as another fellow named Allan. He'd probably use one of those guys, but it would be interesting to see how Julie handled herself under pressure. Putting her on Lazer was fine in theory, but he still had huge reservations about using her in an actual race. Christ, he didn't want her to get hurt.

She hadn't even won at a decent track, and he wasn't going to use a jockey who might endanger other horses and riders, no matter how hard she worked in the morning. His gaze drifted back to the green silks. It seemed her first challenge was to wake up her horse for the post parade.

His mouth twitched at the strange sight. While the other runners danced and pranced, Skippy plodded, not even needing the company of an escort pony. Skippy turned his head once, surveyed the crowd and blinked, as though surprised to see so many people.

"Look at the horse the girl is riding," a perfumed lady in front of Kurt said. "I think he missed his retirement party."

Kurt checked his program. Skippy was seven years old but ambled like he was twenty-seven, and pity overrode his amusement. It was hard for a rider to look good on a poor horse. Without a lucky break or benefactor, many talented jockeys floundered in obscurity.

Tired, worn-out horses might be all Julie rode for a few seasons, and by the look of Skippy, she didn't have much chance despite her comment about finishing on the board. Still, Kurt couldn't quite shake the image of her jaunty thumbs-up. She had encouraged Sandra to bet on Skippy too, so she must have reason to believe the old horse would finish in the money.

Kurt raised his binoculars, studying Skippy as the horse plodded past. Julie was making no effort to rev him up, but she should know what type of warm-up suited him best—hell, she galloped the old guy every morning. And horses did run for her. He'd witnessed that firsthand with Lazer.

He yanked his program out and rechecked the gelding's form. Skippy usually broke well. Perhaps the seasoned horse was saving everything for the race. And maybe he was underestimating both Julie and Skippy.

He slid his hand in his pocket and fingered some bills. The old gelding might be worth a show bet. Skippy would pay loyal backers well. No wonder Sandra had rushed from the barn to slap her money down.

The board flashed a warning, two minutes to post. He sighed and stretched back in his seat. Either he'd be shut out at the windows or get the bet down and miss the start of the race. And he had promised Julie he'd watch her ride before choosing a jockey.

A simple promise to watch.

He had to keep it. She might not be able to race worth a damn, but it would be fun to watch her on the old horse, and Kurt suddenly had a good feeling about it all.

He raised his binoculars and fumbled for a second, surprised by his clumsy fingers. Strange to have pre-race jitters. He didn't even train Skippy. But as the horses mingled around the gate, waves banded in his chest and his breath shortened.

He stared through the glasses, watching the gate crew load the horses. Legs appeared below the bottom bar. Color flickered, and two front feet disappeared. A whirl of motion then the hooves reappeared, and the rearing horse stood square again. The crowd murmured. The horses were in.

An expectant hush blanketed the stands. Kurt's breathing grew shallow as he strained to see. The gates sprung, the horses charged out and Julie's veteran was right there, holding his own with the youngsters. That old horse had fooled everyone.

They ran in a bunch, a tight knot of bobbing horses identifiable only by the bright silks. But when the pack entered the turn they stretched out. Bixton was third, two wide, but galloping fluidly. Julie had Skippy galloping fifth along the rail; her horse didn't look at all sleepy now.

They swept around the turn. It was a soft pace, and Bixton easily grabbed the lead. Kurt found Julie's bobbing green silks, tight on the inside, stalking the leaders, her horse comfortably in hand.

At the half-mile pole, the horses in the back edged up. Julie, snug on the rail, had no place to go. Skippy was passed in a wave, boxed in and pushed back to seventh.

"Let's see what you do now, sweetie," Kurt murmured, pressing the binoculars closer to his face.

Off the backstretch, a blinkered horse in front of Julie drifted wide, and she muscled Skippy into the opening. Skippy scudded forward, splitting horses and finding running room.

"Go, baby!" Kurt dropped his binoculars and leaped to his feet, ignoring the curious glance from the woman in front of him.

Now there were only two horses in front of Julie. Bixton still led when they hit the top of the stretch, but he was chased by a fast-closing gray. Skippy loomed two lengths back, gamely battling to catch them both.

Bixton went to his stick, whacking rhythmically, pleading for every drop of energy. But his mount was tired, and the gray edged past. So did Skippy.

What a gallant horse! Kurt watched the old gelding strain for the wire. Julie waved her stick twice but didn't touch him. No one watching the horse could ever doubt his effort. They swept across the finish line, the gray first, Skippy a length back and Bixton clinging to third.

Kurt cheered with the crowd, his admiration keeping him on his feet. Julie had managed to bring a long shot up for second. Skippy wasn't the fastest runner in the field or the most talented, but the old horse was ratable and had tons of courage. She'd given him a good trip too, saving ground on the rail and not bullying him down the stretch. Not surprising the horse ran his heart out for her.

Kurt zigzagged down the steps and dodged a slew of muttering people to join Adam who leaned over the rail, cheering as Julie trotted Skippy back.

The horse was filthy. Dirt smeared his head and chest, but there was a bounce in his step, and he preened for the crowd, obviously energized by the attention. Julie pulled her saddle off, gave the smiling trainer an exuberant handshake and bounced to the scales.

"Thanks for cutting me off back there, Jules."

Bixton's drawl was unmistakable. Kurt stiffened as the jockey strutted up behind Julie and tapped her on the shoulder with his whip. However, she turned, white teeth shining through her muddy face. They walked away together, seemingly the best of buddies.

"Damn good race," Adam said. "Did you have any money on it?"

Kurt jerked his gaze off the two jockeys. "Yeah. But nothing I can cash."

"Too bad." Adam smugly brandished his own tickets. "Julie will be thrilled with that race. First time she's ever finished ahead of Bixton."

"Are they good friends?" Kurt asked, staring at the results illuminated on the giant board, trying to pretend he wasn't at all interested in Adam's answer.

"Yeah, real good friends," Adam said, "but that doesn't mean Bixton likes to lose. He wants the riding title again this year."

Kurt waited, hoping for more, but Adam's head dipped over his *Racing Form*. Real good friends? What did that mean?

He glanced over his shoulder as Julie paused and passed her goggles to a wide-eyed fan. The young girl had braces and a horse photo on her shirt, and she clutched the souvenir in delight, ecstatic with the gift.

Bixton stopped and waited for Julie to precede him into the jockeys' room. The guy was still smiling, cocky as ever despite riding the beaten favorite. Kurt wondered if they sat together between races or if Julie stayed in the female section. The door closed, and they were gone.

"Have you named a jockey for your big horse yet?" Adam asked.

"Not yet," Kurt said, turning his attention back to Adam. "But I'll know by the end of the night."

"If you don't use Julie, Bixton is by far the best rider around." Adam shook his head with grudging respect. "He came up from Montana and was Alberta's Jockey of the Year. Now, Alberta isn't the bellybutton of racing, but you can't win awards like that without a shitload of talent."

"So he and Otto are both Americans?" Kurt leaned closer to Adam. "Do they travel together?"

"No, Bixton's been here for three years. Otto just showed up last spring. What do you think of the three horse?"

Kurt studied the form above Adam's tapping finger. The three horse had speed but usually burned out on the front end. "Looks okay if his rider can rate him," he said. "Probably impossible for the jock to do though."

"Exactly what I thought." Adam scribbled something and flipped to the next race. "I'm not betting Julie in the seventh," he said as he gnawed the tip of his pencil. "Otto's mare doesn't have a hope in hell. Not unless he slips her some potent drugs."

"That would be stupid, with all the testing," Kurt said, watching Adam's face.

"I never said Otto was smart." Adam spoke without lifting his head from *The Form*. "Think I'll put the three horse over the five."

Kurt glanced at the man's program, watching as Adam agonized over every selection. Julie's father was very serious about his handicapping. Cryptic marks and circles slashed each page, but his bets were modest and placed in the spirit of fun.

Unlike Otto's.

Kurt pushed himself away from the rail. "I'm going back to the barn to grab a halter."

Adam just grunted, engrossed with comparing information in *The Racing Form* to that shown in the track program.

Kurt strolled along the path, passing horses being led over for the sixth race. The handlers' faces were taut, as though headed into battle, a stark contrast to the relaxed expressions of trainers leading runners back. He saw Skippy and the horse's dour trainer walking in front of him, so he lengthened his stride.

"Your horse ran a nice race," Kurt said as he moved alongside. "You sure had him ready."

"Thanks." A smile edged beneath the man's moustache. "I thought the race would suit, and the West girl gave him a good trip."

"She sure did." Kurt nodded his agreement and veered off onto the path to G barn. He was still twenty feet from the door when he heard scuffling, a curse, the crack of leather. He eased inside, taut with curiosity.

Otto blocked the aisle, his hand twisted around Country Girl's tender lip as he rammed a ring bit in her mouth. He mashed her ears with the crownpiece and the mare reared. Her shoes scraped the concrete as she desperately scrambled for a foothold.

"Fuck!" Otto grabbed her left ear and twisted, forcing her head back down. His breath escaped in a series of grunts as he buckled the throatlatch then lashed a chain beneath her upper lip, where it clanged against her teeth.

Kurt winced. "Ever tried asking her politely?" he asked.

Otto jerked around. The mare saw his inattention and struck with her right foreleg but Otto leaped sideways, yanking retribution with the chain.

Kurt jammed his hands in his pockets and forced himself to remain silent. The mare wouldn't have to put up with Otto's brutish attention much longer. She just had to make it through the next thirty minutes.

"Get me that fucking Sandra," Otto growled. "She can lead the bitch over."

"She's on her way." Kurt didn't budge from the doorway.

The desperate mare lunged sideways. Otto yanked her back and wrestled her outside, glowering at Kurt as he passed.

*Thud, thud.* The rhythmic beat of a trotting horse grew louder. Probably Sandra. Kurt hoped she didn't mention he had paid her to pick up Country Girl. Otto had no reason to suspect there was a claim on his horse, but still, it had been a risk. Kurt edged closer to the door, straining to hear.

"Want me to lead her over for you, Otto?" Sandra's holler carried into the barn.

"Yeah, but I ain't paying you."

"Let me slip my lead on, and you can take your chain," Sandra said. "Easy, girl."

Kurt heard the scramble of hooves and another curse. Dust billowed through the doorway and he stepped back, covering his nose, trying not to sneeze.

"Fucking bitch," Otto muttered. "She bit me."

"Serves you right," Sandra said.

The knot between Kurt's shoulders eased. Sandra seemed to believe he was only trying to help Julie when he'd paid for an escort. She didn't realize he'd dropped a claim on Otto's rebellious mare. Their voices faded, and Kurt headed down the aisle to grab a halter.

The door of Country Girl's stall was open, and he poked his head in. Filthy, dark and depressing. Poor horse. It hadn't been cleaned since Kurt's night visit, and the manure had compacted in dense layers.

He closed the door on the stinking stall, hoping to keep the odor contained, then continued down the aisle. Jerked to a stop. The door to Otto's tack room was ajar and definitely unlocked.

A rare opportunity.

He checked the aisle. Two people whooped with laughter as they sponged a horse. A stable hand pushed a heavily laden wheelbarrow while humming off-key to blaring music. No one watched. Everyone was absorbed with their own activities.

He slipped into Otto's tack room.

A snarl of equipment hung off hooks fashioned from crude nails. An X-shaped chain complete with leg bands jangled under his curious fingers. Draped next to it were a homemade war bridle and a casting harness.

He blew out a sympathetic breath for Otto's horses. The devices were useful tools in an expert's hands, but he doubted Otto had much finesse. With Otto, it was merely cruel.

A dented steel box squatted in the corner. Kurt tugged at the padlock. Locked. But with time and the right instrument, he could open it. A faded army blanket was folded on a chair and littered with pocket castoffs: a mixture of American and Canadian coins, a clump of wrinkled betting tickets and an empty tin of chewing tobacco. Nothing illegal. Nothing murderous.

He blew out a sigh and headed back to the paddock, telling himself it didn't matter. Soon he'd own Otto's horse. Soon he'd have answers.

# CHAPTER TWELVE

Sandra slouched on her horse in a cozy huddle with the other pony people. The escort horses stood outside the paddock, heads down, tails swishing, looking as relaxed as their riders.

Kurt paused by Sandra. "Guess you persuaded Otto's mare to make the walk over. Any problems?"

"Nothing I couldn't handle, but that mare is sure scared." Sandra turned in the saddle and gestured at the paddock. "She used a lot of energy and is completely lathered. Julie won't have much horse left for the race." Sandra flicked her ponytail off her shoulder and grimaced. "Too bad I already laid my bets."

"The mare might not win any money," Kurt said, "but the crowd loves her." He walked over to the saddling enclosure where onlookers squeezed around the rail, gaping with morbid interest at the rebellious mare.

An official tried to check her tattoo, but when he reached for her mouth, she lashed out with a protective leg. He dodged in time, but his clipboard hit the dirt.

Otto yanked the mare's nose sideways, grabbing her left ear. The official sidled back to the subdued horse and flipped her upper lip. He checked his list, nodded and moved on to the next horse.

Kurt's eyes narrowed as he watched the identification process. Every racehorse had a unique tattoo so unless the official was part of the conspiracy, Otto couldn't be substituting ringers. Probably her real value was for legitimizing Otto's border crossings between Canada and the States.

But what the hell was he moving?

Kurt was still pondering the smuggling concept when Julie's valet appeared with saddle and cloth draped over an arm. The mare trembled, her body slick with sweat, but she was locked in place by Otto's ear twist. The valet laid the saddlecloth on her back, followed with the tiny saddle then gingerly reached around to buckle the undergirth.

The man standing to Kurt's left chuckled. "The guy with the seven horse will have trouble now. He doesn't have much help, and when he lets go of her ear that mare will explode. She's a death trap."

Kurt edged forward, watching as the valet stepped around the mare and quickly tightened the second girth. Too quickly? The image of a slipping saddle and Julie vanishing beneath a horde of hooves made his gut wrench.

The paddock judge bellowed, "Riders up!" and Kurt sucked in a breath, wishing the race were over. Judging by the mare's panicked appearance, Julie was about to have the ride of her life.

Otto released his twist on Country Girl's ear. She leaped from the enclosure like a scalded cat. The crowd chortled when she snapped out with both legs and seesawed in the air.

Otto yanked at the reins, using brute force to pull her to the ground, and someone stepped up and boosted Julie into the gyrating saddle. The mare arched her back and crow-hopped, putting the crowd in another titter.

Kurt's mouth compressed as he jammed his hands in his pockets. Idiots. Didn't they know how dangerous this was?

"Ride 'em, cowgirl!" someone yelled, and cold beer sloshed his arm as two men joined their plastic glasses in a clumsy toast.

"I'd like to ride *her*," the second man said. "Can't see her face but the body's prime."

Something pulsed in Kurt's head, but he turned slowly, deliberately, raking them with a scowl perfected from nine years' of police work. The two drinkers averted their heads. Turned silent.

He dismissed them and dropped his completed claim in the box, then watched the horses as they paraded from the ring toward the patient group of escort riders. Sandra slipped her lead around the mare, took control from Otto and ushered Country Girl and Julie onto the track.

The mare kicked at Otto in a last show of defiance then quit bouncing and shoved her nose into Okie's mane, as though relieved to see a barn mate. Except for her washy appearance, nothing indicated she was the unruly animal who had entertained the paddock crowd.

Kurt slipped through the spectators to a spot in front of the grandstand but kept his gaze on Country Girl. Had the mare's behavior sparked Connor's interest? She nursed an uncommon hatred for Otto but Connor had never been much of a horse enthusiast. It was unlikely he'd picked up on her odd behavior.

Kurt blew out a sigh, reluctant to admit he might be guilty of tunnel vision and that perhaps the investigation was off target. The results of a vet check could even shift his focus. He wanted the mare to incriminate Otto, would feel no remorse about nailing such a man, but he needed evidence.

Julie's yellow silks broke away from the parade of horses as she cantered Country Girl past the grandstand. There was a slight hitch in the mare's gait, but no scratches were announced. She'd made it past the track vet.

"Julie's going off at big odds," Adam said as he joined Kurt. "Maybe I should bet on her after all." But his voice had a ragged edge, and his furrowed gaze hung on the moving spot of yellow, tiny now against the stretch of brown dirt.

Kurt scanned his program. Country Girl's form wasn't much worse than the bunch she raced against—fillies and mares, non-winners of three—but her erratic behavior would trouble even the most optimistic of bettors. She still had to face the pressure of the starting gate, normal race jostling as well as the boisterous Friday-night crowd. Otto had the mare cranked so tight she was a bomb waiting to explode.

He swallowed, trying to ease his dry throat, and his gaze shot to the ambulance. It always followed the riders, was usually a reassuring presence, but tonight the sight of the familiar orange and white vehicle only increased his edginess.

"Otto's horse isn't that bad." Adam pulled off his Stetson and a drop of sweat slid along his forehead. "The race is only a sprint. Those bush horses are tough. All she has to do is stay on

her feet. Just get home safe. With her rider. All she has to do."
He wiped his glistening brow and clumsily readjusted his hat.

"Let's watch from the grandstand," Kurt said, unable to
resist the compulsion to view the race from a proven spot. His
superstitions always kicked in when he was helpless to affect the
outcome. Both Julie and Skippy had come home safely when he
watched from section twelve, row eighteen.

They climbed the concrete stairs. Adam turned and checked
over his shoulder every second step. By the time they reached
Kurt's spot, high in the grandstand, the man's brow dripped with
sweat, and he once again readjusted his hat.

"Julie has the outside hole. She'll have to boot and scoot."
Adam's voice cracked. "Or she'll be hung out to dry on the turn.
Damn, I hope that mare will run the hook. One of Otto's horses
crashed through the rail last year. Charged through, never slowed
a step. Jock's still in a wheelchair."

*Jesus, man, be quiet.* "At least the mare won't have to stand in
the gate long," Kurt said through clenched teeth. "That's the last
thing she needs." Adam's face blanched so he quickly added,
"But she seems to have the mare settled now. Settled real good."

Julie's yellow silks disappeared into the last slot, and the gate
crew slammed the door.

"She's in," Adam said, echoing the announcer's words.

The doors burst open.

"Look at that mare blast out," Adam said. "She's going to get
the rail. Atta girl, Julie!"

"Nice," Kurt said as Julie coolly took possession of the rail,
riding as though she had complete faith in her mount. Riding as
though her horse was completely sound.

Fear skidded through Kurt but he shoved it back, afraid the
thought of a fall might cause a jinx. He concentrated on the
churning mass of horses, picturing every one of them with four
good legs, four sound legs, and willing them all to come home
safely.

A chestnut filly charged up and joined Julie on the lead.

"She's second by a neck. Keep that horse outside. Make
them work for it, Julie!" Adam hollered and jumped and
punched his fist.

"Here they come now," Kurt said as horses switched positions along the backstretch. "Bixton is four wide, but shit, he's got her. Look at that move." Bixton was wide on the turn but his chestnut filly cruised past Julie and easily grabbed the lead.

"Julie's still third. Hang in there," Adam said.

At the top of the stretch, Country Girl slogged it out for third, while Bixton's horse drew away from them all.

"Shit, they're coming in a wave. Hang on, baby!" Kurt hollered, not sure if he was calling to Julie or the mare.

Julie switched her whip to the right hand and waved it by Country Girl's eye. The brave mare responded, crossing the finish line and clinging to third by a neck.

Kurt's knees were weak, and he glanced at Adam. "That mare's gutsy. Just like your daughter. She's good, Adam—real good. Hard to watch though."

Adam tilted his hat and wiped his brow, a weary gesture that spoke volumes. "This can't be good for my heart."

"No, it can't be," Kurt said. His own breathing was still ragged. He'd never been so nervous, not even with his first-time starters. He wasn't used to trainers like Otto, pseudo trainers with ill-prepared horses. And riders like Julie, forced to take all the risks.

They trudged down the steps to the rail and waited for the horses. Adam reached in his pocket and hauled out his ticket. Stared at it for an incredulous moment then chuckled, the tension in his face turning to triumph as he brandished the betting stub. "Look at this. I forgot all about the triactor. Hell, that'll pay good. Did you make any money?"

"Haven't cashed a ticket all night," Kurt said. The loudspeakers crackled, announcing that Country Girl had been claimed, and he wryly tapped the halter slung over his shoulder. "But I did claim a horse."

"Otto's mare? But why? Wouldn't the horse Bixton rode be a better claim?"

Kurt didn't like the curious gleam in Adam's eyes but merely shrugged and turned toward the group of pony riders milling on the other side of the rail.

"Hey, Sandra," he called. "Can you lead my new horse back?"

"Yeah, sure. I just heard the claim." She edged Okie closer to the rail, her voice turning reproachful. "Now I know why you hired an escort. You could have told me the truth. It's not like anyone else wanted that mare, and I'm always very discreet. Just don't expect Otto to be happy."

The tote board flashed the payouts. She glanced up, and happiness carved her face. "Oh, God," she breathed, her smile widening. "Color me rich."

Kurt chuckled, enjoying her win as though it were his own. The numbers on the board were huge; Julie was going to be a very popular rider with long-shot bettors. He vaulted over the rail, leaving Sandra and Adam gleefully comparing their winnings. They both had the triactor, and the money was juicy.

Several trainers had already picked up their horses, but Otto was still rooted, holding Country Girl while Julie dismounted. His face strobed from pale to purple when he spotted the halter slung over Kurt's shoulder

"You bastard!" His hammy fist jabbed the air, and tendons corded on his neck. "What the hell do you want with my horse?"

"Watch your language," a voice said as a racing official slipped a red claiming tag on the mare. "Take this horse to the paddock and remove the bridle. Ownership has legally changed."

Otto glowered but stopped talking and yanked at the mare, barely giving Julie time to pull off her saddle. The mare was too exhausted to protest and teetered after Otto, flanks heaving, nostrils pitted with red.

Relief clogged Kurt's throat as he watched the plucky mare struggle to walk. Julie had been lucky. Otto hadn't cared enough to get Country Girl in shape. He'd thrown her in a sprint, hoping the animal would gut it out. This time it had worked.

Kurt turned to follow Otto and the spent mare but Julie's hand stopped him, gentle on his arm.

"That was good of you to claim Otto's horse," she said. Grime streaked her face but her eyes sparkled, and she'd never looked so beautiful. "She's too much of a fighter to get along with Otto. He'd have killed her. It was a nice thing you did."

Her approval pierced him, releasing a groundswell of guilt. If she knew the reason behind the claim, she wouldn't be looking at him with such warmth.

"I'm not here to save abused horses, Julie." His voice was gruff. "It was purely a business decision."

"A business decision. Sure," she said, her eyes luminous, "I know you worried about the mare. You were always watching her."

She smiled then, a brilliant smile, and for a moment he felt like a giant. But he was really just a fraud and when he tried to smile back, the skin on his face felt so tight it cramped his mouth. "You're right," he managed. "I was worried about her. But I'd rather talk about your riding. May I buy you dinner later?"

Her eyes widened in dismay.

"And we can talk about Lazer," he added, determined not to let her brush him off any longer.

"All right." she said slowly. "We're all going to Champs afterwards. It's only a few blocks away."

An official yelled for her to weigh out. She gave Kurt a cautious smile before hurrying to the scales. He crossed his arms and watched her go, fighting his self-loathing. He'd always intended to use Lazer as bait, and his personal regard for Julie didn't change a thing. He needed private time with her, time away from the track, and socializing with her was the quickest way. If she thought he was a nice guy, that really wasn't his fault.

But he had a sour taste in his mouth when he joined Otto in the paddock.

"What took you so fucking long?" Otto yanked the bridle off, rattling the mare's teeth. She flattened her ears at the callous treatment. Her nostrils still flared, but her respiration had steadied, her lungs no longer desperate for air, and she looked to be rallying for another battle.

Kurt quickly buckled the halter, afraid he would have a tiger on his hands if he didn't get the mare away from Otto.

"I'll take good care of her," he said, although it was doubtful Otto even cared. He led Country Girl to Sandra, who watched the exchange with open interest. Kurt winked as he passed her the line, but Sandra looked at Otto's dark face and prudently held her wisecracks.

Kurt trailed Sandra along the walkway to the barn, his smuggling suspicions reinforced by Otto's anger. Otto could claim a better horse with the money received for Country Girl, so it appeared the mare's value was measured by much more than just racing. At last, it seemed, there was some headway in the case.

# CHAPTER THIRTEEN

"The walk back was easier than the walk over." Sandra gave Kurt a saucy grin as she flipped him the mare's lead line. "Just what you need, a hot woman to spice up your life." Laughing, she wheeled her horse and trotted back to the paddock.

The mare twisted at Okie's desertion and gave an ear-blasting whinny.

"It's okay, sweetie," Kurt said. "New owner, new deal."

She trembled, reluctant to enter the barn. He waited. She lowered her head, took a tentative step then stopped, her liquid eyes seeming to peer into his soul. Finally she gave a weary shudder and followed him down the aisle.

He led her into the airy box stall next to Cisco where she sniffed at the generous straw, stuck her head out the window then buried her nose in the sweet hay. He lingered by the door, watching her eat, enjoying her contentment but concerned by her appearance.

Her ribs were visible, her neck and hindquarters hollow, and she clearly wasn't used to regular meals. A few weeks at Adam's ranch should add some weight. Give her a fresh outlook on life. The mental vacation alone—

The mare wheeled, ears flattened. He jumped back as her rear hooves smashed against the stall door. Christ! She'd almost nailed him. Maybe she *was* beyond help. She looked enraged now, like the horse he'd seen in the paddock, like she was when Otto was near.

Understanding slammed him, and he twisted, leaping sideways as a shovel whipped the air. It missed his shoulder by scant inches. The steel clanged from its lethal impact on the concrete.

Kurt stared at Otto, stunned by the ferocity of his attack. The man's lips curled, exposing a darkened tongue and a ridge of stained fillings. "Teach you to fuck with my stuff!" Otto pulled the shovel over his shoulder, holding it like a baseball bat. His face contorted, and he swung again.

Christ!

Kurt dodged but not quickly enough. Numbing pain shot down his arm. Adrenaline charged him, and he dove under Otto's arms, grabbed the wooden handle and rammed the butt into Otto's throat.

*Woof!* Otto grunted with pain but bulled forward and locked his arms around Kurt's neck. Kurt buried a flurry of fists in Otto's stomach but couldn't loosen the chokehold.

They did a macabre waltz around the aisle, slamming into stall fronts, sending horses scrambling. Kurt's lungs ached for air; he struggled to breathe. Desperate, he head-butted Otto then drove his fist into the man's jaw. The big hands loosened, and he wrenched free. He kicked Otto's legs out as gasping breaths stuck in his throat.

Otto rose, grinning and confident in his strength. Lowered his head and charged.

*The guy is nuts.* The knowledge fuelled Kurt, sweeping aside his reluctance to fight and perhaps draw a suspension. Fuck it. He wanted to do some damage of his own. He held his ground and rammed his boot into Otto's face, then jabbed three brutal kicks to his stomach. Otto dropped to his knees, sputtering.

"What the hell is going on?"

Kurt wheeled toward the voice, still in a crouch, still punchy with fight. Nick. The farrier shook his head with disgust and smacked a long metal rasp against his leather apron.

"Shoeing horses is hard enough without grown men leaping like apes. Scaring them." Nick twirled his rasp with the authority of a nightstick. "I suggest you take your argument off track, or I'll call security."

"Sorry." Kurt straightened, pulling back his control. The last thing he wanted was for Otto to be suspended; he needed the man close. But pain seared his throat, and it was hard to speak. "Everything's fine," he managed. "A small disagreement but Otto and I are...finished. Right, Otto?"

Otto scowled. A bruise darkened his chin but he opened and closed his fists, clearly less than finished.

The barn turned eerily quiet. Even the horses watched, unmoving, their ears pricked toward the three men. Kurt heard his own breathing, still rough, as he balanced on the balls of his feet. But this time he was ready.

Nick stepped forward and stood beside him, a stalwart force with a big rasp.

Otto jerked back. Cursed and stalked from the barn.

Nick chuckled. "Looks like you licked the red off his candy. Better watch your back though. He's an odd one."

"Thanks, Nick," Kurt said simply.

The farrier nodded, but his expression turned pensive as he eyed the shovel and the fresh groove cut in the floor. "Don't expect Otto to play fair. He's built like a gorilla but not quite as smart."

Behind them, Country Girl churned in her stall, poking her head over the door, staring, then circling again.

"It's okay, sweetie," Kurt said. "He can't hurt you anymore."

"What's wrong with that horse?" Nick asked as he picked up the shovel and propped it against the wall.

"Don't know. I just claimed her from Otto, but she gets upset when he's around. Her reaction saved me tonight."

"You bought a cheap claimer?" Nick shook his head and slipped his rasp in the long side pocket of his apron. "Thought you Woodbine guys were strictly big league."

"I run all types, and she did come third tonight." Kurt paused, sensing the farrier was the type who liked to fix things. "Even with messed-up feet," he added.

"Messed-up feet?"

"Yeah." Kurt nodded. "And she sure could use an expert."

Nick rolled his eyes but gestured at Country Girl. "Quit the sweet talk and bring her out. Horse deserves a break if she's been with Otto very long. The man insists on doing his own shoeing. Always fucks it up."

Kurt led Country Girl into the aisle. Nick ran his hands down her front legs. The mare trembled but lifted her feet, making no objection to Nick's attention, and Kurt's opinion of her intelligence rose another notch.

"Not so bad." Nick crouched, eyeballing her left hoof. "The angles are off, and the toe should be shorter."

"Check her hind end."

Nick bent over the mare's back legs then rose and stared at Kurt with a bleak expression. "Sorry, but you can't race this mare for a while. Looks like she was the practice horse at Farrier School, and every kid took a turn with the hammer. Let's see how she moves."

Kurt led the mare down the aisle. Her hooves clicked as Nick stroked his chin and watched.

"Okay, that's enough," Nick said. "Bring her back."

He slid his hand along her left fetlock and lifted her leg. Lines fanned the edges of his eyes as he stared at her hoof. He spoke slowly, almost to himself. "Looks like she was shod three or four times over the last couple of weeks. Dry feet, couple quarter cracks. The wall is weak, damaged from all the nails. But the aluminum racing plates she wears now aren't the same shoes she had earlier. Those shoes were heavier and needed bigger nails."

When he pressed her sole, the mare flinched and tried to pull away, but Nick kept a firm grip on her leg. "I think she had rubber pads on her back feet." Nick glanced at Kurt. "Her soles are mushy, like they've been covered for a while. Dump some iodine on them. If she ran a third with these kind of feet, she's brave enough. I'll pull these shoes off now. She'll heal faster barefoot." His voice lowered as he expertly cut the nails and removed all four shoes.

Kurt stepped closer, eager to hear every word this gentle man said.

"Her angles are screwed up," Nick continued. "I think the other shoes were too thick, and she pulled some ligaments. She moves stiff, like a girl wearing high heels too long. There shouldn't be any permanent damage though. Her tendons aren't bowed. Damn lucky." He rose and flipped the old shoes at Kurt.

"Those weren't put on by an expert. Some of the nails were a little high. It's a wonder she let me handle her feet at all."

Kurt studied the aluminum shoes while he mulled over Nick's comments. Nothing odd about these. However, it *was* odd to use heavy steel shoes on a racehorse. He felt Nick's curious gaze and gave a quick shrug. "Thanks for looking at her," he said. "She's leaving the track tomorrow, but I have two other horses that need shoeing. Think you can do them?"

"Yeah, I'll pencil them in somewhere. Working nights is a bitch, but it means a new truck by fall." He headed down the aisle but paused and swung around, his eyes alight with interest. "I'd like to see the shoes on Otto's next horse. Maybe they have a new trick south of the border. They're always experimenting with ways to make their horses run faster."

"Otto was probably trying to save money," Kurt said quickly.

Nick only shrugged and turned away.

Kurt watched until he faded into the far recesses of the barn, until he could no longer see Nick's outline, could only hear the solitary tapping of his hammer and the humming of a melancholy tune.

The announcer's voice crackled over the barn speakers. Two races left. Kurt walked to the front of Otto's now vacant stall. According to the police report, Connor had stood in this exact same spot. Talking to Julie. Looking for Otto.

But why?

Otto's frustrated attack confirmed the mare was the link. So far though, all Kurt had discovered was a bad shoeing job.

Shaking his head, he carried the shoes into his tack room and powered up his laptop. The keyboard clicked as he finalized his report to Archer and stressed the need for a border alert. The thought of Otto's heated reception the next time he entered Canada filled Kurt with perverse pleasure.

Laughter and shouts rocked the barn, so he shoved the laptop back into his briefcase and stepped into the aisle.

"Hey! Join the celebration." A grinning Sandra yanked a can of beer from a dented blue cooler and lobbed it in the air.

"Did someone win a race?" He snagged the beer and snapped open the tab. Beer foamed over the top, and he covered it with his mouth, savoring the taste.

"You don't have to win to make money," Sandra'said. "I'm up three hundred and seventy-two dollars from betting, and I ponied every race. So it's a big payday. Help yourself, Martin." She shoved the cooler toward Martin with the side of her boot.

"Whoa," Kurt said. "How old are you, Martin?"

Martin's hand stalled over the cooler. "Almost fifteen," he mumbled, averting his eyes.

Sandra's mouth straightened in displeasure. "Martin can have a drink. There's no damn cop around. And it's my beer."

"And he's my employee," Kurt said.

Martin's shoulders slumped and he lowered his hand. Kurt felt his disappointment; nothing tasted better than a cold beer after a day of dust, dirt and horses, but Jesus, he wasn't even fifteen. And the kid already had social problems.

Kurt glanced at Sandra who cocked her head and glared, as though they'd just entered into an undeclared power contest.

"You don't look the type to care about a little alcohol," Sandra said, her eyes narrowing. "Quite the opposite. And there's no reason to worry about Martin. His mother is a close friend of mine. They live walking distance from here."

Everyone seemed to be a close friend of Sandra's, and Kurt didn't like the speculative gleam in her eyes. Didn't want her natural nosiness turned on him. Sometimes he felt like he had 'cop' tattooed on his forehead.

"One beer, Martin," he said. "But make sure you feed on time in the morning. And I'll drive you home."

"We'll walk him home," Sandra said, clearly unwilling to relinquish her hard-earned status as boss mare. "It's on the way to the pub. Grab a cold one, Martin."

Martin needed no second invite. He pulled a beer from the cooler and popped the lid. His throat gurgled as he drained half the can. Kurt had an ugly image of young drivers and car crashes and resolved to make sure the kid got home safely, regardless of what Sandra said.

And maybe he could meet Martin's mom. He didn't intend to get involved with the people here—never did when he worked a case, not anymore—but Martin was like a sponge and if he wanted a career at the track, there were a few programs that could be helpful.

Awareness crackled through him seconds before he heard Julie's voice, and his pulse quickened. He turned toward her but could only gape.

She swept down the aisle, looking vastly different from the rider he saw every morning, hidden behind a helmet and vest. Tonight, jeans hugged her hips—his hands could probably span her waist—and a white shirt scooped over her breasts. Lovely, full breasts. He took a hard gulp.

Her hair swirled loose, freed from the usual ponytail, and it gleamed under the lights. No obvious makeup other than a hint of lipstick, but her skin was flawless and those killer cheekbones were free of dirt. Nothing fancy, just jeans and a shirt, but her feminine curves made him drool. Christ, he had it bad.

He fumbled a greeting, somewhat mollified to see Martin's eyes had also bugged. The kid even spilled some of his precious beer.

"Julie!" Sandra called, raising her can. "Thanks to you, Okie will get a new pair of wraps. Your dad and I made a chunk of money. Sadly, Kurt wasn't a believer and missed out." She spoke with the smug tone of one who'd successfully backed a long shot.

Julie glanced at Kurt, her gaze steady.

"I had faith in you," he said, "just not enough in your horses. You did a great job tonight."

He realized belatedly his voice sounded gruff, but no one else seemed to notice. Martin had straightened his beer and now pretended to be studying the small print on the can. Kurt wasn't fooled. He saw the kid peeking at Julie. Didn't blame him a bit.

Sandra pressed a beer into Julie's hand. "I saved the last can for you. What a night. A second and third. Gary was so surprised when you passed him, he nearly fell off. And did you see Otto's face when Kurt claimed his horse?"

Sandra did a series of imitations, grimacing and pumping her fists, making everyone laugh, but Kurt was too distracted to pay much attention. His thoughts had already veered back to Sandra's comments about Julie. She didn't date much, but Sandra hadn't said why.

Probably because she didn't want a demanding relationship. He totally understood that. In fact, Julie's position suited him perfectly—he was only here for a short time anyway. His gaze kept sliding back to her. She was looking at Sandra but kept glancing at him. When he winked, she flushed and looked away, but he caught the hint of a dimple.

"Okay. Beer's gone." Sandra abruptly rose, and he suspected she'd caught their glances. Cans clattered as she tossed the empties into the cooler. "Time to get to Champs. If we hurry, we'll catch happy hour."

"I'll meet you over there," Kurt said, looking at Julie. "I need to stay a bit and settle the new mare. She's still hot."

"We'll see you later," Sandra said, grabbing Julie's arm and tugging her down the aisle. "Martin can give you directions to the bar," she called over her shoulder.

Sandra would make an excellent drill sergeant, Kurt thought. Without Julie, the barn had lost some sparkle, but at least he was alone for the next ten minutes. He needed to take some cautionary measures.

He turned to Martin. "I'm moving Lazer to the stallion stall further down the aisle. Please put Ace beside him, and Cisco can go in the stall on the other side of Country Girl."

Martin grabbed Ace's halter, his tone apologetic. "Does the new stall have a bigger window? I didn't notice the mare was hot."

"She's fine." Kurt hesitated, but the kid looked truly concerned. "I want to switch horses in case Otto holds a grudge. He'd recognize Country Girl in a line-up but probably can't pick out my other horses. Not if they're in different stalls."

Martin's eyes widened. "You think he'd deliberately hurt them?"

"It's just a precaution," Kurt said. "Otto was upset when I claimed his mare. He's probably calmed down now. It's just a precaution."

But as he repeated the words, he had the unsettling notion he was really trying to reassure himself.

# CHAPTER FOURTEEN

A swinging sign with large black letters proclaimed 'Champs Bar, Where Winners Meet.' Kurt pushed open the heavy door and stepped into a room swollen with conversation, laughter and the yeasty smell of beer. Clearly a track hangout, racing pictures decorated every inch of wall. A dartboard hung in a mock winner's circle. It wasn't the type of bar that had a dance floor.

Sandra's purple shirt was visible at a table on the far side, and he strained to see her companion. Not Julie, a man. Looked like Gary Bixton. Good. He wanted to talk to Julie alone, away from Sandra and her troublesome mother-hen tendencies.

He spotted Julie perched on a bar stool next to a cowboy in a red striped shirt. He moved in, ignoring the man's resentful frown.

"Hi, Julie." He kept his voice low, using the background noise as an excuse to dip his head close and absorb her fresh smell of sunshine and flowers. She tilted her head, her smile much wider than it had been in the barn. Obviously she was keen to discuss Lazer. Regret pricked him—her warm welcome was based on his horse.

"I thought maybe you couldn't find the place," she said, still gracing him with that big smile. "You must be hungry."

"Starving. I stopped to talk to Martin's mother for a minute." Kurt took the menu she passed him, stared down the cowboy in the striped shirt and further staked his territory by wedging his knee against Julie's stool. "What's good here?"

"The pictures." She shot him a teasing grin. "But if you're starving, everything tastes good." Her laugh was throaty, and he automatically leaned closer. She made a half-hearted effort to straighten her stool, but his leg kept it locked. "Maybe we should move to the table with Sandra and Gary." She pointed across the room. "There'd be more room to eat."

Her gesture lacked its usual grace, and when her hand brushed his chest, she jerked her fingers back. His gaze narrowed, automatically assessing her condition. Bright cheeks, flushed eyes, somewhat inebriated. Perfect. She was tiny and didn't eat before a race. Naturally, alcohol would have a big effect.

It would be simple to ply her with another beer before ordering food. Maybe even switch to something more potent. He'd been trained to encourage people to drink, then listen when they blabbed, but that idea seemed repugnant now. It was hard to be a total asshole with someone like her. One thing was certain though; they were *not* going to move to Sandra's table.

"We can move to a table later," he said. "Food service will be faster here." He leaned over the bar and gestured at a waiter, deliberately brushing his arm over Julie's shoulder, testing her reaction. A shiver of awareness. All good.

"It's good to see you off track," he said, leaving his arm so close he could feel her heat. "You work both sides of the clock."

She swiveled on her stool, and he could smell her skin again or maybe it was her hair. Whatever it was, he liked it.

"It's not work," she said. "Being paid to ride is a dream. I wanted to do that since I was four." She brushed her hair back. Like him, she wore no ring.

"It's probably harder to be a trainer," she added. "You have to attract owners, just like I'm trying to attract trainers." Her eyes widened. "I didn't mean it like that," she said quickly. "Not that you're running around trying to attract owners. Or that I'm trying to attract trainers. Well, of course, I suppose I am—"

She bit her bottom lip and looked so flustered he squeezed her hand. "Already done," he said.

"What?" she asked. "What's already done?"

"Attracted."

"Want the usual, Julie?" A waiter with a shaved head and protruding ears appeared, brandishing his order sheet and a stubby brown pencil.

She grabbed the diversion like a lifeline, ignoring Kurt's comment as she turned her attention to the waiter. He listened to her order, noted her too-careful enunciation. She reminded him of a drunk at a breathalyzer. Obviously she'd had several drinks before he'd arrived, in addition to the beer at the barn.

Convenient, of course. But he didn't want her wasted. Sometimes witnesses tried so hard to remember that they conjured up things, even padding stories to please their interrogator.

Not that Julie would lie. And he didn't like to think of himself as an interrogator. This could be as pleasant as she let him make it. But there simply wasn't much sense in loading her with liquor—relaxed and talkative was all he wanted.

He listened while she talked with the waiter, and it was apparent the guy was smitten, asking if she wanted her fries crisp or her bun toasted. Kurt's mouth tightened. It shouldn't take that long to jot down an order, although maybe she was the one prolonging the conversation. Maybe she wanted to avoid being alone with him.

He took a thoughtful sip of beer. There was no way she could have guessed he was a cop. Archer was anal about secrecy, and only close friends and family knew the kind of work Kurt had been doing. The race world thought he'd spent the last nine years working at an obscure breeding farm. Still, the Internet was pesky.

The waiter must have realized he couldn't linger by Julie any longer and reluctantly moved on to Kurt. "What 'cha want?" he asked. He didn't mention the three kinds of cole slaw or the sweet potato fries.

Kurt gave his order to the disinterested waiter. "Better hold the onions," he added with a pointed glance at Julie.

The waiter frowned as he walked away, and Julie elbowed Kurt in the ribs. "Double onions for me," she called, not missing a beat.

"Ouch." Kurt gave her his best hurting smile, perfect for skittish women. An old girlfriend once said it made her want to take him home, feed him chicken soup then bonk his brains out.

It didn't seem to have the same effect on Julie—she rolled her eyes. "Stop teasing the waiter. He's always a big flirt. Not that it matters." Her voice trailed off.

"Of course it matters," Kurt said. "This is the third time I asked you out. I don't like to share."

"I don't remember being asked out. And this is just grabbing something to eat, a meeting to talk about Lazer." She crossed her arms. "That's all it can be."

There was a finality in her voice, and he leaned forward, genuinely puzzled. He liked her, and she may not have realized it, but she'd touched him three times tonight. Dinner, a few drinks, some pleasant company. He didn't understand why it was such a big deal.

He mentally reviewed her file. Single. Her mother, also a jockey, had been killed in a car accident. Julie had never been married, and the researcher hadn't dug up a boyfriend. But something made her ball her napkin in agitation.

She tossed the paper wad at his chest, eyes sparkling with such mischief he decided he was over-analyzing. "Good catch," she said as he grabbed the napkin in midair. "And this is a meeting. And I'm paying for my own food. So don't lay on the charm or tease about onions. Gosh, you Eastern trainers are cocky." A smile softened her words, but her back had straightened, and her chin had a challenging tilt.

Best to lighten things up. The last thing he needed was to stir her stubborn streak. And, of course, he already had something she really wanted. Something she wanted desperately.

"Not cocky at all," he said mildly, "but there are certain Eastern traditions that must be observed. Especially the one that says a jockey must let her trainer pay for dinner."

"Really?" Her eyes widened. "You're kidding? I'm riding Lazer?"

Something kicked in his chest. Her happiness was infectious, and he didn't feel quite so battered and chewed up. "I liked the job you did tonight," he said gruffly. "You held your ground but weren't dangerously aggressive. You knew when each horse was giving all they had. It was good riding. Smart riding. And, yeah, I want you to be Lazer's jockey."

She was almost hopping on her stool now, but her leg was touching his, so he wasn't going to complain. "It's nice of you to give me this chance," she said. "I've never ridden a good horse before."

"Julie, don't tell a trainer that. And don't admit you're new, like you did with me the first day. Fake it until you make it." He couldn't stop grinning. My God, she was sweet. After years of working with creeps and scum and everything in between, it was refreshing to be around someone so utterly honest.

He slipped a hand around her hip and gave an impulsive hug. She didn't pull away, probably still distracted about Lazer, so he left his arm draped around her, wanting to feel her reaction to his next question.

"Speaking of trainers," he said, watching her face, "I heard a friend of Otto's was murdered last week. Did you ever meet the guy?"

She nodded, but he felt no telltale stiffening. Nothing she wanted to hide. "Yes. I talked to him in the barn. The police said I was the last one to see him alive."

Heaping plates were slammed on the counter in front of them. The smell of fried food, after a diet of coffee, bagels and sandwiches, made his mouth water.

"Enjoy," the waiter said as he plunked salt, ketchup and two kinds of spicy sauce in front of Julie. Kurt received a plastic fork.

Julie looked at Kurt, and her dimples flashed. "Since this has been such an excellent meeting," she said, "I'll share my ketchup."

"A deal," he said wryly, wishing the food hadn't come just as she was talking about Connor. Still, they were both hungry. Better to finish this conversation later and let her eat in peace.

She bit into her thick, dripping hamburger without a touch of reservation. He liked that and turned to his own food. The burger was big, delicious and filling. He left half his fries, watching in surprise as she continued to eat.

"Guess you didn't have lunch," he said ruefully.

"Or breakfast. Too nervous to eat." She paused, mid-bite, slanting him with a conspiratorial smile. "Guess I shouldn't

106

admit to nerves either. Fake it until you make it, isn't that what you say?"

"No, Julie," he said quietly. "Don't change a thing." He liked everything about her—her honesty, her dedication, even her temper, and he also liked the sensuous way her mouth moved as she enjoyed her food.

"So," he said impulsively, "we should have another meeting tomorrow. You can show me one of Calgary's famous steakhouses."

Her eyes darkened, and he was certain he saw regret. "I'm sorry." Her voice lowered. "We both know it's stupid to mix business with pleasure. Even though you're horribly attractive." She stopped talking and even under the muted lights, he could see her cheeks flush.

"Don't stop now," he said. "I like that word." He also liked her company. All in all, he was very much enjoying the evening.

"What word?" She gave a hopeful smile. "Horribly?"

"No. The other word."

"Attractive then." She waved her fork, dangerously close to her eye, not seeming to notice when he gently guided it away from her face. "But men and horses always look better after a few beer, and I really do prefer horses right now. No time for anything else."

"Maybe you should consider time optimization," he said, feeling his mouth twitch. "Men and horses, together at the track. You can use me for a test drive, kind of like a morning gallop."

She laughed and bit the end of a fry. "You like teasing, don't you. I didn't see that when we first met." Her nose crinkled in memory, and she tilted her head. "Actually, you were different, harder."

"Really?" He forced an exaggerated chuckle, somewhat irked she'd picked up on his earlier mindset, back when he'd been suspicious of her involvement. It was odd she could read him so well. She was fresh, unspoiled, but like her dad, rather astute. Something he needed to remember.

She was also intoxicated and shouldn't be driving. It took her three attempts to spear the last fry, but she chased it around the plate with single-minded determination.

"I can drive you home tonight," he said, watching her fork with concern. "I just have to pick my truck up at the barn."

"Thanks, but there's no need. I'm staying at Sandra's."

His disappointment rocked him. And he needed to get back on focus. This was about Connor, not about his own interest in an attractive woman, a woman who regrettably was more interested in horses than men.

"I talked to your dad about hauling Otto's mare tomorrow," he said. "He thought it'd be a nice day to ride in the mountains. Can you show me where your place is? Maybe guide me around after? I can bring Cisco."

"Sure." She wiped her mouth and absently pushed her empty plate toward the lurking waiter. "A trail ride would be fun." Her eyes narrowed as she tried to peer over his shoulder. "I wonder where everyone is? I haven't seen Sandra all night."

He shrugged but wasn't surprised. His arm draped the back of her chair, his hip moored her stool and the hardy souls who had ventured in her direction had been deterred by his flat stare. Even the cowboy had moved on. He lifted his hand and traced a path across her smooth cheek. "You have a bit of ketchup, right there." He wiped the fictitious spot, watched her eyes and the way she looked at him. Could feel her slight shiver.

"It's late." Sandra's voice was sudden and authoritative. "We gotta go."

Julie jerked back. He lowered his hand, smoothing his expression before turning toward Sandra, surprised he hadn't noticed her approach. "It's not that late," he said.

"Close to midnight, and we peasants have to get up early." Sandra crossed her arms, looking at them both with an amused expression. "Do you still want your two-year-old ponied tomorrow?"

"Please," he said. "I'm hauling the new mare after Julie gallops Lazer." He picked up the bill, stilling Julie's hand as she reached for her purse. "I'm paying," he said softly. "It was just a dinner meeting."

She let him take care of the bill, and he figured it was a major accomplishment. "Do you need a drive?" he added.

"No," Sandra interrupted, her voice loud as she gestured in an indeterminate direction. "We're walking. It's only a couple blocks west. Gary's staying at my place too."

Kurt digested that news as they walked toward the door. He wanted to see Julie home. Conversation was beginning to flow, and it was painfully difficult to talk to her at the track.

He pulled open the door, holding it open for both ladies, then followed them outside. A lithe shadow unfolded from the wall. Bixton.

"Congratulations," Kurt said, remembering Bixton had ridden three winners earlier that evening, a laudable feat at any track.

"Thanks, but Julie is the real star," Bixton said. "She didn't have much horsepower but got both her mounts up for a piece of the money." He looped his arm around Julie, his teeth gleaming wolfishly under the streetlight. "You rode smart, Jules. But a couple things need improving. We can discuss riding strategy at Sandra's."

Julie turned toward Kurt, calling out a goodbye even as Gary propelled her down the sidewalk. Their conversation shifted to talk of whips, the best time to switch hands and then Kurt could no longer hear their actual words, only her low laugh.

His jaw clamped as he watched her walk away.

"Jocks always rehash each race." Sandra blew out a sigh. "And it's *your* fault they didn't have a chance to talk earlier. Now they'll keep me up all night."

She pointed in the opposite direction. "That's the fastest way to your motel. Two blocks, then cut through the first alley. No one in his right mind would try to mug you. Especially the way you're scowling." She grinned but not unkindly. "See you tomorrow, dark and early."

She hurried off in the direction of her friends, leaving him unclenching his jaw and feeling like someone had just claimed his favorite horse. This sucked. He'd noticed Bixton flirting happily with almost every girl in the bar, yet somehow the nimble jockey had snagged Julie right off his arm.

Obviously Julie and Bixton had some sort of relationship, albeit a loose one. He could just imagine the type of riding strategy they'd be discussing. A steamy image of Bixton with Julie made his chest kick.

He rammed his hands in his pockets, wheeled and headed toward his motel, searching for a positive note. He'd turned up goose eggs tonight, but at least when he'd mentioned Connor, she hadn't been evasive. And though she professed not to date, she clearly had some time for men. Understandably, she avoided demanding relationships, didn't want anything to interfere with her career.

All fine with him. He only needed a little chunk of time anyway, just enough to chat her up. And tomorrow they would be alone—no distractions, no interruptions, no Bixton.

Equanimity restored, he cut across the gravel to his motel. Reached in his pocket, searching for his room card but paused, hit with a familiar sense of danger. Something was different.

He stilled, staring at the unit window. The curtains had been closed when he left, but now a two-inch gap loomed. And the room was dark. He'd left the desk lamp on.

A horn blasted from the street and he jerked, his reaction intensified by his rushing adrenaline. From the adjoining room, a television droned. Its whitish light cast surreal shadows. He flexed his hands, focusing on his own room.

It was silent. But maybe not empty.

He eased onto the shadowed walkway that fronted the motel, his mind scrambling. It was unlikely the cleaning staff had made a second visit today. But someone had been in his room. Otto? Or perhaps the person who'd shot Connor? He doubted it was Otto who had pulled the trigger. Otto was the type to use his fists; Connor hadn't had a mark on him other than the bullet holes.

Kurt lingered in the shadows, questioning his instincts, trying to soothe his innate wariness. So far, he'd played everything low key. A few questions to Julie, but nothing that would connect him to Connor. Unless someone had burned him.

The air was crisp, but sweat beaded on his forehead as he remembered another job, another surprise. Of course, that debacle had been his fault. A little pillow talk with Anne Marie, and his identity had been blown.

But there was no gang and no Anne Marie. Archer and his assistant were his only contacts, and Archer didn't make mistakes.

Kurt's heart thudded more evenly. His breathing steadied. Besides, whoever was in there was sloppy.

He edged to the door, watching the folds of the curtains. Nothing moved.

The door to the motel office slammed. Someone laughed. Steps jolted along the walkway. He grabbed the diversion, eased back then tramped forward and rapped on his own door.

"Pizza's here!" he called.

No response. *Knock, knock.* Nothing.

He fingered the doorknob. It skewed uselessly in his hand, the deep grooves rough beneath his fingers. Clearly not an ambush. He shoved the door open with his foot, reached in and switched on the light.

Goddammit! The room was a shambles of clothing, plastic and glass. He stepped over the television cord, covered with shiny shards of glass, and checked the room—bathroom, closet, beneath the bed.

Empty.

He scooped up a leather sleeve, torn from his jacket. A pair of jeans was intact but his suitcase had been split, the hinges broken. He tossed the clothing aside and moved into the bathroom.

Glass, remnants of the mirror above the sink, crunched beneath his boots. His toothbrush and container of allergy tablets floated in the toilet. A wad of tobacco left a streaky trail and clumped on the tiles, a calling card left to taunt.

Damn. Otto was one crazy fucker.

Kurt gritted his teeth as he bent over and scraped the tobacco into a plastic bag. An intrusion always felt personal, but at least the damage was minimal.

Obviously the mare was the trigger, and Otto was unraveling. Besides, he told himself, no real harm had been done. His gun and briefcase were locked in the room safe, and his laptop was in the truck. He had nothing else of value.

Oh, Christ. He jerked upright. The horses! His innocent, unprotected horses.

He sprinted to the motel office and reported the break-in, fielding the clerk's questions with brusque replies. No, he had no idea who'd trashed his room. No, nothing was stolen. The flustered night clerk passed him a blue garbage bag and called the police.

Kurt rushed back to his room, scooped up some clothes and the gooey tobacco evidence. Stuffed them in the bag, tossed it over his shoulder and ran toward the track.

"Gathering trash?" the guard in the security booth asked with a snide snicker.

Kurt didn't answer. Wasn't in the mood for jokes and didn't like the man's attitude. This guard wasn't the pale-faced skinny kid, but a paunchy guy with a tired uniform and the bored expression of someone who didn't like his job.

Kurt flipped his pass out, hurrying, yet trying to control his dread. The horses were fine. Just fine.

"So many people chugging back and forth. Don't understand how those overpriced animals get any sleep. What'cha doing here so late anyway?" The guard tilted back in his chair and fiddled with Kurt's credentials.

"Let's hurry it up," Kurt said softly.

The guard started to protest but saw something in Kurt's expression and pressed his mouth shut. He shoved the ID through the grill and started writing, suddenly occupied with paperwork. "Go on," he muttered.

Kurt jogged to G barn. The pathway seemed darker, lonelier. His stomach churned with apprehension. He shouldn't have left the horses alone. Should have done more than switch stalls. Should have guessed Otto was unstable.

He controlled his urge to barge into the barn and paused outside the door. Heard nothing but the benign chewing of hay and a restless horse shuffling in the straw.

He walked down the dim aisle. A few animals poked their heads over their doors, watching with curious eyes. He blew out a sigh of relief when he stepped on some hoof trimmings that dotted the floor. Nick must have been shoeing late. Good old Nick. The horses hadn't been alone for long.

He headed toward Cisco's stall—his least expensive horse but the most precious— searching for the App's wide forehead, his intelligent eyes. Couldn't see him and Kurt's breath caught. But when he leaned over the door, there was Cisco, lying in the straw, eyes placid and heavy with sleep.

Cisco flicked his ears when he saw Kurt, as if questioning his presence at such a late hour, and debating if he should get up. Kurt edged away, weak with relief, not wanting to disturb him.

He visited each horse. All were fine. Lazer, Ace and Otto's mare were on their feet but blinking and groggy with sleep. He checked their pulse, listened to the familiar rumbling of their gut. Everything was normal—no colic, stress or injury. Even the mare was content, surprising him with a low nicker.

The tightness in his shoulders eased, replaced with a bone-aching tiredness. He unlocked his tack room and stretched on the cot. The mattress was thin and lumpy, but the horse blanket was soft and warm. Slowly his mind settled.

It hadn't been such a bad night. With a couple nudges, everything was now rolling. Otto was losing his cool, bound to make a key mistake, and tomorrow Julie might provide insight as to why Connor had followed Otto.

He would have the whole day to work with her, just the two of them. All alone. He hoped they would get along very well.

# CHAPTER FIFTEEN

Clanging buckets prodded Kurt awake. Someone shouted, and hungry horses nickered and stomped as they called for breakfast. He hauled the blanket over his head, blocked out the noise and went back to sleep.

He didn't know how much longer he dozed, but persistent knocking jerked him out of a deep sleep.

"Kurt, you in there?"

He muttered, the words unintelligible even to him. Sandra's voice poked at him from beyond the door. "Want me to pony Lazer too? Julie has a headache."

He jerked awake, surprised he'd slept through the feeding racket. Rose, yawning, and opened the door. "Morning, Sandra. You finished with Ace already?"

"Yup. Martin got him ready." Her gaze swept his chest and she gave a saucy wolf whistle. "Yum. Enough muscles to make a girl like me stutter."

He scooped his shirt from the floor and yanked his arms into the sleeves.

"Don't worry." She rolled her eyes. "I'm too tired to jump you. Gary and Julie kept me up way too late. Now please hurry. I want to go home and grab some sleep."

He fumbled with his shirt, still groggy and feeling slightly out of synch. He was also intensely curious as to Julie and Gary's relationship. Not technically any of his business, of course, but one never knew when little details might help a case.

He followed her into the aisle, still tucking in his shirt. "Where's Julie now?" he asked. "She's supposed to show me the way to her dad's ranch."

"Dunno. I banged on their door earlier this morning, but they didn't get up. They're probably mainlining coffee in the kitchen now. Neither of them can hold their liquor, not like me." Her smile was smug. "Come on. Get your horse ready. Or should I ask Martin to do it?"

"No, I'm coming," he muttered, hoping his dismay over their sleeping arrangements didn't show. He readied Lazer and led him down the aisle to Sandra. "I put a bridle on him in case he gets strong."

"Okie and I can handle him," she said. "You want a mile and a half?"

"Two. And give him a shot down the lane."

He followed her to the gap, watching as Sandra guided Lazer onto the track. The colt bit at Okie's neck, but Sandra snapped his nose, and he straightened with an air of resignation. Clearly Lazer was in capable hands.

Kurt turned and walked to the kitchen. He bought a coffee and leaned against the counter, scowling and surly. Spotted the two jockeys nestled in the corner, heads pressed together over a large carafe of coffee.

He weaved through a cluster of people. "Good morning," he said, addressing them both but looking at Julie. Dark shadows lined her eyes, and he couldn't resist adding, "Late night, I hear?"

She glanced up, her smile fading when she saw his face. He knew his mean look was intimidating but hell, he felt mean. He told himself it wasn't her chumminess with Bixton that bothered him, more that she was hindering his job. Yanking his chain.

"Want me to gallop Lazer now?" She picked up her vest from the empty chair, but her enthusiasm was clearly forced, and she looked pale.

"Nope," he said. "Sandra's looking after him." Julie shouldn't be galloping horses anyway. Not today. Christ, she looked exhausted. "You okay?" He softened his voice.

"Perfect."

He raised an eyebrow.

"My stomach's a little queasy," she added, "but not too bad. I don't usually drink like that. But we were celebrating." Her gaze drifted to Bixton, who gave her an indulgent wink.

Kurt stiffened, resenting that wink, resenting Bixton's satisfied smile. He usually didn't begrudge another guy's action, but it wasn't surprising the man always looked so damn happy.

Bixton pushed back his chair and rose, still wearing that satisfied expression. "Glad I'm no apprentice," he said. "My head hurts too much to be bounced around by a horse. I'm going home to sleep this off. Sorry you can't come with me, Jules." He gave her shoulder a possessive squeeze.

He sauntered toward the door but was only halfway across the room before a brunette in a cropped shirt and skin-tight jeans grabbed him. Julie seemed totally accepting of his defection, even as the girl tugged Bixton into a chair, leaning so close her breasts almost brushed his face.

Kurt automatically edged sideways, hoping Julie wouldn't see how the brunette was plastered over Bixton. Hopefully she didn't like Bixton too much; it appeared the jockey managed women as deftly as he did the horses.

"Sorry to interrupt your socializing," he said, "but the trailer is hooked up, and I'm in a hurry." He swallowed hard but couldn't remain quiet. "You shouldn't have stayed up so late." She pushed her chair back, grimacing at the harsh sound, and included him in her sweep of displeasure. "I'm ready," she said. "But if you're going to be grumpy all day, I'll draw you a map and catch a ride home later."

He picked up the coffee carafe, topping up both their cups. "I'm not that grumpy," he said. "Just sorry you had such a rough night." He passed her the cup and glanced over his shoulder. The brunette was still draped over Bixton like a wet blanket. Julie had to see them, yet wasn't reacting, and Kurt's hope flared.

"No need for a map," he said, his voice almost cheery. "I expect my mood will improve."

116

# CHAPTER SIXTEEN

"Just twenty more miles west." Julie shifted in the passenger seat but kept a wary eye on Kurt. The dark stubble on his jaw looked menacing, and she wondered why he hadn't shaved. Maybe he'd gone bar hopping after they'd split. Met someone and didn't make it home.

Her chest tightened, and she pressed her shoulders against the seat. Didn't like her spike of jealousy. Sure, he was attractive, mouth-wateringly attractive, but he was a trainer. Her boss.

And he had dark corners that popped up when she least expected them. Like this morning. The easy charm she'd enjoyed yesterday had vanished. Today his eyes were tight, like he had much on his mind.

"Are your horses okay?" she asked with sudden concern.

His head swung, his flat gaze pinning her. "You expect them not to be?"

"No." She shook her head. "But you seem preoccupied." She was used to forceful men but his grim stare was unnerving, and he knew how to use it. "I just thought maybe Lazer or Ace," her words tripped in confusion, "I thought maybe something…"

A smile softened his face, and he looked at her with such gentleness that her uneasiness disappeared, replaced by the rapid thumping of her heart.

"I apologize," he said. "You left so quickly last night. I was disappointed."

"Oh," she managed as her heart kicked with delight. So, he hadn't been joking. He really did want to go out. She didn't know what to say, didn't know yet what she wanted. It had been a while since she dated. Maybe it was time.

She wet her lips and drew in a shaky breath. It was easy to flirt in a dark bar, blame it on beer, but this was cold hard daylight. No alcohol in sight.

And Kurt was not a good idea. He was a trainer and there was a critical line between being friendly and inviting disaster. It was hard enough for women in racing—no need to make it harder.

She pointed out the front window, grasping for safer conversation. "That's the front range of the Rockies. They used to be small acreages, but the city stretched."

"Yeah, it's bulged out a lot since I was here."

"When was that?" She relaxed slightly, reassured by the conversation shift. His attention was on the road, and she could study him, unobserved. Could watch the way his big hands held the wheel, the deft way he handled the truck.

"Had some work here a few years back," he said.

"Racing business?"

"No, another type of business. I've always worked with the family stable but started training full time." He paused, as though choosing his words. "I needed a career change. When my father retired, he made me an offer I couldn't refuse." He glanced at her, his expression inscrutable. "I had some nice horses handed to me."

"Nicer than Lazer?"

He paused a moment. "Yeah."

She swallowed as she imagined the quality of his animals. Lazer wasn't even his best. She felt inexperienced, gauche and slightly jealous. Her own family had worked so hard, struggled on the fair circuit. Sacrificed so much.

She stared at the green hills, trying to untangle her feelings. At least it was Kurt. If someone was born to privilege, she was glad it was a man like him. He was kind to his horses and, when he chose to be…kind to people as well.

She turned back, able to tease with hardly any rancor. "So you really are another spoiled Easterner, always handed the easy road."

118

"I'm not spoiled, Julie. But I am an Easterner." His gaze lingered on her lips, and she felt an odd tingle before his attention swung back to the road.

He was probably an excellent kisser. He had a thin upper lip, much fuller on the bottom, but it softened when he smiled, like he was doing now—

Her gaze shot to his eyes, and she blushed. He was watching her again, comfortable with the fact she'd been studying him, and, oh God, maybe he even knew what she'd been thinking. He always seemed to know.

"What did you do before training?" Her voice sounded breathless.

"Whatever I was told," he said. "What about you?"

She gathered he hadn't liked some of his orders and she wanted to hear more, but there was a finality in his voice, in the abrupt way he'd turned the conversation.

"I wanted to be a jockey since I was three," she said. "Mom rode and taught me a lot. But she wanted me to go to university. Wanted me to have options."

She tapped her fingers on the edge of the window, not wanting to think about the last four years—the sheer exhaustion of university courses, ranch work and the need to hone her riding skills. She'd been reduced to racing on the bush, unable to break into Calgary's elite jockey lineup. But now she had the time, the opportunity to prove she had enough talent to ride with the pros.

She calmed her hand and pointed out the window. "The Millarville track is past those poplar trees. That's where I rode my first race."

She didn't add that it was a stock horse race. No starting gate. No rules. If he knew much of her experience was at small tracks and local fairs, he wouldn't want her. Kurt's background was blue blood—no backyard tracks in his pedigree.

A fat gopher darted across the road and Kurt shifted the wheel. She leaned forward, checking the side mirror as the gopher emerged intact behind the long trailer.

Skill or luck? If it was skill, he was a helluva driver. And soft enough to care about a gopher. How sweet. Her heart gave a little sideways shuffle. She checked his hands, large capable hands with big fingers which Sandra swore corresponded to a big dick—Julie quickly slam dunked those thoughts and averted her head, staring into the fierce eyes of a red-tailed hawk perched on a post.

"Good hunting for hawks," Kurt said, as the truck and trailer rumbled by. "Gophers are everywhere."

She nodded, surprised he even noticed the bird. "I wanted more hawks after one of our horses stepped in a gopher hole," she said, surprised she was sharing the story. It still hurt to remember how her favorite yearling—a last gift from her mother—had broken his leg, and her words stumbled, rusty at first, but coming faster as he listened in empathetic silence.

"I took my rifle and sat for an hour in the back pasture," she concluded. "Wanted to rid our field of gophers but couldn't take a shot. Decided they were part of living here."

"It's hard to kill," he said quietly.

"Yes." He was a good listener, but she didn't want to babble his head off anymore so she relaxed in the seat and admired the vast stretch of looming mountains. Their jagged teeth were stark against the sweep of blue and except for an occasional pump jack, the view was timeless.

Her father only rode in the fall, on his hunting weekends, but when she was young, she and her mom had enjoyed countless rides. Life had been full of fun and horses and long chats. God, she missed her.

She realized Kurt was talking and jerked around, blinking away the sting in her eyes. "Pardon?"

"What kind of rifle do you have?" he repeated.

"Mine is only a twenty-two, but we have racks of guns. And a pistol."

"I see." He stopped talking, studying the view as the truck and trailer bounced along the rutted road. Ranches dotted the hills, intermingled with stands of aspen and spruce, and she thought it was the prettiest spot in the world.

"Turn left at the next driveway," she said, breaking the silence.

He swung to the left of the cottonwoods and followed a rail fence that flanked their property. Some posts had been replaced, and the green color contrasted with the weathered rails. She lowered her window and shouted at the blue heron standing in their trout pond, but the bird remained unruffled, legs hidden in the dark water.

Kurt laughed at her frustrated groan. "We'll make a scarecrow. See if it keeps him out."

Her heart jerked at the easy way he linked them, and she leaned forward on the seat, fingering her seatbelt, as she directed him up the driveway to the barn.

"This place must be a lot of work." His eyes narrowed as he studied the fields of cattle and horses. "Just you and your dad here?"

"It's not so bad now," she said, "now that I've finished my degree."

"It must have been tough driving into the city every day."

Her face tightened in a defensive reflex. She couldn't remember telling Kurt she'd commuted, and it had been a sore point—her dad had wanted her to live in residence. However, he'd needed her too much, both physically and emotionally. "I only went part time," she muttered.

Kurt was watching her with that interested expression so she shrugged and kept talking. "Mom had just died. The drive wasn't so bad once I got used to it."

"So you put your life on hold for a while," he said as he eased the truck and trailer to a stop.

She blinked, jolted by his statement. No one had ever said it so succinctly, but that's exactly what she'd done. And no wonder. Her selfishness had caused her mother's death. She waited for the customary rush of guilt but felt only sadness. The heavy guilt had ebbed.

"You're right. Guess I did put it on hold." She pushed open the door and leaped to the ground, feeling much lighter.

He lowered the ramp and backed Country Girl off the trailer. Cisco's plaintive nicker resonated behind them and the gelding strained to see his travel buddy, unhappy at being left alone.

"This way," she said, and Kurt led the mare down the lane, following her to the empty paddock. He unbuckled the halter, released Country Girl and joined her beside the gate. The mare dropped to her knees, rolled luxuriously in the grass then galloped along the rail, bucking and calling to the other horses.

She peered at Kurt's face, trying to figure his thoughts. She'd done the bulk of the talking today and while he knew much about her, he was still an enigma. He'd stretched his arm over the top rail, looking relaxed and clearly enjoying seeing the mare run free. His expression was satisfied, almost triumphant.

His elbow brushed her arm, but she didn't edge away as she generally did when men moved too close. Didn't want to.

"My vet will drop by," he said, breaking the easy silence. "Take some blood, run a few tests."

"Is something wrong with her?" She stared up at him in alarm. She'd hoped the mare would race later in the month, especially after running such a brave third. With Kurt as her trainer, the mare would no doubt improve. Heck, she'd almost won last night, even hampered by Otto.

"It's just a routine check I run on all my new horses," Kurt said, but she noticed he didn't look at her. "It helps me work out their feeding program."

"How long will she be here? I can gallop her in the evenings. Keep her in shape." It would be great for both of them, and the mare would be even better after a break. "I wouldn't charge you," she added when he didn't answer.

She saw him swallow and then he turned to her, his eyes regretful. "I'm sorry. I'm not sure if she'll ever return to the track. I know she was one of the horses you rode. But if she does run again, I'd definitely want you to ride her."

"Oh," she managed, moved by his empathy almost as much as by the loss of the mare. She tried to force a smile, but her lower lip quivered.

"Damn. Please. Don't look like that." His voice roughened. "You have Lazer. And you can ride Ace too, if you want." He wrapped his arm around her in a reassuring squeeze. "But this mare shouldn't race. She's had a tough time."

Oddly she wasn't that upset, her disappointment tempered by the knowledge he was right. There had been something wrong with the mare, and it was nice he was a responsible owner. Nice that the mare was free and eating grass. Nice that he'd kept his hand splayed around her hip.

She could feel the heat of his body, smell his minty breath, and if she turned her head a few inches...a quiver of anticipation shook her.

"The mare is going to like it here," he said. His warm breath fanned her ear, sending little shivers down her spine. "Peaceful, no bugles."

He lifted his hands to her shoulders and gently turned her around. His eyes darkened as they settled on her mouth, his desire so obvious her pulse jammed into overdrive. She knew she should remind him, remind her, that she absolutely never dated trainers. Absolutely never.

She could stop this thing right now. But the intensity that pulsed from his big body was too magnetic, too overpowering and it was impossible to do anything but rise on her toes and slide her arms around his neck.

His head dipped and his mouth covered hers. A hand slid beneath her hair to cup the back of her neck. His mouth was firm and hungry and coaxing. Her lips automatically parted and when his tongue slipped in her mouth, her brain seemed to shut down. She clung to his hard shoulders, conscious of nothing but his kiss, the way his tongue mated with hers, the way he feasted on her mouth. Sensations rocketed through her, and she was only dimly aware of his bold hand as it drifted over her rear and tucked her between his hips.

Her world shifted and she had no conception of time, but when he finally lifted his head, she clung to him with a shameless sigh.

"Julie," he breathed, his voice husky, his eyes a darkening gray. He dragged a thumb over her lower lip, and she saw him swallow. "Is your dad home?"

"His truck's here," she managed but his thumb traced a sensual path along her neck, lingering over her collarbone, and it was difficult to speak.

"Let's grab you a horse then." He lowered his hand and brushed her mouth with a quick kiss. "Remember where we stopped."

She stared, blinking in disbelief. Her legs were weak, her brain still stumbled, and he was thinking of riding? "We stopped," she muttered, "just as I was about to say this was a bad idea."

He tilted her chin, his breath ragged. "*This* is a damn good idea. And I'd really like to be alone with you right now."

"We sort of are," she said, amazed at how the touch of his hand on her neck could cause such a ricochet of sensations.

Steps pounded beyond the barn, and she jumped. Kurt gave her a rueful smile and stepped back just as her dad, hatless and frazzled, charged around the corner. The brisk wind ruffled his gray hair, and he looked half dressed without his Stetson.

"Glad you two are still here. I need some help." He jabbed a thumb over his shoulder.

"What's wrong, Dad?" she asked, adjusting Country Girl's halter over the post, afraid that if he saw her face, he'd know she'd been kissing Kurt. And, in fact, wished they were still kissing.

"Got a mare in for breeding," he said, "and she ain't cooperating." His voice was thick with impatience, and he vanished behind the barn.

She looked at Kurt but he'd already turned to help her dad, and she followed them both, weaving through the outbuildings until they reached the round pen where Dude paced the fence in a frenzy of anticipation.

"Nice-looking stud." Kurt's warm gaze flickered over Julie's before turning to her father. "Foundation breeding?"

"Yeah, Joe Cody bloodlines. Dude's offspring are real versatile, great in reining and cutting. You interested in Quarter Horses?"

"Where's the mare?" Kurt asked.

Julie hid a smile, admiring how he'd averted a long pedigree conversation. Her dad had the fanatical zeal of a breeding enthusiast and would have talked for hours. She always found it boring.

124

"It's Nick's, the farrier's mare." Her dad retrieved his dusty Stetson from the dirt and slapped it against his leg before placing it carefully on his head. "I put her back in the barn, first stall on the left. She's a first-timer. Needs a chain. Almost kicked Dude's head off. Mine too."

Julie turned to get the mare, but Kurt touched her shoulder. "Relax. I'll get her," he said quietly.

Minutes later, he reappeared leading Nick's horse, a pretty bay with four white socks. Julie had seen Nick rope with the mare. She was agile and quick, but lacked power, and the farrier hoped for a foal with more size than his dam.

Kurt led the mare into the pen and adjusted the chain over her nose. The mare stared at the stallion, trembling in response to his hopeful snorts. Her tail was wrapped, and she squatted slightly.

"She looks ready," Kurt said.

"She doesn't know what she wants," her dad said. "I teased her with him earlier. She was responsive then, but changed her mind."

Their blunt words made Julie flush. She'd helped with countless breedings, but Kurt's presence and his hot kiss left her strangely self-conscious. Her gaze drifted back to him; she studied his body while he was busy with the mare.

His arms were big—he was almost as muscled as Dude—and his biceps rippled when he patted the mare. When he reached up to adjust the halter, she glimpsed his ridged stomach. Her breath quickened, and she clambered up on the top rail, figuring she might as well enjoy the view. Most of the men who brought mares for breeding were potbellied and ancient, almost as old as her dad. Kurt was a vast improvement. And he sure could kiss.

"Ready?"

Her dad's question pulled her attention back to Dude who pawed and stretched his head, curling his upper lip in response to the mare's odor. He nuzzled her flanks. Julie felt a rush of sympathy as the fully erect stallion swung up and entered the mare with a savage thrust.

Dude covered her, biting her urgently on the neck, then signaled jerkily with his tail. He withdrew with a satisfied grunt.

"All he needs now is a cigarette," Julie said, oddly irritated by his contentment. Tomorrow he'd be just as eager to breed the next mare led into his pen.

Kurt chuckled, but her father shot her a reproachful look as he guided the stallion through the gate. "I'll rinse off his penis," he said.

Her face warmed. She jerked her head away, awkward again now that she and Kurt were alone. She slid off the fence, reluctant to meet his eyes. "I'll walk the mare around a bit," she said.

"I'll do it, honey," Kurt said. "You go catch your horse."

Honey? She'd always thought that word sounded patronizing. Had never let anyone at the track call her that. Even Otto had backed down after saying it once too often. But they weren't at the track now, and it didn't really annoy her. In fact, the easy way it rolled from Kurt's mouth kicked her body into a tingling awareness.

She shoved her hands in her back pockets and sauntered toward the pasture, pretending a nonchalance she didn't feel. Certainly she couldn't deny the attraction, but events were moving much too fast. And a man who could kiss like Kurt was dangerous. She didn't like her mindless reaction. Needed time to think. Time to regroup.

Unfortunately she had the disturbing feeling she was no longer the one in control.

# CHAPTER SEVENTEEN

Kurt unwrapped the mare's tail, staring over her rump to watch Julie trudge toward the south pasture. Her head was bent; she appeared deep in thought. He hoped those thoughts included him. Her passionate kiss had left him hard with need and if she wanted a little fun, he'd be more than willing to provide it. In fact, he intended to shove any thoughts of Bixton right out of her stubborn head.

"Thanks for the help," Adam said as he walked up and stroked the mare's neck.

Kurt smoothed his expression before turning and tossing Adam the rolled bandage. Julie's father always seemed to be creeping up on him. It was a bit unsettling, especially when he'd been eying Julie with distinctly carnal thoughts.

"Going to be a nice day." Adam fingered the tail bandage and scanned the sky with an expert eye. "Be nice to go with you, but I'm helping a neighbor shuffle some cattle."

Kurt nearly choked on his relief. Much as he liked Julie's dad, three would be one too many for this trip. He nodded, making a sound that he hoped passed for disappointment.

"Did you get your mare settled?" Adam asked.

"Yeah." Kurt nodded, happy to change the subject. "She's in the middle paddock next to the buckskin. I wrote down her feeding directions and an emergency phone number. Be careful. She's lost faith in people. A vet is dropping by for a routine check. How do you want the board handled?"

"You can pay later when I figure out her costs. Let's go back to the house and grab a coffee."

Kurt followed Adam into the cedar home. The screen door slammed behind them, and a huge mottled shadow stalked down the hall.

"Sit, Blue," Adam said, using a bootjack to pry off his muddy boots. "Don't pat the dog. He's not real chummy."

"What kind of dog is he?" Kurt asked, noting the dog's raised hackles. "Coat looks like a seal."

"We don't have many seals in Alberta." Adam's eyes glinted with amusement. "Julie found him when he was a pup. Probably part coyote with some heeler and Australian shepherd mixed in. He's great with the stock, tougher than a badger. Doesn't like many people, but he's a helluva dog."

The "helluva dog" made Kurt uncomfortable. Blue sat obediently, but his strange eyes glowed as he watched Kurt tug off his boots.

"Want me to let him out?" Kurt asked.

"Sure," Adam called, already halfway down the hall. "Julie might want help with Dusty."

Kurt pushed the door open. The dog paused then brushed by with an air of disdain as though a stranger was beneath his notice. "You're welcome," Kurt said.

Blue's head swung. Kurt wasn't sure if it was the words or the amusement in his voice, but the dog definitely looked annoyed. He yanked the screen door shut leaving Blue on the other side. Their eyes locked as they measured each other through the mesh.

"I'm on the veranda," Adam called.

Kurt turned, forgot the dog, and followed Adam's voice and the welcome smell of hickory coffee.

Adam passed him a warm mug. They relaxed in wooden chairs—surprisingly comfortable despite their hardness. The veranda gave a sweeping view of the tidy pastures, the hayfield and the darker dirt oval. Something moved, and Julie came into view on the ridge, leading a white-faced sorrel.

Kurt took a hasty gulp of coffee then set his mug on the table. "I'll help her load."

"It's okay. She has plenty of help." Adam pointed at Blue trotting down the driveway and marking every fencepost. The dog shoved his head in the air then bolted, a streak of gray against the bleached gravel. Nose down, he followed Julie's trail.

The dog's boisterous greeting almost knocked her down; the horse she led pivoted, pinning his ears at the dog's raw enthusiasm.

Adam chuckled. "Dusty is ornery when he knows he's going to work, but Blue will change his mind pretty quick."

It was obvious the sorrel wasn't looking forward to leaving his comfortable pasture, and when Julie tried to lead him onto the trailer, he planted his feet. Her words weren't clear, but her hand signal was.

Blue sprang forward, nipped Dusty on a hind fetlock and easily avoided the retaliatory kick. The horse humped his hindquarters, but the dog slid in again, punishing the resistance with another nip.

Dusty lowered his head, trotted up the ramp and joined Cisco in the trailer.

"Not bad." Kurt smiled with approval. "We could use that dog behind the starting gate."

"Yeah," Adam said, "he's handy to have around. Dusty hates the trailer but walks right on when he's heading home. Usually Blue goes with Julie so there's never any trouble loading."

Kurt's smile faded. Shit. Blue was certain to be protective, and just the thought of the dog watching them with those odd blue eyes made him uneasy.

"But today I need Blue's help moving cattle," Adam added.

"Of course." Kurt quickly set down his mug and rose, afraid he'd end up with a chaperone if he lingered any longer.

"Saddlebags are on the table," Adam said. "Julie asked me to throw some food together."

Kurt slung the nylon bags over his shoulder and gave Adam an appreciative 'thanks.' Julie's father was a good example of western hospitality, and Kurt hoped Julie would be just as obliging.

He joined her by the trailer and checked the ramp, but she'd already bolted it in place. Blue sat by the back wheels, tongue lolling, wearing the eager expression of a dog anticipating a road trip.

"Handy dog," Kurt said. "Too bad your dad needs him today."

"Yes, but he's worth three riders to Dad." She scratched Blue behind his ears. "You stay here, fellow. You'll have more fun working cattle."

The dog whined and pressed against her legs, but his steady gaze followed Kurt, watching as he tossed the saddlebags in the back and opened the door for Julie.

She gave Blue a final pat and climbed in the cab, and he closed the door with a sense of relief. Girl, horses, food—they were ready. He carefully eased the truck and trailer from the yard, checking for the dog in the side mirror. Blue sat, still as a statue, until he was swallowed by their dust.

Kurt glanced at Julie. "I was sure he'd follow. Must feel good to have devotion like that."

"Of course it feels good." She settled against the seat and gave him such a beautiful smile it sucked his breath away. Now that he'd tasted her mouth, he wanted more.

He reached over and squeezed her hand. "I can make you feel good too," he said. He ran his thumb over her palm, gently rubbing the calluses left from years of riding.

"Probably you could," she said lightly, "but I don't imagine you heel quite so well."

He didn't intend to be deflected with humor and let his gaze roam her body, making no attempt to hide his appreciation. She pulled her hand away, a blush coloring her face, reaching all the way to the top of those elegant cheekbones.

"Best we don't go too fast," she said. "Dad says you're interested in buying some land." She pointed out the side window, clearly determined to change the subject. "Be nice to have you as a neighbor. Especially if you have a starting gate. I'd love a neighbor with a starting gate."

"I have three," he said.

It wasn't a joke but she rolled her eyes and relaxed, and that prim tone disappeared. He liked listening to her voice, didn't even have to pretend as she entertained him with tall tales about wacky neighbors. He nodded with a buyer's interest as she pointed out acreages where the water supply was poor and absorbed her comments about soil and rainfall.

But his conscience wouldn't shut up.

She believed he was moving here, had devoted a rare day off to show him around. She was a smart guide too, quick to pick up on the type of land that interested him—a mix of flat and rolling land. Of course that was a sham but if he *was* moving here, that's what he'd want.

He averted his head, needing a second to maintain his façade. Connor would have laughed, told him to suck it up, and Kurt shoved away his regret. Work was work. You did what you had to do.

They rattled over a string of Texas gates. "Sure a lot of cattle guards," he said, eyeing the bouncing trailer in his mirror and watching Cisco's ears flick in displeasure.

"We need the gates," she said. "Cattle are summered on crown land. Moved up in the spring and brought down in the fall." She pointed to their left. "Park there. It's a rough trail but it's isolated, and we'll see more wildlife."

He eased onto the gravel lot. There were no other vehicles, and there was plenty of room to maneuver. He backed the horses off and tied them to the trailer, and they quickly saddled.

"Do you have everything from the truck?" he asked as he grabbed a blanket and attached it to his saddle.

"Yes, but I'm glad you brought a slicker. The weather's always unsettled here. The only consistent is the mist hanging over that mountain."

It's good to be prepared, he thought, filled with a sense of anticipation. It had been years since he'd taken a girl and blanket into the woods, and he was as eager as a teenager. He didn't know how this was going to go, but he definitely wanted to enjoy her mouth again. He knotted his latigo, yanked it tight, then followed with Cisco. Reached Julie before she placed her boot in the stirrup.

He slid his hand along her back and tugged her to him. "We're alone now," he said softly.

She smiled then rose on her tiptoes. Her mouth was sweet and fresh, but he coaxed her to open and soon she clutched at his shoulders. He deepened his kiss, molding her closer until her breasts flattened against his chest. Goddammit, she felt good, smelled good, and the way her tantalizing body pressed against him made his heartbeat rev. He couldn't get enough.

*Honk!* Gravel crunched as a truck wheeled past, and a man's voice yelled ribald encouragement.

"Christ. Sorry, honey." He lifted his head, shocked at his lack of control. He pulled his eyes off her mouth and stepped back, trying to hide his ragged breathing but he could have stood in the parking lot for another hour, holding Cisco with one hand, Julie in the other. "Where are we going anyway?" he asked, his voice husky.

"Just to the hunting campsite." She swung gracefully into the saddle, looking much cooler than he felt. "It's a nice ride. We can eat there, and there's grass for the horses."

"Good. Let's go," he said gruffly as he mounted Cisco. She was throwing him off stride, and he needed to get his mind on the job. "While we're riding, you can fill me in on Country Girl. I don't know much about her, and Otto isn't going to tell me anything."

He followed her up the path, listening as she talked about how Otto never bought bedding, how he often ran out of grain and about the time he'd tried blinkers.

"Country Girl really didn't like them," Julie said. "She almost flipped twice. Even Otto admitted it wasn't a good idea."

He squeezed Cisco's sides and jogged alongside Dusty. Julie spoke faster now, her face indignant as she relayed how Otto didn't seem to have any real training plan and that he often left it up to the rider. Kurt banged his knee against a tree trunk. He winced but stayed beside her on the narrow path.

"What about the owner?" he asked, studying her expression. "There must be someone else involved with the horse. Someone that makes decisions."

She tugged at her lower lip which didn't help his concentration. "No," she said. "There's nobody else. Just Otto."

So she didn't know the man with the accent. Not good. He ducked under a low-lying branch, considering a different approach. "I heard that horse owner who was killed knew Otto."

"He wasn't an owner." Her face shadowed. "Not even a race fan. He was just backside looking around."

"Otto's friend? He must have been some prize." Kurt forced a snicker, feeling an ache in his chest. Forgive me, buddy, he thought. "Was he an asshole like Otto?"

"Oh, no. He wasn't like that. And he wasn't Otto's friend either. He was just interested in the mare."

"Oh?" That was new information. The police report merely said Connor had been looking for Otto. There had been no mention of his interest in the mare. "What did he like about the horse? Had he seen her before?"

Kurt's hands tightened around the reins as he studied Julie's face. If she knew why Connor had followed Otto to the track, it could be a major breakthrough—the thread that might unravel the entire mystery.

But she only shrugged. "Maybe he saw the mare racing at another track."

"Or maybe he met Otto and the horse before?" Kurt squeezed Cisco again, moving his horse a few feet ahead of Dusty so he had a better view of Julie's face.

She looked puzzled, her nose wrinkled in thought. "I don't think so. Otto had already removed the mare's shoes and left to unhook his trailer. The guy didn't even know which horse belonged to Otto. He just asked if Otto had taken off the shoes."

"And had Otto?" Kurt heard the sharpness in his voice, knew it was too strong. Ease up, man, he chided, but he sensed she knew something. Was exceedingly grateful for this opportunity to get her alone and probe.

She gave him a curious look but nodded. "Yes. Otto removed the back shoes as soon as he arrived. He went in the stall with tongs and a clinch cutter. I couldn't see in, but there was quite a racket. That mare was feisty from the moment she arrived."

"What time of night was that?"

"Just after ten. I had a ride in the last race and had to meet with the stewards. I dropped by, hoping to catch Sandra. Otto was surprised there was anyone else in the barn and upset that a shoe was falling off."

A chill attached to the back of Kurt's neck. "Probably best not to surprise that man, Julie," he said, trying to sound casual but, Christ, she could have been hurt. It was different for him. For Connor. They'd known the risks. Sometimes they'd been in such deep cover, it had been difficult to remember what side of the law they were on.

The horses filed under a low-lying branch, and he waited a minute before continuing. "So," he said, "Otto hauled in late with a horse from the States, removed her hind shoes and left. And all this guy wanted was to find Otto? Did he say anything else?"

She twisted in the saddle, and her eyes looked sad. "I already told the police everything. They talked to Otto. He didn't know the guy. I wanted to help, but I didn't talk to that poor man more than a few minutes." Her voice faltered. "I got the feeling he wasn't used to horses. He didn't seem comfortable in the barn."

"Yeah," Kurt muttered but his throat constricted. Connor hadn't really minded animals, but he did hate the smells. Kurt had often teased him about his sensitive nose, joking that he was better than a drug dog.

He let Cisco settle behind Dusty and tried to blank his emotions so he could sift through the facts. One detail was confirmed—Otto had lied to the police. In Connor's last call to dispatch, he'd reported helping Otto with a flat. Something had aroused his suspicions, prompting him to follow Otto. But where had Otto gone after he dropped the mare at the track?

Frowning, he pushed Cisco back up beside Dusty. "Do you think this fellow caught up to Otto? Maybe in the parking lot?"

"I don't know. He might not have been quick enough." Her eyes narrowed. "Why do you care so much?"

"Curious." Kurt shrugged. "I own the mare now. Maybe the guy knew something about her, something that would explain why she acts so weird. You were the last person to see him alive. Think." She flinched at his words, and he gentled his voice. "It's always hard to talk about stuff like this...I know."

Her eyes were a troubled green as they clung to his face, and she spoke slowly, almost reluctantly. "The police said he signed in with the security guard. He asked for directions to Otto's barn.

I talked to him around ten-thirty." Her voice caught. "Sometimes I wonder if there was something I could have done. Something I could have said that might have made a difference. I just directed him to the parking lot. Maybe I should have gone with him."

"I doubt anything you did or said would have changed things." Kurt reached over and gave her shoulder a reassuring squeeze. "But did he mention why he wanted Otto?"

She shook her head. "We didn't talk long. He was in a hurry, and so was I."

"Even something insignificant might help."

"I've gone over everything he said, three or four times. I even showed the police where he stood, where Otto dropped the horseshoes and—"

"Wait. You're saying you saw Otto's shoes?" Kurt's voice turned so sharp, Cisco flattened his ears.

She nodded. "They were in front of the stall. That man, Connor O'Neil, looked at them. He asked if Otto had just taken them off. When I said yes, he smiled."

"Describe his smile," Kurt said.

"What do you mean?" She jerked her head around.

"Was it a smile a man gives an attractive lady, or was it a smile like he'd found something?"

"That's silly. It was just a smile."

"Please, it's important."

"Guess it was a satisfied smile."

"Describe the shoes," he said, his voice hardening.

"They weren't aluminum race plates," she muttered and her chin now had a mutinous tilt. "Just normal shoes."

"Were they extra thick or heavy?"

She shook her head.

"You sure?"

"Yes." She snapped the word over her shoulder and pushed Dusty into a jog.

He let her go but felt the disappointment. Damn. Normal shoes were too thin to be hollowed out. Unless the mare's vet check revealed something, his smuggling theory had just crashed. And his list of suspects was down to zero.

They were both silent as they climbed the steep path and entered a stand of spruce. The horses seemed affected by their riders' moods and plodded with gloomy ears and labored breathing. The trees filtered the sun's rays, and the stink of rotting vegetation cloyed the air.

Cisco jammed to a stop. Kurt stared at the trees snarled across the path, like a giant game of pick-up-sticks.

"Can your horse cross that?" Julie asked as she studied the mess. She didn't look at him, and it was clear she was annoyed with the way he'd grilled her. "If they get a leg caught and panic," she added, "it could be quite a wreck."

"Cisco will be fine," he said quietly, still nursing his disappointment. "Want me to cross first?"

Her expression turned smug as she eyed his App, and she even had the gall to sniff. "I better go first. My horse is bred for this. Dusty's one of our best trail horses. He doesn't need a groomed track in the city."

She kicked Dusty forward, and Kurt smiled in spite of his failure to uncover any useful information. He should have guessed she'd interpret his words as a challenge—and of course, any self-respecting jockey would want to lead the way. Despite the blanks he'd shot today, he was still glad to be spending the day with her.

Dusty's head lowered, and the horse picked a careful route over the deadfall. In some spots, the branches were so high they scraped her stirrups. Dusty was almost safely across when his hind leg snagged in a vee of branches. *Crack!* A tree shifted, tilting under his belly and pinning his front legs.

The rim of his eyes flashed white. He leaped in the air and charged forward, tossing Julie onto his neck. *Smack!* The saddlebags whacked his ribs, scaring him even further. When he finally scrambled to the other side, he was wide eyed and trembling.

Kurt exhaled in relief. Not many riders could have stayed on through that kind of rodeo. Even Cisco had been entertained, his ears pricked as he watched Dusty's odd contortions.

Julie leaped off and ran her hands down the horse's legs. "He's okay," she said, color returning to her face.

136

"What's that on his hoof?" Kurt leaned forward, staring at the dark mark on Dusty's left hoof. He'd noticed it before but had assumed it was dirt.

"Hoof brand. A friend of Dad's has a grazing permit. Some of our horses are turned out in the summer. The brand makes it easier to identify the carcasses," she wrinkled her nose, "in case of animal attacks. What do you think? Want to try to cross, or should we find you an easier way around?"

She gave a saucy smile, and he knew he'd cross much more than a deadfall to join her. He clucked and Cisco stepped forward, carefully easing each leg between the downed trees. He gave his horse plenty of rein, letting Cisco pick his footing. The saddlebags were silent.

"Not bad." Julie gave a reluctant salute when he reached her side. "But you have to remember I went first and showed you where to step."

"Or where not to." He smiled at her competitive nature, resolving to enjoy the rest of the day. Tomorrow he'd find another suspect. His gaze lowered, and he forgot their banter and simply stared. The chilly air had left her nipples pointed and outlined against the fabric of her shirt. Lust curled deep in his belly, and he jerked his gaze away.

"Come on." She wheeled Dusty, urging her horse up the last slope. "It'll be a lot warmer in the valley. Better view too."

"The view here is perfect," he said, his voice husky, but he followed her into the grassy meadow. "Is this where we're stopping?"

"Not yet. There's a river further up where the horses can drink. Lots of grass too."

He forced his eyes off Julie and studied the mountains still topped with snow. "They're beautiful. Like a movie backdrop. Thanks for bringing me here," he added quietly.

"It's beautiful, isn't it." She grinned like a proud parent. "This is one of my favorite seasons too. The big animals haven't left for higher country, and that lovely spring smell is everywhere. Look." Her voice hushed. "There's a coyote. She must have pups somewhere." A gray shadow slipped through a stand of pines with something brown and unlucky dangling from its mouth. "If we follow, we might find the den," she added, her voice bubbling with excitement.

Kurt's eyes drifted back to her chest. "I think we should get to the campsite and relax. My horse is hungry."

He pushed past her and across the meadow. Cisco balked—unusual for him—but Kurt was in a hurry and forced him forward. The Appaloosa stepped out but humped his back. Three steps in and Kurt heard an ominous sucking sound. Cisco floundered, sinking so fast Kurt's stirrups buried in the swampy ground.

"Fuck!" The menacing bog stretched around him. Beautiful, green, deadly. He helped Cisco gather himself for a powerful effort, and the horse wheeled on his haunches. Mud flew as Cisco scrambled back to firm ground.

Julie laughed and recoiled her lariat. "Thought I'd have a chance to use my rope. I do believe that horse is smarter than his rider."

The horse is a gelding. He's not distracted, Kurt thought, as he leaned down and studied the brown muck clinging to Cisco's belly. "A good guide would have warned me." He straightened, watching as she fingered her rope as though hopeful he might make another attempt to cross the bog. "And put that damn rope away," he added. "You're scaring me."

"Greenhorns should stay behind their guide." She stuck her nose in the air. "Or maybe I will have to rope someone today."

"I promise not to pass anymore," he said. "Scout's honor."

"I doubt you ever were a Scout," she said, still smiling. "This way, silly."

He wasn't in the habit of letting people call him silly, but he followed her around the treacherous ground and even let her lead. Besides, despite the disappointment about Connor, he was having fun.

They lingered at the edge of a clear river to let the horses drink. When Dusty lifted his head, Julie spoke with a renewed air of command. "We can cross on that shallow bar but stay behind me...greenie."

She looked like a Nordic princess as she walked her horse into the water although she was taking this guide thing much too seriously. He felt like he was back in school again, where life was simple and fun. However, the name calling was getting out of hand.

He studied the swirling river, then trotted Cisco across the shallow side channel, catching up to Julie and Dusty just as they entered the gravel bar. He positioned Cisco directly behind her, timing it so his horse's legs kicked up a sheet of water.

The frigid spray sparkled as it hit her back, and her startled squeal made him grin. "It's freezing!" she said. "Move up beside me."

"Ah, but I was told to stay behind the guide."

She turned, protesting, but water splashed her chest, and the shock on her face was so comical he laughed like a kid. She kicked Dusty into a lope, soaking herself even more. Both she and her horse were drenched by the time they clambered onto the opposite bank.

Sputtering, she wheeled Dusty around. Her chest heaved, and she swiped at her dripping face, too mad to even talk. Dusty shook himself, spraying water everywhere, looking just as pissed.

Kurt was still laughing, and even Cisco walked with more of a swagger. But Julie was much wetter than he'd intended. Even her front was soaked, the shirt plastered to her chest.

Her mouth opened and closed. "I should leave you here," she sputtered, "but probably Cisco would show you the way out."

She spun her horse and trotted into the campsite, dripping a trail of water.

Kurt followed, trying to flatten his grin. He dismounted beside a stack of firewood and a blackened ring of rocks. "I'll unsaddle for you, honey," he said, careful to keep his mouth flat.

"Don't 'honey' me," she snapped, and it was obvious she spotted the twitching of his mouth. "I can unsaddle my own horse. The exercise will warm me up."

She really was soaked. Her shirt and bra were transparent. Completely transparent. He swallowed and pulled off his own saddle before leading Cisco deeper into the meadow where there was less chance he could sneak away. Cisco was wily and could move fast, even with hobbles.

On the way back to the campsite he passed Dusty, now hobbled and contentedly ripping off sweet blades of grass. Julie sat cross-legged on the ground but didn't look nearly as content.

He stopped by his saddle and untied the blanket. The sun would dry her thin shirt, but her jeans were drenched and plastered to her legs. He walked over and lowered himself beside her. "I really am sorry," he said quietly. "Sometimes I don't think."

"One of my friends always pulls that trick too." She shook her head in exasperation. "Why do guys have to soak girls whenever they're around water?"

He cocked his head, pretending to give it serious thought. "Guess it's the squeals we like, those helpless little cries. And when they come from a jockey, one of the most dangerous and toughest professions in the world, no man can possibly resist—"

"Enough." She smiled but the word trailed to a shiver.

"Spread your jeans in the sun," he said. "You can wrap yourself in the blanket while they dry. I'll grab the saddlebags and see what's for lunch."

He rose and gathered the bags, trying to keep his back turned but couldn't resist a few peeks. Saw her struggle with the boots, the slow peel of her drenched jeans. Cute pink underwear. She didn't remove her shirt.

He waited until she was wrapped in the blanket then slung the saddlebags over his shoulder and returned to the campsite.

"Warm enough?" he asked, dropping the bags and sitting down beside her.

"Yes. But on the way back you're crossing the river first. The deadfall too. I don't think I should trust you."

"No," he said. "You shouldn't." She was looking at him with big eyes, so he picked up the edge of the blanket and gently blotted her hair. "I didn't mean for you to get this wet."

"Yet you laughed," she said. But she tilted her head and let him dry her hair, even the tiny tendrils at the nape of her neck, and he liked how the sun glinted on her lighter strands. He also liked that she didn't stay mad for long. Some women sulked for hours, maybe more. He really didn't know how long they sulked, because he made a point never to see them again. But Julie wasn't like that. She was reasonable.

"This reminds me of when we first met," he said. "You were mad then too."

"You were laughing then too," she said.

"Yeah, well, guess you do that to me." He reached under the blanket and checked her t-shirt, still damp against her skin. "Do you want my shirt?" he asked, his voice low.

"Better keep it on," she said, her voice just as low.

Julie leaned against Kurt's chest as he blotted her hair and told herself the shivers were from the water and not from the little curls of desire spreading through her body. She wasn't really cold though, how could she be, not with the heat his body radiated.

And then he wasn't using the blanket any more, only his warm fingers, and she tilted her neck as his hand stroked her cheek, as though memorizing her face.

"Love your dimples," he said, his voice so low, it moved like liquid along the back of her neck. She quivered but knew it wasn't from the cold. His touch had changed, turned sensual, and his thumb moved in a slow circle, sending tingling sensations along her skin to her breasts, and lower. A hum of pleasure escaped her throat.

"Honey," he breathed, and the way he wrapped that word with such longing, such desire, made her breath skip. She tilted her head an inch, only an inch, but it was enough. His warm mouth lowered, and his tongue slid in her mouth, slow, smooth and seductive.

It was the most erotic kiss she'd ever experienced, and she pressed against him, needing to get closer but he kept a hand cupped around the back of her neck, the other splayed around her jaw, stroking, always stroking.

Her nipples tingled, and she made an impatient sound. Slipped a hand beneath his shirt, slid her fingers over that rippled chest. She hadn't wanted to borrow his shirt earlier, hadn't wanted to be tempted by his undoubtedly gorgeous chest, but she was way past that now. She arched up, pressing her breasts against him, and finally his hand brushed the bottom of her breast. Seconds later, his thumb grazed the tip of her nipple but so languidly she thought she'd explode.

She pulled back. His eyes were dark, unfathomable, the sun shadowing his face. "Touch me," she said.

He whipped her shirt off then effortlessly flipped her onto the blanket, unhooking her bra in an easy motion that revealed years of practice. She felt a twinge of jealousy for those unknown women, but then his bold hands covered her breasts, and she stopped thinking. His mouth sucked gently at her nipple and she groaned and arched upward, until he obligingly cupped the other one. His knowing touch filled her with sensations, and she tilted her neck, reveling in the feel of his lips, his hands, the slight graze of his teeth.

His hand slipped into her panties, and she squirmed, but she really couldn't move because his mouth was over his breast, and the stubble on his chin rubbed her skin, and it was so erotic she could only grip his shoulders.

And then he pulled away. Cool air brushed her chest as he leaned back. She heard his zipper, felt him reaching in his pocket, and he tossed some packets of condoms by her head. He was already rolling one on. Good. She hated this part, didn't know if she should help or look away, and the whole thing felt awkward. Although he wasn't a bit awkward, not like Joey who had struggled just trying to open the plastic.

And how many condoms had he brought? She twisted her head, blinking. Three? Good God. And then he was back over her, tugging down her panties, positioning himself above her.

He cupped her with a knowing hand, stroking until she quivered with longing. "Open up, sweetheart," he whispered, kneeing her thighs further apart. And then he pushed and the intrusion was so sudden, so sharp, she gasped and pressed her hands against his chest.

"Oh, yeah," he murmured, his expression one of intense bliss. She clamped her mouth shut, determined not to make a sound, but he jerked his head down, absorbing her stillness, the way her hands pressed against his chest.

"Julie?"

"Just finish up," she said.

But he stared at her, the cords of his neck rigid. Sweat gleamed on his forehead. "Fuck," he said and rolled off.

He lay on his back, his forearm over his face, as though shielding his eyes from the sun. She tugged the blanket around her and shot a quick look at his massive erection. "You could have finished," she muttered.

"Finished?" His tanned throat rippled as he took a hard gulp. He sat up but didn't look at her, just reached out and tugged her to his side, carefully tucking the blanket around her.

"I'm sorry," he said. "I should have moved slower. I uh…had the wrong impression."

He sounded so odd, she reached up and patted his arm. "It's okay. It's been a while," she said, "and I never liked it much anyway."

She thought he flinched and glanced up, but he was staring straight ahead, his expression inscrutable. He had his arm around her, but his touch was different now, polite and reserved, and his utter silence made her eyes itch.

And then he plucked a blue wildflower from the grass. Stuck it gently behind her ear, and the gesture made her heart kick.

"How long has it been for you?" he asked.

"High school." She looked down, tightening her nervous fingers on the blanket, and the flower dropped from her hair.

He nodded as though he understood, but of course he didn't. "I shouldn't have rushed you like that," he said. "I should have gone slower. Could have made it better."

She gave a dismissive shrug. "It happened so fast. It's not like it was planned."

He coughed and was silent for a minute. "Your last boyfriend was in high school?" he finally asked. "No one since?"

She averted her head at the incredulity in his voice and picked up the little flower, unable to keep her hands still. "My mother was killed in a car accident," she said, plucking out a small blue petal. "I was supposed to drive her home but wanted to stay with my boyfriend. I never felt much like sex after that."

"Ah, honey." He blew out a regretful sigh. "That was a head-on collision. The other car crossed the line. You couldn't have changed anything."

She glanced sideways, surprised he knew about the accident. Sandra must have told him. However, even Sandra didn't understand the extent of her guilt. Nobody knew how the phone had rung and rung, and how she and Joey had laughed and continued pulling off their clothes. How they'd turned off the insistent phone.

Her mother had clung to life for five agonizing hours but had died before Julie made it to the hospital.

She swallowed then held Kurt's gaze. "Dad called me," she said, her voice scratchy. "I was in bed the whole time. The phone was two feet away. Was enjoying myself too much to answer."

His arm tightened and he reached up, pressed his gentle finger to the sides of her eyes, wiped away her tears. She hadn't even realized her eyes were wet.

"Guilt doesn't help," he said. "You can't beat yourself up about it. Easier said than done...I know," he added, and his voice was so understanding she kept talking.

"If I had been driving, the accident might not have happened. Maybe I would have reacted more quickly. She rode nine races and was exhausted. She wanted a drive home. I was too selfish."

"Or you might have been dead too," he said quietly. "That's why you don't date?"

"Maybe. I don't know. It's the riding too, I guess." She blew out a breath. "I hope you don't feel used. This was meant to be a sightseeing tour not a sexual experiment." She gave him a teasing poke, determined to move on. "Although you sure brought a lot of condoms."

"I did," he said, but his voice sounded so odd, she straightened. "I always carry them," he added, but he wouldn't look at her, and an alarm niggled in her head.

She automatically tightened the blanket around her shoulders. Her throat had constricted, and she didn't know why. "You said you had the wrong impression. What did you mean?"

144

"I'm not sure." He shrugged. "I don't remember the context."

He sounded too much like a lawyer, and she reached for his hand, needing some reassurance. "If I ask you a question—one question—do you promise to tell the truth?" she asked.

He squeezed his eyes shut as though she were asking an impossible thing, and his fingers tightened around her hand.

"P-please, Kurt. It's important to me." Her voice caught but it was his expression that scared her the most; his face was twisted almost in agony. And then it abruptly straightened to that god-awful mask she hated.

"I promise," he said, his voice bleak.

She swallowed. "Did you really want to look at land today? Because you never asked about prices and that last acreage was so beautiful."

He made an indeterminate gesture with his head.

"You didn't think it was beautiful?" she asked hopefully, her words coming in a rush, because if he was shaking his head to the first question, there was only one other reason why he'd ride up in the mountains with a pocketful of condoms.

"I didn't really want to look at land today," he said, his diction perfect. Perfect and very clipped.

She slowly released his hand, didn't want him to feel her trembles. Squeezed her eyes shut but couldn't stop the wobble in her mouth. "So why did we come up here?" she asked, her voice so low she wasn't sure if he could hear.

"Truthfully, I wanted to talk to you, Julie," he said and she laughed, almost hysterically, because she knew then he was lying.

"I see. 'Talk to me.' Well, I'm sorry I gave you the wrong impression." She raised her chin, gathering her dignity. Hoped he wouldn't notice the devastation in her voice. "Please l-leave now so I can get dressed."

She waited until he left the clearing then rose and gathered her jeans. They were dry and stiff, but she yanked them on, following with socks and boots, warm and toasty from the sun. It took longer to hook her bra than it had taken Kurt to unfasten it, and she swore in frustration, then yanked her shirt down and smoothed it with her hands. There, everything was back to normal. Good to go.

She could hear the pounding of an ax, sharp and almost violent as it bit into the wood. Sounded like he was splitting a year's supply of firewood.

She wasn't ready to face him yet so turned and stalked up the animal trail trying to manage her pain. She swiped her cheeks, angry at him but even more angry at herself. She wished she were home, wished he was gone, and she fervently wished she hadn't been so easy.

Would he say anything at the track? Just the thought made her groan. Gary had cautioned her about stuff like this, had stressed how important it was to keep personal affairs separate. Be squeaky clean, he'd warned. A whiff of gossip could sink a jock.

She swallowed the lump in her throat and tried to reassure herself. Kurt might consider himself a prize stud—he definitely knew his way around a woman's body—but he didn't seem the type to blab. The real mystery was why he had targeted her.

Had he planned this because he liked her or because he wanted a quick bang? He must be disappointed. It was a damn long way to ride for some shitty sex. She kicked a rock and kept walking.

# CHAPTER EIGHTEEN

Kurt trudged back to the campsite with the axe in his hand and a load of wood balanced in his arms. Julie's jeans and boots were gone, and so was she. He blew out a sigh and let the wood tumble to the ground. She hadn't passed him which meant she'd followed the trail upcountry.

He hoped she didn't walk far, but she was mad, hurt and confused. Goddammit. He never would have touched her if he'd known how innocent she was. He cursed under his breath. He'd been taught to lie and misrepresent, and he was good at it, but when she'd looked at him with those luminous eyes, it had been impossible to lie. And then he'd hurt her worse.

Cisco's nostrils flared with pink as he stared up the narrow trail; no doubt he was tracking Julie too. Kurt glanced at Dusty, who was still head down in the grass, and continued up the path, reassured. As long as one horse was hungry, it was unlikely the other would wander far.

Unlikely but possible.

He checked his watch, resolving to return within twenty minutes. Some hobbled horses could cover a lot of ground, and Cisco was one of them.

He walked fast, spurred by his ballooning guilt. Something moved, and he spotted Julie's proud back. She was only twenty feet ahead, her steps hushed by the carpet of moss and lichen. He closed the gap but remained a polite distance back, giving her plenty of space. He couldn't understand why he hadn't been able to lie. Wasn't yet certain of the best way to herd her back to the horses.

His hope flared when the trail led into a meadow filled with flowers. This might cheer her up—pull her out of her funk much easier than his clumsy words. She loved spring; here it was, at its finest.

Flowers dotted the grass. Snow lilies and paintbrush swayed in the breeze, creating a lush backdrop, their brightness exaggerated by the deep blue sky, the green mantle of grass, the scattering of bleached bones.

He edged around a speckled alder, his eyes narrowing. Dirt and boulders had been thrown over the meadow, their moist brownness at odds with the vivid colors, like unexpected graffiti that warned of a gang presence.

*Snuffle, snuffle.* His heart jerked in horror. A massive grizzly dug for lily bulbs only a stone's throw away. Her shoulder hump shook as her long claws tore out clumps of ground. A cub mimicked her actions.

Kurt forced his stiff legs to move. He reached for Julie, rooted to the ground. His clumsy hand grabbed hers, and together they backed away. But they were moving too slowly, breathing too loud. And then it was too late.

The grizzly raised her head. She thrust herself up on hind legs, like a heavyweight fighter readying for battle. Dirt streaked her face, masking her eyes, as she sniffed the wind for their scent.

"Don't move." Kurt's tongue felt thick, his words ragged. He reached out and gripped Julie's waist. "If she charges, I'll distract her. Run for Cisco. Ride out for help."

"Don't look in her eyes." Julie's voice was low and urgent.

The bear's growls deepened. She stretched higher. Her cub circled and scooted for the safety of the trees, jarring the air with his frantic bawls. Kurt scanned the meadow, desperate for a log, stick, anything. But the brilliance of the flowers mocked him. Far off, too far off, stood a stand of spruce.

Fuck.

Julie stood in front of him. So small, so innocent, and he was swept with a warrior's need to protect.

"I'm not leaving," she whispered. "I have—"

The grizzly charged.

He grabbed her waist and jammed her behind him. "Run!" he yelled, jerking back to face the bear.

The grizzly's head swung. Surely she wouldn't pass him to chase Julie? Panic galvanized him and he waved his arms, yelling with a voice like a stranger's. The bear's head turned, and her attention locked on him. Oh fuck, this wasn't going to be fun.

Every muscle tensed as he struggled to remember everything he knew about surviving a grizzly attack.

The bear was deceptively fast. Fifteen feet away, she swerved and bolted in the direction of her bawling cub.

*Oh, God, thank you.* Weak with relief, he wheeled, almost running over Julie who was frozen behind him. She hadn't followed his directions, had been too scared to move. Understandable. Adrenaline had a weird effect.

He slung her over his shoulder and rushed down the trail, ignoring the prickling of his neck and the compulsion to glance back every second stride.

Cisco's ears pricked as Kurt rushed past with Julie mute in his arms, but the horse turned his attention back to the grass. The pounding in Kurt's chest eased. Cisco's behavior confirmed the bear wasn't following.

He wrapped Julie in the blanket—her cheeks so colorless her green eyes were a vivid slash. Knew he looked as shaken. The mountains loomed around them, heightening his sense of insignificance. He lit a fire, craving its ageless comfort.

"We're okay now." He lifted her onto his lap and rubbed her stiff arms.

"Some guide I am." She managed a shaky smile. Her hands were fisted, and she clutched a small red can in her fingers.

"What's this?" He pried opened her fist. "Bear spray?" His voice thickened as he scanned the label on the canister. She hadn't run at all. He should have known she had too much gumption to run. She'd had his back—and he couldn't have asked more from any partner. "You always carry that mini-can in your pocket?"

She squeezed her eyes shut and gave a shivery nod. "A promise to Dad. Did you see the size of her claws?"

"Those claws are miles away now." He gave her hand a reassuring squeeze. "I should have paid more attention to Cisco. I think he smelled her earlier."

She tilted her head, breath still shaky. "You realize you just stared down a charging grizzly?"

"So did you, Julie," he said.

Their eyes locked in mutual respect, and he impulsively leaned down and kissed her mouth. Kept it quick but she tasted good, too damn good, and he dragged his head away, and pressed his face into her silky hair.

"Thank you, God," he muttered, feeling achingly alive. She was fine, he was fine, life was fine, and every one of his senses pulsed with gratitude. A squirrel scolded from a pine tree, a hawk circled lazily. Her lips stroked his throat

"You're so warm," she whispered.

He didn't move, could barely breathe as she continued a slow exploration with her mouth. Up his neck, under his jaw, the side of his throat. Her breasts, her hip, every feminine curve pressed into him, seeming to scald his skin. He clenched his jaw, heard his teeth grind.

She dipped her head, tracing slow circles on his chest with her fingers, and his whole body jerked to attention, waiting on her mouth, her touch.

He trapped her hands, his voice ragged. "You better stop."

"I don't want to stop." She pulled away and continued her slow torture.

He didn't move, kept his hands clenched at his side, but his pulse beat erratically and his jaw throbbed. Her mouth was all over him now, hitting every sensitive spot, and it felt so good it hurt.

"Stop acting like a statue." She gave him an impatient nip.

"I just want you to be sure." Christ, he couldn't believe that was him talking.

"Do I strike you as someone not sure?" She pulled off her shirt. Then reached down and tugged her boots off, tossing them aside with two quick thuds.

He groaned and tugged her to him, cradling her face, devouring her mouth with primal hunger and then it was

150

impossible to get close enough, to touch her enough. He hauled her jeans down, removing them with single-minded desperation.

The skin on her stomach was soft and warm, even warmer between her legs but when her breath caught, he froze.

"It's okay," she said, gripping his shoulders and tugging his shirt off. She pressed her mouth back against his, but it felt like she was trying a little too hard, and he knew he should stop. Shoved away the thought.

He forced himself to linger, caressing her with his finger, rhythmic and insistent until she arched against him.

The zipper on his jeans stuck and he yanked at it, then ripped open a condom and rolled it on. Curved an arm under her hips and slowly, carefully, guided himself in. Her eyes clung to his, and he didn't know what he was saying, but he didn't stop murmuring assurances, didn't stop kissing her precious face.

She deserved more time but when she impatiently arched her hips, his control shattered. He pulled her legs around his thighs and deepened his thrusts. She matched his passion, rising to meet each stroke.

She was hot, tight and wonderfully responsive. Little noises escaped her throat, and he gasped and strained until her walls convulsed around him. Seconds later, he burst inside. Shuddered and collapsed with barely enough strength to roll over and pull her on top.

He closed his eyes, spent and content. Her hand caressed his damp chest and he held her tight, wanting to stay lodged inside. Maybe have a quick nap.

"Now I know why people think so highly of sex," she whispered.

He pried his eyes open. Her head was on his chest, her face relaxed and dreamy. "It's not always this good," he said. Always good but not this good. He closed his eyes again, hoping she'd stop talking.

"Why not?" she asked. "If both people...take their time."

He cracked his eyes open, accepting that a nap wasn't going to happen. It was always a mystery why women turned chatty afterwards, and he only wanted to sleep. "You didn't like sex with your boyfriend," he said, feeling slightly smug.

She wrinkled her nose and looked skeptical. "Joey and I were both young. And guilt about Mom didn't help. It bothered Joey too."

"You know what," he held her hips in place, feeling a surge of resentment for the unknown Joey. "We don't need to talk about this stuff." History was history. He didn't want to hear about her old boyfriend. About what they did or didn't do. "Just accept that sex would be no good with anyone else," he added, giving her a teasing squeeze.

"Or maybe it would be better."

"Don't be cruel," he said. This type of conversation was always best avoided and besides, he was more interested in her sleek curves. He palmed her breast, keeping her impaled as he skimmed a finger over each nipple, leisurely admiring her sleek body now that the rush was over.

Amazingly though, he felt himself harden. "Don't wiggle," he said.

She smiled. And squeezed again.

"Goddamn," he breathed. There was no danger of him slipping out now. He'd never had anyone with such tight muscles. She licked lazily at his chest, sinuous as a cat, and he mumbled something but didn't know what he was trying to say. Could feel himself swelling inside her.

"You okay?" Her eyes sparkled with mischief.

"Yeah," he managed, his voice gruff. Her mouth skimmed his chest, and she continued doing that vise trick with her muscles, muscles incredibly toned from riding. Somehow he managed to keep breathing, to stay still, but it wasn't easy.

"Goddamn." His voice trailed off to a croak as she tightened again, and he couldn't remain still any longer. He slid his hands around her hips and thrust. She flinched, and he stopped, guessing she was sore, but seconds later she squirmed in encouragement, her breasts beautifully accessible. And all his.

He sighed in appreciation and drove upward, holding her hips, rocking her against him. Her fingers pinched his shoulders, and she whimpered. She's going to come again, he thought. Her sounds rose to a crescendo and he palmed her buttocks, holding her in place as her walls shuddered spasmodically around his grateful cock.

She collapsed on him, boneless.

"Damn," he said. "You're a fast learner. Little Joey was a fool."

She nipped his chest in rebuke but he liked the feel of her teeth—liked everything about her—and he chuckled as he adjusted her in the crook of his arms. "You're quite a woman, honey," he said, pushing back a lock of hair and gently kissed her forehead.

She lifted her head, eyes radiant, and the emotion that spilled across her face was unmistakable. Damn! He squeezed his eyes shut. So much for simple, uncomplicated sex.

The tip of her finger twirled around some chest hair, tickling as it settled on a faded scar. "What's this mark? Looks like a bullet hole."

He had a good hunting story he used in situations like this, but he was reluctant to shovel out any more lies. Not to her. "A shooting incident," he said, his voice creaky as an abandoned swing.

He felt her interest but kept his eyes closed. "It must have hurt," was all she said. Her hand skimmed over the tattoo on his left arm. "Kind of a scary tat. You ride a bike?"

"Used to," he mumbled, thinking of the scum gangs and the things he'd done. The things he'd ridden. Anything to keep his cover.

He grabbed her hand, feeling dirty and exposed. Vulnerable. But her warm lips continued exploring, and he didn't want to stop that, not when they drifted down his ribs. She reached a knife scar, propped herself up on an elbow and stared in concern. "You need to take better care of yourself, Kurt. Or else find nicer friends. How did you get all the scars?"

He opened his eyes but kept his face impassive. Personal questions were okay when he stuck to the script but for some reason he couldn't lie to her, and that was a dangerous thing.

"Guess you don't feel like talking," she added. Her words were steady, but the hurt in her voice was unmistakable, and he felt like a shit.

He stared at a hawk circling in the darkening sky, wishing he could escape so easily. Knew he had to shut her up before he blew everything. "Why would I feel like talking when there's a naked woman on top of me?" he finally said. He forced a chuckle and even brushed her nipple with a lazy finger. "A naked, willing woman."

She flinched and even to him, the words sounded crude.

"And you always accommodate willing women?"

"Always," he lied.

"I see." Her voice was small with just a hint of a quaver, but she rallied well. "Well, it's late. We better get out of here before the sun drops." She disentangled herself and pulled away.

Perfect, just what he wanted. But he felt mean and hollow with an empty hole where his heart should be.

"I'll get the horses." He yanked his clothes on and strode across the meadow, not wanting to look at her pinched face any longer.

It had to be done. Her feelings might be a little hurt, but even his relaxed code couldn't justify a relationship with someone so fresh and innocent. Not while he was in undercover mode.

He stalked along the path. It had been a mistake to have sex; the kicker of it was he liked her, liked her a lot. He glanced over his shoulder, his steps slowing as he blew out a regretful sigh. Maybe he should admit what was going on. Let her decide if she wanted to spend time with him.

He cursed and thrust aside that option. No, he couldn't let anyone in again. Julie was too honest, too easy to read. She'd slip up with her friends. Sandra was nobody's fool, and neither was Bixton. His cover would be blown in half a day. And someone at that track was involved in Connor's murder.

He bent down and unbuckled Cisco's hobbles. The horse must have sensed his frustration and followed dutifully, not even trying to snatch grass when they detoured for Dusty.

He led the horses back to the campsite and silently saddled. Julie was snuffing out the smoking fire and didn't look up. Had probably already written him off as a fuck-head.

154

The realization made him yank the cinch so tight Cisco flatted his ears, indignant at the treatment, but Kurt flipped his stirrup down and scowled. No way around it. He had to keep his hands off Julie. See her at the track but keep it professional.

Exactly what she'd wanted in the first place, and his guilt grew.

He didn't like the feeling and was determined to control it. Besides, keeping his distance wouldn't be a problem. He already had everything she knew about Connor. He didn't need her anymore. The knowledge didn't make him feel a bit better, and he cursed as he led the horses toward her.

The side of her neck was reddened, and her lower lip looked swollen. He blew out a regretful sigh. "Julie—"

"You must be hungry," she said, cutting him off. "Seems we missed lunch." She tossed a granola bar across the chasm that separated them.

He pocketed the food and tied on the saddlebags. They mounted and silently headed down the trail. He edged up beside her, but she raked him with such a contemptuous stare that he pulled Cisco behind and fell in line.

A flinty wind chilled his neck as they rounded the ridge. He turned and glanced over Cisco's rump. The sunshine had drained from the day, and the grassy spot where they'd lain was now shadowed. He sucked in an achy breath, knowing he was giving up something precious yet absolutely certain nothing could be done about it.

Kurt glanced across the cab of the truck, watching as Julie fought to stay awake. They'd talked in monosyllables since loading the horses but for the last half hour, silence had replaced their stilted conversation. Now her eyelids drooped until another bump on the road jerked them open again.

She was clearly exhausted. And before dawn, less than seven hours away, she'd be galloping exuberant horses. He couldn't ignore her struggle and reached out, pulling her closer. "Just sleep," he said. "I can find the way to your place." She argued of course, but he tugged her against his lap, and she fell asleep mid-sentence.

He automatically stroked her hair, disentangling a stubborn blue petal, then wrapped both hands around the steering wheel. He shouldn't be touching her like that, not when he couldn't give her the honesty she deserved. But his hand kept drifting back to her hair, her neck, and he finally gave up and let it remain. It didn't matter. She was asleep. But tomorrow, for both their sakes, he'd be much more disciplined.

It was dark when his headlights panned the driveway of the West's ranch. He eased to a stop. Julie jerked upright, stared for a moment then scooted to her side of the truck, rubbing her eyes and yawning.

"Relax. I'll get Dusty," he said.

He lowered the ramp and backed off her horse. She stepped from the truck, and a growling dog shot from the dark, spooking the horse.

"It's okay, Blue," she said but the dog continued growling as he shouldered his way between her and Kurt. "That's odd. He met you earlier. Usually he only growls at strangers."

"Guess he doesn't trust me," Kurt said.

He shut his mouth, but the words hung in the brittle silence. She stared at him for a second then gave her dog an approving pat. Took Dusty's lead and walked catlike toward the pasture, seemingly unhampered by the darkness, her tiny silhouette flanked by the larger shadows of dog and horse.

Kurt followed, closing the gate as she slipped the halter off Dusty. The sorrel trotted into the dark, ground thudding beneath his anxious hooves as he searched for his pasture mates.

"Want a coffee for the drive back?" she asked. He guessed by the sound of her voice that she'd just stifled another yawn.

"No, I'm fine. Thanks for everything, Julie. I'll see you tomorrow."

He wanted to add that it had been one of the best days of his life, but their camaraderie had chilled like the night. She probably would have misunderstood anyway. So he remained silent, watching until she and Blue reached the house, and the screen door slammed.

He blew out a sigh, climbed in his truck and headed toward the city.

His mood was pissy when he reached the track, and he circled the parking lot, scanning the vehicles with his headlights. Otto's pickup wasn't there. A shame. He would have enjoyed a late-night altercation.

Martin had already prepared Cisco's stall and feed, and the App dived into his food. Kurt checked Lazer and Ace then wearily unhooked the trailer. Another day with little to show. Now that Julie had sunk his shoe theory, they had nothing on Otto but a break and enter.

Heavy with frustration and another emotion he didn't want to analyze, he drove back to the motel. Detoured to the front desk to pick up a new room key.

"Good evening, sir." The night clerk sounded much too cheery. "Your room is cleaned and the lock repaired. There's also a message from the police."

He passed Kurt a pink slip and a new key card. Kurt folded the message and checked his own phone as he followed the walkway to his room. An update from his racing assistant. Four calls from Archer.

Damn, he'd completely forgotten to send his report. It was late and there was a two-hour time difference, but he pressed Archer's number.

Archer yawned, his voice crusty. "We haven't heard from you in forty-eight hours, and your damn phone was off. What do you have?"

"Not much," Kurt said. "But I still think Otto Laing is good for it. He lied about meeting Connor. Had a temper tantrum when I claimed his horse."

"What horse?"

"The horse that was on the trailer Connor followed." Kurt locked his door and did a quick inspection of the room. Television, mirror, clock—everything was replaced. Otto's visit was like a bad dream.

"What do you mean? Claimed it?" Archer sounded wide awake now. "Can you do that?"

"If it's a claiming race. The trailer was clean, so I'm checking out the animal. Owning her was the only way to get a good look...she was cheap."

"My idea of a cheap horse is vastly different from yours," Archer said. "And I don't recall giving authorization."

"Maybe you'll remember once you wake up."

Archer cursed, but curiosity overrode his annoyance. "So what did you find?" he asked. "Drugs?"

"Nothing yet. The vet was scheduled to run some tests today. The results will be called directly to you."

"What about the other one? The jockey? She was the last one to see Connor," Archer said. "You pushing her?"

Kurt's chest squeezed. "She's not involved," he said. "She just happened to be around that night. It has to be Otto. But he's only the muscle. Get some surveillance on him, and we might flush out his partner."

Archer turned silent, and Kurt paced a crooked circle.

"We need reasonable grounds," Archer finally said. "And the girl is still a suspect. There's a three-hour time gap when no one saw her."

"She thinks of nothing but horses, lives in the country and doesn't even like Otto," Kurt said.

"Even so—"

"Get some surveillance." Kurt paced again, eager to divert Archer. "Quick as you can."

"It'll take twenty-four hours to get something in place. You know that." The groggy murmur of Archer's wife sounded in the background.

"Fine, but alert the border guys. Otto spoke about another trip to Montana. We can nail him when he crosses into Canada. Tell them to tranquilize any horse he's hauling. Check mouth, ass, feet, everywhere."

"Okay." Archer said. "But watch your back."

"Sure." Kurt disconnected, tossing his phone on the bed. He'd been so hot for Julie, he'd forgotten that she was a suspect, at least in Archer's mind. Another good reason to keep his distance.

He yanked off his boots and tossed them against the wall. Tomorrow wasn't shaping up to be a very fun day.

# CHAPTER NINETEEN

Streaks of red bruised the eastern ridge when Kurt rushed into the barn. Forecasting this high-altitude weather was a skill he hadn't yet mastered but it smelled like rain, and he wanted to get his horses on the track before it turned into a mud hole.

"Good morning," he said to Martin who was diligently scrubbing water buckets. Sandra had Okie in the aisle, making some sort of tack adjustment, but he was disappointed Julie wasn't waiting by Lazer's stall.

He looked at Sandra. "How did Lazer feel yesterday?"

"Like a train. He dragged my horse around the track, and Okie's no featherweight. Might have to raise my ponying fee."

"Forget it," Kurt said. "There shouldn't be any charge if your horse had a free ride."

She laughed. "No freebies, ever. I might bet your horse though. He's feeling wicked. Did you decide on a jockey yet?"

"Julie's riding him." Speculation sharpened Sandra's face, so he turned and addressed Martin. "Did you feed all the horses?"

"Julie's riding Lazer!" Sandra squealed. "She must be ecstatic. Did you decide that at the bar?"

"No." Kurt shook his head, aware Julie would hate any innuendo that a personal relationship had landed her a horse. "It was decided after I saw her ride two good races. And after consultation with the owner."

"*The Racing Form* lists you as the owner," Sandra said.

Kurt's mouth twitched. "*The Form* is correct."

Sandra grinned and started whistling, a catchy tune, but one he couldn't identify.

"I fed the horses and cleaned all three stalls," Martin said, his wary gaze shooting from Kurt to Sandra and back to Kurt again.

"Good," Kurt said. "Run a brush over them. I'll see if I can find Julie. We're already running late."

Julie stood in the stirrups and eased her mount to a trot. Her heart slammed against her ribs when she spotted Kurt leaning against the rail, talking to the bay's trainer.

She headed reluctantly toward the gap, toward the familiar rumble of his voice, the voice that had whispered such intimacies yesterday. Her hands felt damp around the reins and she was sure her cheeks were flushed, but she squared her shoulders. She'd just galloped three horses, only natural she'd look flushed.

"He felt even, Barb," she said to the bay's trainer. "No sign of weakness in that left front."

"Good. We'll put him back into light training. Can you take him out tomorrow?"

"Sure." Julie unbuckled her saddle and pulled it off, turning to Kurt as the trainer led the bay away.

"Good morning," she said.

"How you feeling?" He stepped closer, his voice lowering. "You okay?"

"Fine." She waved at Harrison who was walking by and spoke quickly, trying to hide her embarrassment. "I just picked up another horse. That bay I was on…he's coming off an injury though, so it'll be a while before he's ready."

She knew her nervousness was making her babble, but it was okay. Kurt was no longer looking at her, his attention caught by a flashy chestnut colt. "I can gallop your horses now, if you want," she said, shifting her feet and balancing her saddle in the crook of her left arm.

"I prefer to gallop Lazer on a freshly harrowed track," he said. "But this will have to do since you weren't available earlier."

"But I was here." His unfair criticism stung, and her voice rose. "I dropped by your barn an hour ago. Martin said you hadn't arrived yet."

"Well, I'm here now. And my horses are ready if you are." He strode toward G barn, not even waiting for her to follow.

160

Her breath drained with a whoosh, sucking all her air. What the hell? She gripped her saddle and followed, struggling to pretend this was just another routine morning, and she really didn't have the urge to pick up a rock and drive it into his stiff back.

Despite her exhaustion she'd lain awake much of the night, analyzing his every word. His every gesture. And though it was clear sex meant little to him, she'd assumed he'd be civil. Had assumed they would still have a professional relationship—a bit strained maybe—but at least civil.

She hadn't prepared herself for hostility. Had imagined many scenarios but not that one.

"Hi again, Martin," she said, walking into the barn with forced vitality, hoping no one would see that her insides had shriveled. Kurt was already in the stall adjusting Lazer's bridle and didn't look up.

"I forgot to tell Kurt you were here earlier," Martin mumbled as he helped position the saddle on Lazer's back. "You look really, um, nice today."

"Thanks." She tried to smile at Martin, but her face was so tight she feared it resembled a grimace. A ball of hysteria circled her chest as she remembered the extra effort she'd taken to dress. Twenty extra minutes that could have been used for something more important. She could have filled three water troughs, cleaned two stalls. Now she'd have to do it tonight or worse, worry that her father would rush and try to do it all.

Kurt led Lazer into the aisle, remaining silent as he legged Julie into the saddle.

*What an asshole.* "What do you want done today," she asked, struggling for an even tone as he led the prancing horse outside.

"Twice easy. Breeze three furlongs," he said.

She nodded, her face hot as she stared over his wide shoulders. Only twelve hours ago, she'd hugged and kissed and stroked those shoulders. Dumb, dumb, dumb. Obviously, yesterday meant nothing. He'd wanted a willing woman, and she'd certainly been willing. Regret consumed her—a sharp searing pain that chewed a gaping hole in the middle of her chest.

Feeling small, wounded and worthless, she pasted on a smile but was numbingly oblivious to everyone she passed.

"Hey, Julie! Drop by my barn later," a man called. "Got a young horse I want you to gallop."

She stared in the direction of the voice. A laughing, shiny-haired guy, D barn. She had a vague memory that he owned several gyms, but his name was lost in her miserable haze.

"And tell Sandra I've got cold beer waiting," he added with a grin.

She nodded, barely registering his words. Kurt's indifference ripped at her. The walk to the gap had never felt so long or oppressive.

But finally they were there. Kurt silently released the eager colt and stepped back, and she guided Lazer onto the track, desperate to go anywhere as long as it was away from him. Lazer sidestepped and bucked, taking advantage of her inattention, and she knew it was critical to regain her composure.

Obviously, Kurt regretted yesterday too. It had been rash to ride with him, but it really galled her that she'd been so keen to have sex. So keen she'd been the first to whip off her clothes.

Lazer's ear flicked at her miserable groan.

"It's okay, fellow." She gave his neck a reassuring pat. "It's not your fault you have a prick for a trainer." He tossed his head as though in agreement, and his sheer exuberance made her feel better.

She blew out a long breath, knowing she couldn't blame it all on Kurt. "Touch me," she'd said. And he certainly had. It was foolish to combine business with pleasure, and she'd been a fool. With minimal effort he'd persuaded her to board his mare, take him on a trail ride and top it off with a bout of sex.

She'd done it all gleefully, a gullible apprentice eager to please. He'd probably chuckled all the way home, he and his unnaturally clever horse. But he didn't have to be so mean afterwards.

A tear welled, and she yanked her goggles down. At least she'd had some good sex. No doubt about it, he'd been adept. His fingers, his mouth. Who could have resisted that?

162

No one, she decided. And he had put her on a very nice horse.

A sour thought nagged her. Had he used Lazer as a lure for sex? Maybe he had no intention of letting her ride in a real race.

No. He wasn't sneaky, she decided. A jerk, yes, but an honest jerk. She just had to accept she was insignificant to him. However, she wasn't insignificant as a rider. He liked the way she rode, and that's what mattered. Personal feelings couldn't enter into it. Combining business with pleasure was fun, convenient too, until it blew up in your face.

She exhaled a deep breath and pushed away her resentment. It wasn't her nature to wallow in self-pity. In guilt, but not pity. She was on a nice horse, doing what she loved. Really, nothing could be better.

From his position at the rail, Kurt watched the slender figure guiding his horse. Lazer had seemed ragged at the start, but now he floated around the track—until a horse passed him and it was clear the colt's stride roughened.

Julie settled him quickly though. She was a helluva rider, and he would've put her up on Lazer, even at Woodbine. However, the colt's inability to stay focused was troubling. The horse had lots of potential but was too distracted by animals around him. And horses didn't run races alone.

He met Julie at the gap and snapped a line on Lazer. "That looked pretty good. How did he feel?"

"Very nice," she said, her voice cool. "He switched leads when asked, relaxed well, then put out good effort down the lane. There were a couple strides when he lost his focus, when that other horse was alongside him. Other than that, he was a real pro."

Kurt nodded. Her report was also pro. She seemed to have shoved aside yesterday's intimacies. Christ, he'd been so eager to see her this morning, and all she'd talked about was a new horse she'd picked up.

And that was perfect, of course. Just what he wanted. Easier for both of them if she accepted he was a first-class prick. But the notion left him deflated.

"So concentration is the problem," he said. "Guess that's the trainer's job to fix, not yours." He scanned her face for a shade of yesterday's friendship, but she just sat there, haughty and aloof, patting his horse, and he had the perverse need to grab her attention. "If you're happy with my horse," he said, "quit slapping him."

"I'm not slapping him." She looked at him then, mouth tight with indignation. "As you can see, I'm patting his neck."

"It's a slap when it can be heard back at the barn."

And that got her attention. She stared at him now, eyes wary. "So sorry, *sir*." She reached down and stroked Lazer with exaggerated gentleness.

He turned, hiding his amusement as he led them back to the barn. Her irritation was preferable to indifference, and it was some consolation he could so easily annoy her. "Are you able to gallop Ace now?" he asked.

"Of course. You know I never refuse you anything."

Ouch. He wanted to hide his smile so let that comment go, but damn, he enjoyed her company. She filled his senses, made him feel alive. "We'll switch horses at the barn," was all he said. They passed Sandra heading the other way. She waved, still whistling the catchy tune he'd heard earlier, but didn't slow.

They reached the barn, and he stopped Lazer in the aisle. Julie dismounted while Martin held Ace, and they switched her saddle with smooth efficiency.

"What do you want done with Ace?" she asked as Kurt boosted her up. His hand lingered on her boot, and he yanked it off.

"Once at a jog," he said gruffly. "Easy gallop twice around. Work on hitting his leads. Then take him for a walk by the grandstand. We'll school in the paddock tomorrow."

"Hi Jules, Kurt."

The cocky drawl was unmistakable. Gary Bixton. Kurt nodded but noticed Julie reacted with considerably more enthusiasm. Her dimples even showed, something he hadn't seen all morning.

"Hi, Gary," she said. "Gosh. Another early morning?"

"Look out, hotshot. I'm rustling up mounts. My business is hurting since an apprentice beat me on Saturday." He rolled his eyes in disgust. "A girl apprentice."

She laughed. "I imagine trainers are dropping you like a rock."

Kurt's mouth tightened. They obviously had a close relationship, just not the type he'd imagined. Poor information, poor inference. Or maybe he'd used it as an excuse to grab what he wanted. Spoiled, she'd called him.

Bixton was all business as he turned toward Kurt. "Have you decided on a jock for your three-year-old? I can give him a whirl. See how we get along."

Kurt folded his arms. Gary Bixton was an excellent rider, experienced, savvy and the top money earner on the circuit. He glanced at Julie and saw the raw anguish on her face. She thought he'd swap riders, even after he'd committed the horse. Didn't trust him a bit—smart girl—but the knowledge stung.

"Thanks," he said. "But Julie has agreed to ride him."

"See what I mean?" Bixton shook his head. "She's hogging all the best runners." But he winked at Julie in tacit congrats. "Not a bad decision, I guess," he added reluctantly. "Guess I'll move on to the stakes barn. Nothing good left here."

Kurt watched as the jockey sauntered away. The guy had an odd way of popping up— never staying long, but not missing much either. Curious.

Julie perched on his horse, waiting. He turned Ace and led them toward the track. She didn't speak, but her silence didn't feel quite so heavy. He removed his lead line at the gap, and for a stark moment their eyes met.

"Be careful," he said.

Julie wiped her warm forehead and raised her goggles as she walked Ace in front of the grandstand. The gelding eyed the sprawling clubhouse, the rows of steps and bright garbage cans, but showed no inclination to spook. He'd galloped well too, staying balanced in the turns and switching leads when asked. Still, she was exhausted.

Already she'd galloped five horses, and riding was demanding work. There was also a slight ache between her legs, but she didn't want to think about that.

Hooves pounded. Sandra galloped up, brandishing her phone and a curious grin. "We haven't talked since yesterday," she said. "You and Kurt took a long time to move the mare. His trailer was gone all day."

Julie carefully composed her face. "We went on a trail ride."

Sandra finished her text and shoved the phone in her pocket. "You guys looked tight at the bar too. And now I hear you're Lazer's jockey. Come on. Give me the dirt."

Julie stroked Ace's neck, stalling for time. Sandra was like a badger at digging up gossip. And though she could be trusted to keep her mouth shut, Julie didn't think she could talk about Kurt, not yet, not without revealing her hurt. As a friend of her mom's, Sandra was already too protective. Luckily, the quickest way to steer her away from a subject was to bore her.

"Oh, we helped Dad a bit." Julie kept her voice monotone. "Looked at some acreages then rode into Mist Mountain. Weather was okay. Horses were good. Dusty got caught in some deadfall. They built a new cattle guard, and the parking lot is widened. Nothing too interesting." She topped it off with a long shrug.

"Really? Then what's that red mark on your neck?" Sandra asked.

Julie whipped her hand up with a guilty start while Sandra howled in delight.

"Gotcha! I used that trick on my little sister. Worked every time." Sandra clutched her stomach, still giggling. "So Kurt kissed you, and the sky didn't fall in. See, it's okay to have men in your life. Get out there and enjoy. Be happy."

Julie tried to smile but the muscles around her mouth were exhausted, and Sandra's comments only whipped up the pain. She wiped some imaginary dirt off Ace's rippling shoulder and swept away a stubborn fly.

Sandra prattled on. "If you want advice about when to have sex with someone that looks like Kurt, I'd say now. But since that's not your style, how about the tenth date or fifth horse, whatever comes first."

Julie's breath leaked out in a regretful choke.

Sandra turned silent. "Oh, dear," she said, finally. Gently.

"It just happened so fast." Julie blew out a miserable sigh. "The first time was a mistake but the second time it was me—"

"Second time!"

"It was just that I got wet in the river, and then we surprised a grizzly. Things blew out of control."

Sandra doubled up, hooting. "Hell—when you decide something, you sure don't mess around. Don't bother telling me all the details. Unless you want to, of course," she added hopefully.

A horse jogged by, and the rider called a greeting. Julie grabbed the diversion and turned Ace along the rail but Sandra followed, eyes bright with interest.

They walked half the oval, with Sandra shooting curious looks, before Julie spoke again. "We had sex yesterday. I think I wanted it more than him. But it was a one-time thing. He made that clear. Although obviously I like him." She sighed, but somehow the admission made her feel better.

Sandra stared up the rail to where Kurt waited beside Gary. "You picked a tough one. Not my first choice for you. Half the girls in the city would be delighted to unbuckle that man's belt." She gave a knowing shrug. "But men are like horses. The good ones are worth some aggravation. Play it cool, see what happens."

"Whatever I do just makes him scowl." Julie's temper flared, and she shot a glare in Kurt's direction. "He's really cranky."

"Cranky can be another word for jealous." Sandra gave a worldly flip of her ponytail. "And there are some guys here who'll thank him for proving the best part of a man isn't always his horse. It's been a long, dry spell for you," she went on. "I know your mom would be glad you're finally living a little. So no regrets, okay?"

At Julie's nod, Sandra relaxed and started whistling.

"Stop it." Julie said, darting a glance at Kurt, praying he wouldn't hear. "That song is old, and it's not funny."

"Then I'll sing it instead." Sandra belted out a few bars of 'Julie, Do Ya Love Me.'

"Your singing sucks, and it's scaring my horse." Julie leaned down and slipped off Okie's bridle. "Now forget the song or you don't get this back." She waved the bridle in the air. "And Okie looks frisky today. Even friskier if I slap him."

Sandra giggled but stopped singing. "At least you've got your gumption back. Now give it back before the outriders see." She grabbed her bridle, looped the reins over Okie's neck and together they walked toward the gap.

Kurt listened intently as Gary Bixton spoke about a horse he'd ridden in Montana—a kind, sweet-tempered mare called Country Girl.

"I couldn't believe it was the same horse." Gary shook his head. "Poor girl. I don't know what Otto did, or why, but he turned her into a psycho."

Why? Probably so no officials at the border would inspect her, Kurt thought. It had to be smuggling. He turned as Julie returned on Ace. Sandra walked beside her, riding without a bridle; her horse looked naked with his bare head.

"How was he?" Kurt asked Julie as he attached his lead to Ace.

"Perfect," she said. "And I'll be here at five thirty tomorrow in case you want your horses out first."

"Hurry up, Julie," Sandra called. "Cody finally got his trainer's license, so he's pretty happy. Only took him three tries." She smacked her lips. "He has a truckload of beer."

"A bit early to start drinking, isn't it?" Kurt frowned. Alcohol and drugs were a jockey's worst enemy. Julie didn't need the wrong kind of encouragement.

"Maybe it's early for you," Sandra said, "but I've been up since four."

"Julie will be busy with me for a while." Kurt tightened his grip on Ace's lead.

"Oh, I'm sure Cody will wait for her. He's waited this long," she added with a snicker. "Want a ride over, Gary?"

Bixton lithely swung himself up behind Sandra. Her horse didn't seem at all perturbed by the second passenger and continued his steady walk.

"See you later, Jules." Bixton gave a roguish grin. "Beer first, sauna later."

Kurt's mouth tightened. Those two jokers were a bad influence. Bixton might be able to handle alcohol, but Kurt already knew Julie couldn't. And if her reactions were a fraction too slow, if her decision making was the least bit faulty... He glanced up, chilled with sudden fear.

"We apprentices don't drink as much as the old guys," she said quietly.

His apprehension eased, but he blanked his face, wondering how the hell she knew what he was thinking. No need to worry anyway. She valued her career too much to place it in jeopardy.

Already she'd bumped him from ex-lover to trainer. He'd been deliberately cool this morning, guessing anger would help her move their relationship back to an impersonal footing; instead she could give him lessons on how to dump a lover.

He pretended to adjust Ace's lead as he studied her face. She looked good, her cheeks flushed, her lips pink and full. Not as thick and pouty as they'd been after their lovemaking. Not as soft.

He wheeled away and spoke without looking. "You did pretty good with this fellow. I think he's ready. Want to ride him in his first race?"

"Yes! Yes, of course. Thanks," she added. The happy bubble in her voice made him feel better than he had the entire morning.

Once inside the barn, he called Martin. "Put a sheet on Ace and cool him out. Come with me please, Julie."

She followed him into his tack room, waiting while he thumbed through his condition book.

"There's a maiden race for two-year-olds, four furlongs, on Wednesday night. Ace is in shape and should be able to handle the hook. You comfortable with that?"

She nodded, her eyes still sparkling. "Sure. He was balanced on the turns. A bit curious in front of the grandstand, but there shouldn't be a big crowd on Wednesday."

"Okay." Kurt tore his gaze off her mouth. "Tomorrow we'll take him out with Cisco, spend more time in the paddock and by the stands."

"We're finished then?" she asked.

"Yes." His hands tightened around the condition book and he kept his head averted, pretending to be absorbed with the fine print. "See you tomorrow, early."

"All right," she said and left. He heard her call a cheery goodbye to Martin, then her steps faded to silence. Probably off to party with the others.

Scowling, he tossed the condition book onto the cot. Damn, he liked that girl. However, he wasn't here to socialize. His goal was to build a case that would convict Connor's killer.

He strode toward the security gate. Archer was putting a tail on Otto. Julie knew nothing about Otto's friends. It was time to use other means to track down Otto's secretive visitor.

The pale, skinny guard was on duty.

"Good to see you again." Kurt gave the kid his best buddy smile. "I need your help. My cousin is dropping by to look at a horse, and I need to make sure he can get back to the barns."

"Of course. But he'll need credentials to go backside."

Kurt blew out an exaggerated sigh and propped his arm on the front of the ledge. "But that takes so much paperwork. Couldn't you let him through? It would only be for a minute."

The guard gave an emphatic head shake.

"Well then, could I sign him in here?" Kurt asked.

"Sorry, sir. You have to go to the race office and apply for a visitor's pass."

"But he's not staying long."

The guard shook his head, still polite, but his face was beginning to flush. "We used to let people in, but the office tightened up. Now everyone needs a pass. It's a rule."

"But this will be late at night. No one needs to know." Kurt pulled out his wallet and waved some bills. "Let's work something out."

"No exceptions," the guard snapped.

"Come on. Just for five minutes. I'll be with him the whole time."

"Sir! Get a pass like everyone else." The guard's face was now a blotchy red. Color even stained the tips of his ears, and his Adam's apple jerked spasmodically.

"Okay, okay." Kurt backed up, raising his hands. "I'll go to the office." He gave the flustered guard a soothing smile and turned away, satisfied now that sign-in rules were strictly enforced. There would be some record of Otto's visitor.

Kurt walked into the austere race office. The receptionist was sleek and composed, simultaneously typing and talking on the phone. A spectacular array of rings sparkled as her nails clacked over the keyboard.

"I can mail the group information," she said, her voice clipped, "but it would be easier if you could check our website. We're very busy." She cut the connection and glanced up at Kurt, her frown turning to a welcoming smile.

"Good morning." She pushed a stack of forms aside and leaned back in her chair and didn't look at all busy.

"Hello," he said. "You look like someone who can help."

She also looked experienced, poised and accustomed to male attention, the type of woman he usually preferred, someone who knew the rules before the game started. And it was always helpful to have a contact in the race office.

"It's so busy in the spring." Her pretty sigh made her breasts heave. "New trainers, not enough stalls, riders complaining about the track—everyone wants endless attention." Her skirt had a slight wrinkle, and she smoothed it before crossing long slim legs. "I haven't seen you before." She studied him with such blatant approval, he almost squirmed. "You're obviously new. Too rugged to be an owner, too big to be a rider…must be a trainer?"

"That's right." He nodded. "One of those guys who wants endless attention."

"I see." She arched a shapely eyebrow. "Well, maybe I can help. What exactly do you need?"

"It's kind of personal."

She leaned across the desk and for a second her blouse draped open revealing creamy skin and an intricate lace bra. He pulled his gaze up and locked it on her face. "Why don't you just sit down and tell me," she said, her voice turning throaty.

This might be easier then he had thought. He eased into the hard visitor's chair. "There was a guy at the barn last Tuesday night," he said, leaning forward. "Wanted me to call if I sold my trailer. But I lost his name and phone number so…" He checked her desk for a nametag.

"Tiffany, Tiffany Gates," she said.

"Glad to meet you, Tiffany. I'm Kurt." He shook her hand but deliberately left his arm on her desk and inched his chair closer to her computer. "So, Tiffany, I need someone who can check the visitor passes that were issued that evening."

Her mouth curved, revealing perfect teeth. "That's easy. Who signed him in?"

"Otto Laing."

Her nails clicked, and she stared at the computer screen. "Sorry, nothing was requested by Otto Laing. And that's odd, because security is really tight this year."

Shit. Kurt's optimism plunged. "But how else could he have got through? Is there anything else on Otto's file. What about a groom or owner's license?"

She scanned the data. "No, nothing…wait. There was a license issued last spring for a Marcus Friedman, but it expires at the end of the month. Was that the guy's name?"

"I think so. But if I saw the picture, I'd know for sure."

"Sorry, but I can't give out information like that." She glanced over her shoulder at the corner office then shot him a coy look. "You don't want to get a girl in trouble, do you?"

"Not at work. But the man really wants my trailer, and I'd hate to disappoint him. What could it hurt?" He gave her what he considered his most persuasive smile. "I would really appreciate it, Tiffany," he said.

Her eyes flickered sideways, but she turned and pressed some keys then tilted the monitor toward him. "Is this your friend?" she whispered, shooting another glance down the hall.

Blue eyes, brown hair, patrician features. Possibly a European accent. The name read Marcus Friedman, and his age, forty-seven, fit the voice in the barn.

"That's him." Kurt memorized Friedman's address a full three seconds before she turned the monitor away.

"I can't give you his address, but I'll write the phone number down." She jotted on a business card and handed it to him with a confident flourish. "My home number is on the back as well."

"Thank you," Kurt said. "Marcus and I both appreciate this."

"Betting tips are a nice way to show appreciation." She leaned toward him, and her silk blouse gaped again. "A drink after work is even nicer."

"Sure," he said, already calculating how long it would take to drive to Friedman's house. "How about tomorrow?"

She checked her calendar and made an exaggerated moue. "Sorry. I'm busy."

"Some other time then. I have your number." He stuck her card in his pocket, but he already had what he wanted. "Now who do I see about entering a horse?" he asked.

# CHAPTER TWENTY

Kurt slid into his truck and punched in Archer's number. An automated voice requested he leave a message. He recorded his destination, flipped the phone shut and entered Friedman's address into his GPS.

Thirty minutes later he was in Elbow Valley, on the west side of the city.

The address matched a luxurious home perched on a rolling hill overlooking the city center. He drove to the bottom of the manicured lawn and parked on the gravel shoulder. A stooped groundskeeper tended a bright garden, and he raised his head as Kurt walked up the drive.

"I'm lost." Kurt sagged his shoulders.

"Wha'cha looking for?" The man creaked to his feet, peeled off soiled gloves and wiped a liver-spotted forehead.

"Olympic Hill," Kurt said. "I must have missed the turnoff."

The gardener shook his head. "Nah, just get back on the highway. Head west another five minutes. You can't miss it."

"I was told I wouldn't miss it earlier, but I ended up here." Kurt casually inspected the property. No sign of horse ownership. "Nice house," he added, trying to peer around the back. "You've got a great view of the city."

"Oh, this isn't my place. I just look after the flowers. Look good, don't they?"

"Yeah, they do," Kurt said with a spike of longing. The fresh spring smell reminded him of mountain meadows, lusty sex and Julie. The old man was staring at him, so he flattened his mouth. "Must be an oil man that lives in that house," he added.

"No, Mr. Friedman owns a jewelry shop. 'Pieces of Seven', I think it's called. Can't be doing so good though, because the real estate agent was here last week. Standing right where you are now. She liked my flowers too."

"Yeah, they're real nice," Kurt said. "So the owner is selling?" He bent over and helpfully tossed a weed into the wheelbarrow.

The man stiffened, and Kurt guessed maybe it hadn't been a weed after all. He stepped away from the flowers, and the gardener relaxed.

"Selling out, is he?" Kurt prompted.

"Yeah, the housekeeper said he's moving back to Europe. Selling his house and cars. His wife don't like it here. She already left." He scratched at his thin chest leaving a smear of dirt on his shirt. "Sure hope the new buyer keeps me on."

"Yeah. Wonder why they're moving..." Kurt let his voice drift.

"Dunno. Mr. Friedman don't talk to me much. Housekeeper says he's homesick."

"Homesick, yeah." Kurt nodded. "That's probably it. Well, thanks for the directions. Good luck with the new owners."

Anticipation pulled him down the hill, and it was an effort not to jog to his truck. He did a U-turn, waved at the helpful gardener and punched 'Pieces of Seven' into his GPS.

No such shop existed. He searched every type of jewelry business. Had driven ten blocks east, cutting cross-town, when the screen finally showed a store called 'Pieces of Eight.' Ah, bingo. 37th Avenue, SW.

Fifteen minutes later he stood on the sidewalk in front of a neglected building. Several gold letters had peeled from the sign, leaving its name unreadable. Assorted silver jewelry was displayed in the window, but steel bars blocked his view and three large stickers warned of a security system.

He stared through the window, scanning the pattern on the silver. Designs focused on the city's western heritage—lots of chuck wagons, cowboys and bulls. Odd location for a retail outlet. The stuff might appeal to tourists, but this avenue fringed a residential area. It felt like a shop with no real desire to sell.

He jogged up the three front steps and pushed open the door. A bell tinkled; a lady bustled from the back room. Her pink shirt was tucked into shapeless beige slacks, and silver jewelry matched the type on display. 'Betty', her nametag read.

She eased to a wary stop, staring at him, as though suspicious he intended to rob the place. He gave a reassuring smile.

"Good morning." She relaxed a notch and stepped forward. "May I help you?"

"Probably," he said. "I'm looking for a gift for my girlfriend."

Her head bobbed with eagerness. "We have many lovely gifts. What kind of jewelry does she like?"

"I'm not sure." He glanced around, studying the shelves.

Betty's bracelets jangled as she pointed at a glassed display case. "A chain or a brooch might be nice. What color—"

"Green, and her hair is like honey with blonder streaks."

"I was going to ask what color she wears. Green?"

"No, that's her eye color."

She smiled then, a big approving smile. "Some men have been married for years and still don't know the color of their wife's eyes."

Kurt shrugged. He was a trained observer. Only natural he noticed everything about Julie. "What do you suggest?" he asked.

"We have some popular pendants with a Stampede theme."

His mouth tightened as he remembered Julie's persistent cowboy friend in the red shirt. "Nothing with a cowboy," he said quickly. "Maybe something with a stone."

"I'm sorry, sir. We don't sell those. Our silversmith designs all the pieces here, but he doesn't set stones." She gestured hopefully toward a smaller display. "Maybe you'd like to look at something over there?"

"No stones?" His disappointment was so acute he gripped the edge of the glass case. Another dead end, yet he'd been certain he had it figured. Otto and friend couldn't be smuggling silver; it was much too bulky to conceal on a horse.

"Well, we do have some zircons," Betty said. "But they're not sold out of this shop."

"Zircons?" Kurt blew out his relief, and his fingers did a relieved tap dance on the glass. "Are those the fake diamonds?"

"It's a mineral," she said primly, "and not a fake diamond. Usually they're shipped to overseas customers. But maybe we could find an extra one, just for you. Please wait a minute."

She bustled through the door and reappeared in seconds with a portable display cradled in her arms. "Ted designed these pieces and can add a zircon anywhere you want. The stones are lovely. Not many people can tell the difference between a zircon and a diamond."

"Bet not," Kurt said. "Is Ted the owner of the store?"

"Oh, no. Ted is my son. He's the designer."

"May I talk to him?"

"Sorry, sir," she said. "No one is allowed in the back. Store rules. I'll just fill out an order form and have Ted come out."

"Wait." Kurt worked hard to maintain a solemn expression. "Before I place this order, this *special* order, it's imperative I see Ted in his work environment. It makes the jewelry much more personal. I believe the artist's individuality is the very essence of his creation, so it's important to have a sense of his work."

Betty stared, her mouth slightly open, and he feared he'd overdone it, but then her head bobbed. "Yes, yes. You're absolutely right, sir," she said. "And you do understand the creative process. I didn't realize you wanted a special design. Follow me. But you can only stay a few minutes."

"Of course." He tracked her behind the counter.

"In this door," she whispered. "Ted doesn't mind visitors, but the owner is very...fussy. Teddy!" she called. "I have someone here who wants a special order."

Kurt followed her into a spacious workshop. A young man sat at a bench, engrossed with shaping a strip of silver. An assortment of pliers and snips covered his plastic work surface.

He peered at Kurt over the top of black-rimmed glasses. Acne dotted his face, and a lank strand of hair was shoved behind his ear. His black t-shirt sported music notes, a confusion of foreign symbols and a spattering of shoulder dandruff.

"Working on a ring." Ted gestured with his head as he placed a strip of silver on an anvil and tapped it with a steel rod. His

177

eyes narrowed in concentration. He seemed untroubled and largely oblivious to Kurt's presence.

Kurt scanned the room. On his right there was a jeweler's bench with a more elaborate lighting system. A gold-framed picture hung above it. Looked like Friedman with a smiling woman and a sullen-faced teenager. He eased sideways.

"You can't go there! That's Mr. Friedman's section."

Kurt stopped at Betty's sharp warning. She plucked nervously at the silver chain around her neck. Ted didn't look up.

"Does the owner do the same work as you?" Kurt asked, obediently moving back beside Ted.

"No. He only sets stones." Ted shook his head in disdain, still tapping with his rod. "I design my jewelry from scratch using sterling silver. Look at this."

Kurt looked down at the unremarkable sheet of silver. "Wow," he said.

"This is the silver before I transform it. It's 925/1000 pure. I started designing using copper and pewter, but now I only work with silver."

"Great. Excellent progress." Kurt gave a hearty nod, stealing another glance at Friedman's table. He didn't know the names of the tools and equipment, but the shop seemed exceedingly well equipped.

The door chime jangled. He felt Betty's stare and pretended an absorption in Ted's silver creation. Her footsteps receded as she left to greet the new customer, but he waited until the door clicked shut before he spoke. "Your mother said you could add zircons to a custom-made piece," he said, speaking quickly. "Could I see some of the stones, Ted? I understand there's a wide range of quality on the market."

"I have a few in my drawer, but most of them are locked over there." Ted jabbed at the corner workstation. "Mr. Friedman looks after the settings for overseas customers. But you can pick a stone from this group. Prices are listed on the back." He pulled out a display case and dropped it in front of Kurt.

Kurt tingled with satisfaction as he studied the spectrum of colors. "What did you say the owner's name was?" he asked.

"Marcus Friedman. He's from Belgium or Germany, someplace like that. Last year he saw me selling my pewter at the flea market and hired me on the spot. He pays for all the materials, the tools and the workshop." Ted squared his narrow shoulders in pride. "I get a percentage of sales. Just like an owner."

"I see. And how are sales going?"

"Well, kind of slow." His smile faded. "But Mr. Friedman says it takes time for artists to build a customer base. Anyway, the shipments to Antwerp are going well."

"How often do you ship overseas?"

"Four or five times a year, I guess. Mr. Friedman delivers them himself." Ted adjusted his glasses and glanced around as if expecting Friedman to pop up any moment. "I guess that's where he is now," he added.

"So the pieces shipped always have zircons in them?"

"Either zircons or fake gemstones. They really like that stuff over there."

Kurt muzzled his satisfaction as he fingered a colorless stone. "This one looks like a real diamond. Must be hard to tell the difference."

"Yeah, especially the ones used as diamond simulates. The stones we send to Europe are top quality."

"Where do you get the zircons?" Kurt propped his hip against the table, keeping his voice casual.

"I think they're mined in Australia or Thailand, places like that. They come in brown and green crystals." Ted shuffled through a drawer. "Anyway Mr. Friedman looks after all that stuff. He wants me to concentrate on the silver design and not worry about gemstones."

"Of course." Kurt cemented a bland expression, but his heart thumped with triumph.

"So, did you want a brooch or a pendant?" Ted found a piece of creased paper and extracted a stubby pencil from his drawer.

"What?" Kurt frowned. "Oh yeah. How about a pendant. And stick this rock in it."

"You sure you want a zircon? That'll make it quite expensive."

"Doesn't matter. Can you design a mountain peak and put the rock at the bottom? Use one of those chains out front to hang it on."

"Yeah, sure. I'll feather the mountain and put the zircon right here." Ted sketched an image and tapped the paper with his pencil. "That'll be ready in two weeks."

Kurt peeled a fifty-dollar bill from his wallet and placed it on the workbench. "How about a little extra," he said, "if you finish it in three days?"

"Three days isn't a problem." Ted scooped up the money.

The door tinkled. Seconds later, Betty hurried back. Her eyes relaxed when she saw Kurt lounging harmlessly beside Ted.

"Ted, I just sold a ring." She included them both in a bright smile and looked at Kurt. "Isn't his work lovely?"

"Very nice," Kurt said. "In fact, I worked out an order with him. And I'm happy, extremely happy, with what I found here."

Sales must be slow, he thought, noting the relief that lightened her kind face. But considering the location, he wasn't surprised. He felt a surge of pity for the struggling pair who clearly believed the shop had more conventional business goals.

"Let's go out front, and we'll calculate your deposit," she said. "You really shouldn't be back here. The owner likes everyone to follow the rules."

Kurt followed her meekly. "Is the owner strict?"

She hesitated. "A little, but he gave us both jobs. Taught me to do the paperwork, even though I don't have a bit of accounting training."

Satisfaction edged from the corners of Kurt's mouth, and he didn't even try to stop his smile. This was all excellent information, and he wanted to pick up Betty and give her a big hug.

"I just wish we had a better location," she went on. "We don't have many browsers, and Mr. Friedman doesn't want the store open on weekends. Now, I need your name and phone number."

Kurt reached out and pumped her hand. "Betty, I'm in a hurry, but you've been a huge help." He pulled out a hundred-dollar bill, considering it money well spent. "Here's a deposit. Ted said he'd have the necklace ready by Friday. I'll come back then."

He strolled out beneath the sound of the tinkling bell, ignoring her sputters about receipts, records and strict store policies.

His diesel truck started with a triumphant roar. He drove east, heady with satisfaction. He used a few minutes to process the information, then hauled into the curb at a vacant meter and called Archer. Plenty to report today.

"I just left a jewelry store called 'Pieces of Eight'," he said. "I suspect the owner, Marcus Friedman, works with Otto fencing diamonds. They bring the stolen goods across the border with a horse. Or on a horse." He frowned into the phone. "I haven't figured that part out yet. But Friedman's store is a front. He reworks the diamonds into cheap costume jewelry, and it enters Europe as zircons."

Silence.

Seconds later, Archer's breath came over the phone in a whoosh. "Any chance we can catch them with the stones?"

"Friedman probably flipped the last shipment in Antwerp," Kurt said. "He's winding down. House is on the market. Family moved out. But check the export records from Customs. The value and description will be for costume jewelry, but we can get an idea of the volume he's running. Substitute diamonds for zircons, and we're talking millions. Did you get the vet report?"

"All negative except for internal parasites and some anemia." Archer snorted. "The vet said some of those tests you ordered seemed purely health-related. All you care about is animals, and now we own a goddamn horse." But the satisfaction in his voice was obvious, even though he was two thousand miles away.

"What about the tail on Otto?" Kurt asked, making a mental note to ask Adam to include vitamins in the mare's feed.

"Order's in. And I'll get surveillance on Friedman. We should have them tagged in a day or two once we free up some manpower."

"Push it through," Kurt said. "What about your earlier promise? Something about unlimited support?"

"You don't need unlimited support," Archer said. "As usual, you're a one-man wrecking crew. This was fast, even for you." His voice lowered. "Your cover's okay though? You safe to wrap this thing up?"

"Yeah, but we need to play Otto tight. I overheard them talking about a last shipment. That's why they didn't want to lose the mare. They needed her for a final run."

"Okay but check in every day. And go easy."

"Always," Kurt said, closing the phone on Archer's sardonic chuckle.

He pulled his truck back into the inching traffic. A dented yellow taxi cut in front, but he slowed and gave the car some room. He was in no hurry. It had turned out to be a very good day. Not as enjoyable as yesterday, of course, but definitely a very good day.

# CHAPTER TWENTY-ONE

The spring air was crisp, but the dawn held promise. The track would be good today. Kurt sauntered into the barn, nodded at a bleary-eyed groom and tossed his empty coffee cup into the garbage bin. It dropped to the center of the container with a satisfying clink. The perfect toss.

He strode down the aisle feeling all was well in his world.

"Morning, Kurt." Sandra's cheery greeting stopped him.

He backed up and glanced in her tack room. A box of doughnuts sat on the floor surrounded by crumbs, cups and a cluster of napkins.

A man in black jeans, the same man who had ogled Julie yesterday, lounged on Sandra's cot. His arms bulged beneath the sleeves of his too-small shirt, and his hair was the same color as a sleek wharf rat.

Kurt almost didn't see Julie. She was wedged beside the guy, laughing at something he said. Must have been a good joke, because she didn't look up.

His mouth tightened; he pointedly checked his watch.

"We've already been out," Sandra said, looking absurdly satisfied. "They're harrowing anyway, so it's our eight o'clock break. Cody here has been voted trainer of the week. He brought beer yesterday, coffee and doughnuts today."

Cody gave Kurt an absent-minded nod and gestured at the doughnuts. "Dig in, dude. Plenty for everyone."

"I hope you'll make your weight, Julie," Kurt said, confident his voice showed nothing but professional concern.

"I will." She leaned over and studied the selection then extracted a sticky pastry, glossy with white icing.

"Julie doesn't have to worry about weight. Just look at her," Sandra said as she leaped forward to scuffle with Martin over the last chocolate doughnut.

Kurt was looking. He was looking as Julie took a big bite, was looking as her mouth opened and the tip of her pink tongue licked the corners of her mouth. Was looking as her bottom lip curled—

He glanced away, afraid Sandra might guess the nature of his thoughts. But she'd beaten Martin in the doughnut skirmish and seemed preoccupied with wiping the icing off her fingers.

"Ride my horse," Cody was saying. "He's had about sixty days' training."

Kurt waited until the man finished talking before cutting in. Julie could ride any horse she wanted but not on his time. He'd already booked her for Ace and Lazer—she was supposed to be with him, with his horses.

"I'd like you to ride my horses now, Julie," he said. "After your doughnut and coffee, of course. Ace is entered for tomorrow."

"Certainly. Just let me know when he's ready."

Kurt's mouth compressed. He'd assumed she would watch while he saddled the horse, the way she always did. After another solitary evening, he'd been looking forward to some company. Yet if she preferred to eat doughnuts and giggle with Cody, the so-called trainer of the week, that was fine too.

Exactly what he wanted.

"Lazer will be ready in ten minutes," he said. But he lingered in the doorway, reluctant to move. Cody had shifted on the cot. His leg pressed against Julie's and she didn't inch away, not like she did with Kurt.

"Let's get them ready, Martin." Kurt jerked away from the door.

Martin scrambled off the cot, snagging another doughnut on the way out. Kurt strode to Lazer's stall, Martin by his side, contentedly munching.

"I've already brushed Lazer," Martin said. "He only tried to kick me once."

"You did a good job too," Kurt said as he bridled the glistening colt. "I'll take Cisco and Ace out after we finish with this guy. You've got chocolate on your chin."

Martin ducked his head, wiped his face with his sleeve, then crammed the last piece of doughnut into his mouth. "The double chocolate ones are the best, but these are pretty good too," he said, his words sounding smothered. He swallowed and looked gratefully at Kurt. "This has gotta be the best job in the world. Being around all the horses, all the nice people."

"Yeah, it's nice." But Kurt's fingers turned awkward as he struggled with the buckle on Lazer's blinkers, and he didn't want to look at Martin's trusting, young face any longer. He turned Lazer and led him down the aisle, longing to return to his real racing business where there was no need to lie to good people.

He stopped Lazer outside Sandra's tack room, outside the circle of carefree laughter and easy voices, and wished he could join in. Lazer pawed, and the impatient horse yanked him back to reality.

Dammit. He had a job to do. Hadn't come to make friends. And Julie worked for him. He shouldn't be doing this—delivering a horse to a rider simply because he felt a bit of guilt. In fact, he should fire her ass.

But he sighed and led Lazer even closer to the open door.

"Milady, your mount is ready," he said, resisting the urge to drop a deep bow. "I assume you want to use your own saddle?"

"Definitely." She rose, scooping up her weathered exercise saddle—the one she always insisted on using—from Sandra's rack. "See you later. Thanks, Cody."

They silently saddled Lazer. As Kurt bent to leg her up, a black blur streaked beneath his arm, dodging a path between the colt's legs. Lazer leaped sideways. Clipped Julie's shoulder. She stumbled, almost fell but he reached out and hauled her to his chest.

"Damn cat," he muttered. "You okay?" He sucked in Julie's smell, enjoying the feel of her in his arms.

She nodded and quickly stepped away, while Lazer yanked at the reins, snorting, and scanning the aisle for the terrifying cat. The colt suddenly looked too big, too rambunctious, too dangerous for an apprentice. But she'd already walked back to his side, and Kurt automatically legged her into the saddle.

She glanced down, her gaze steady while she awaited his instructions. "You sure you're all right?" he asked, dragging his hand off her boot.

She nodded again and looked so disdainful he pushed away the unsettling notion that Lazer was too much horse.

"He bucks a bit when he's feeling good." Kurt's voice was gruff as he led the prancing colt down the aisle. "Get him moving right away. Three laps, same as yesterday, but with a little more gas down the stretch."

He wanted to warn her to keep Lazer's head up, to be careful of the colt's stunts, but the haughty tilt of her nose suggested surplus conversation wouldn't be appreciated. He needed her to look at him though, to smile at him the way she had with Cody, and suddenly the reasons for distancing himself seemed unimportant.

Friedman was in their sights. Julie wasn't a suspect and had no new information pertaining to the case. He wasn't going to spill his guts like he had with Anne Marie—no chance of that—so there was no reason why he shouldn't enjoy Julie's company. No reason at all.

He just had a little backtracking to do. A big weight slid off his shoulders. "How's my mare settling?" he asked.

"She's fine."

"Blue isn't hassling her too much?"

"Of course not," Julie said. "He never bothers the animals."

"He looks like a dog who'd enjoy getting close to the stock," Kurt said.

"Well, maybe he heels her a bit," she admitted, with such an adorable flush it was hard to pull his gaze away. "But it's all in play."

"We need to have a chat, Julie."

"It's okay," she said. "Blue won't hurt her."

"A chat about us," he said.

Dismay swept her face. Obviously she didn't want to dredge up Sunday's events. Further words stuck in his throat; no doubt she'd written him off, just as he'd set her up to do. They reached the gap where he fiddled with the bridle, reluctant to let her go.

"Keep a tight hold," he said, pretending to adjust a buckle. "He's feeling good so I switched to a ring bit. And these blinkers are new. Probably why he reacted to the cat. He's had an open cup before, and they didn't help with his focus. But let me know what you think."

Both she and Lazer looked impatient to get on the track, and there was simply nothing left to say. He released the colt and stepped back, joining another trainer watching from the rail.

"Your horse looks fit," the man said. "Good-looking animal."

Kurt pulled his gaze off Julie and turned to the man beside him.

"My name's Red Jollymore. That's my three-year-old coming now, Sweating Bullet." The trainer beamed with pride as he pointed at a big bay. The horse was clearly eager to run, his head bent to his chest as he strained at the bit. "You entering the allowance race Friday night?" the man asked.

"That's the plan." Kurt stuck out his hand. "I'm Kurt MacKinnon."

Jollymore pumped his hand, his mouth stretching in an eager smile that revealed a chipped front tooth. "Yeah, I know. Spent a month at Gulfstream. Saw your horses run there. We're honored to have you in Alberta. You here for the Derby?"

Kurt stalled, pretending to check his watch. The Alberta Derby was a month away. No way would he be around for that. But the Derby was the only race that made sense. Jollymore knew the caliber of his horses and would question why he'd shipped all the way out for a lowly allowance race.

"That's right. I'm here for the Derby," Kurt said as Sweating Bullet charged down the stretch. "Your colt looks strong. I see we won't steal any wins. Guess we'll meet next month."

Jollymore puffed out his chest at the praise. "We'll meet before the Derby. I'm entering for Friday too. It's a good prep. Bull hasn't lost yet, and I've got Bixton riding. Who you putting up on your colt?"

"Julie."

"Julie? The West girl? Isn't that a big race for an apprentice?"

"She can handle it," Kurt said. "She's a quiet rider, a thinking rider. And the horses respond to her."

"No shit. Guess any red-blooded male would respond to that."

Kurt stared coldly at Jollymore. The man sobered and looked away, his chuckle fading to an embarrassed cough.

"Looks aside, she's plucky and a hard worker," Kurt said, easing up on the man. "None of the regular jockeys are out here galloping. And I like a rider to work with my horse going into a race."

"Guess you're right." Jollymore's forehead crinkled in thought. "Maybe I should give her a chance. Be nice to get the weight allowance."

"Well, I'd be using her even if she weren't an apprentice. She's got talent."

Jollymore stared across the track, nodding solemnly.

There you go, Julie, Kurt thought. That should boost your career. And Jollymore was listed as one of the top local trainers. She'd be safer riding for his barn than scrambling for mounts from hobby horse hackers. He turned his attention to Lazer, warmed with a mixture of satisfaction and relief. Finally he'd done something good for her.

Lazer had stretched out, sweeping around the turn. He passed on the outside of Sweating Bullet, who'd slowed before the clubhouse turn.

Kurt stiffened as Jollymore's horse broke away from his rider's hold and chased after Lazer. The two colts matched each other, stride for stride, ears flattened as they galloped in tandem around the turn, both riders fighting desperately to stop the premature duel.

Julie braced her feet in the stirrups, pulling on the right rein and forcing Lazer to the middle of the track. Kurt watched her deftly regain control, settling Lazer back into a steady gallop on the inner rail.

Sweating Bullet, however, continued to power around the track.

"Pull him up! Pull him up!" Red Jollymore hollered, waving his stopwatch as Sweating Bullet pounded past, still flat out.

"Goddammit!" Jollymore's voice quivered with rage. "Strongest exercise rider here and the idiot can't hold my horse." He glanced at Julie with new respect. "I see what you mean. Damn smart rider. Don't know how I missed it."

Kurt smiled and stepped up to the gap. Both Lazer and Julie were breathing heavily, and he snagged the horse quickly so she could recover.

"Good job out there," he said, but his smile disappeared when he saw her pained expression. Something was obviously wrong. Not Lazer, the horse had trotted back fine. But she looked stricken. Maybe her shoulder? Lazer had clipped her when he spooked at the cat. "What's wrong?" he asked.

She leaned down, eyes regretful. "It wasn't all good. At first he wanted to run with Jollymore's horse and really pulled. But it was that chestnut on the outside that slowed him. Lazer started looking around and just stopped trying. I have to say, the blinkers didn't help at all. I'm sorry, Kurt."

He couldn't speak for a moment, weakened with relief. She was fine, just fine. Her concern was with Lazer. And the way she looked at him now, with such empathy, made his breath thicken. She didn't know Lazer was a throwaway, that the race was meaningless. She was pouring her heart and soul into his training, staking her career on a horse that was mentally immature and didn't give a shit about running.

"It's okay." He coughed to hide his gruffness. "Lazer might not make a racehorse. Just remember if he comes last, it's no worse than what he's been doing. He's had enough chances."

"But you didn't drive all the way from Ontario to run last. And Lazer is fast. He just doesn't try." She shook her head, her voice turning thoughtful. "Maybe one of Sandra's magnets would help. They use them on children with attention issues. They helped Sandra's sister, and I've heard they can calm animals too."

Hope blazed on her face, and he gave a quick swallow. She was genuinely concerned about him and his lazy horse. "I'm willing to listen." He coughed again, desperate to clear his throat.

"You can tell me more about these magnets while Martin gets Ace ready."

And I'll tell you a few things too, he thought, setting his jaw.

He led Lazer to the barn and handed him over to Martin. "Cool him out and wrap his legs. We're taking Cisco and Ace out next, but Julie and I need to have a meeting first."

And the meeting would be about much more than magnets. He waited for her to precede him into the tack room then shut the door with a decisive click.

"I've been using magnetic wraps and blankets for a long time," he said, "but I don't know much about this attention thing."

"Well," she waved her hands, eyes eager, "you already know magnets speed healing by helping cells. So if we help the cells in Lazer's brain, it might help him focus." She tapped her forehead, so enthusiastic he couldn't help but grin.

"The magnets are no joke. Just try it." She took a step closer. "There's no bad effect either, and they might really help."

"Okay."

"Okay?" She tilted her head in surprise. "You mean you'll try it? Don't you want to talk to Sandra first?"

"I'd rather talk to you. I want to apologize for the way I acted yesterday. Sort of…withdrawn."

"Withdrawn!" She crossed the small room, her voice rising. "Bullshit. You were rude and mean."

"Maybe," he said. "But at the time I thought we should step back, especially since I won't be here long—you know, since Lazer isn't panning out. I don't want a permanent relationship. You're very inexperienced—I'm not." Her eyes narrowed, and he rushed to deflect her. Didn't want her asking tough questions, didn't want to make up any more lies. "But I'd really like to see you while I'm here," he said quickly. "What do you think? Can you handle that, knowing I'm leaving soon?"

The corners of her lips quivered.

Shit, she was going to cry. Nothing made him run faster than tears. Yet he moved forward and instinctively wrapped her in his arms. Dipped his head to find her lips, comforting her in the easiest way he knew.

190

Damn, she felt good. Her mouth moved under his, and he scooped her closer, drinking in her taste. This was much better than talking anyway. She wasn't even angry, thank God. She'd slid her hand beneath his shirt, skimming her fingers over his chest, dipping along the barrier of his jeans, caressing, teasing.

He closed his eyes wondering where her little hand might explore next. Things were definitely looking up. He'd been nuts to pass this up—

Shit! He jerked his eyes open. Those sweet fingers had just twisted his nipple. Hard. He stared at her, incredulous, unwilling to believe she'd faked that kind of response.

But no, she clearly was all huffy, hands on her hips, eyes blazing and so angry she sputtered. "So you wonder if poor inexperienced me can handle seeing you. For a short while? Gosh, this is such an honor. Now let me think."

He raised his palms and edged back. "I didn't mean it like that."

"Oh?" She stepped forward, rapping a finger against his chest and backing him against the wall. "Exactly how did you mean it?"

"You hadn't had sex for a long time," he said cautiously. "You don't sleep around. That made me think—"

"That I wouldn't fit in with your stable of willing women?"

"There are no other women, willing or otherwise," he muttered, perturbed he couldn't read her quite as well as he'd thought.

"Really. Then why did you say you always had sex with anyone willing?"

His hands felt sweaty. He didn't like the way she chipped away at his feelings, cracking him open, leaving him exposed.

"Look," he said, "I was just talking. You surprised me, okay. And I didn't expect it, wasn't looking for it, don't want it." He crossed his arms, hiding behind a belligerent glower.

But she wouldn't back off and even had the gall to give a scornful snort. "You need to change your method. That bad-eyed scowl doesn't work anymore."

"All right." He lowered his arms. "What method do you want?"

"Honesty, that's all. A little attention. And no mood swings. That's the woman's job." She rose on her tiptoes and gave his chest another saucy jab. "And I'm going to be angry a lot longer than this. You have some major sucking up to do."

His arms snaked out, making her squeal as he pinned her against the wall. "This *is* my major sucking up," he said. "But if you want more attention, I'm prepared to work on that. Quite diligently."

"Diligently?"

"As diligently as you'll let me," he said. "That's a promise."

Her suspicious expression tore at him, but he had to admit her instincts were excellent. He wasn't the kind of man she needed or wanted. However, his attraction to her was potent, and he didn't intend to waste any more time. Time was already in short supply.

"Let's start again," he said quietly. "Just see where this thing takes us. Are you free for dinner tonight?"

She paused so long, he stopped breathing. Finally. "Yes, I'm free."

He blew out a relieved sigh and dipped his face in her hair, hiding his expression as he sucked in her familiar smell. "You don't know how much I want you," he whispered.

"I feel the same when you kiss me," she said. Her voice was so certain, so honest, it frightened him. Good thing she was with him and not that steroid-stuffed Cody.

"Jesus, Julie. Never tell a man that."

"Except for you." She gave a teasing smile.

"Exactly. Now you understand." He stroked a possessive finger over her cheek, watching as her expression turned pensive.

"I'm not sure," she tugged at her lower lip. "Well, I'll probably go right home after dinner." Her words came out in a rush, but he understood what she meant.

"That's fine. Just dinner will be perfect," he said, and to his surprise, he meant it. "Let's get the horses." He pressed a chaste kiss on her forehead.

"You're riding Cisco today?" she asked.

"I want to give Ace a horse to chase and afterwards go for some paddock work. Cisco's company will steady him." And he didn't plan to let Julie out of his sight.

Hooves clattered, oddly close, and they both turned toward the door.

"Sounds like a horse is coming right into the tack room," Julie said.

"That's Ace. He swings his right front out. You can hear a slight hesitation when he walks," Kurt said. "One of the reasons he was cheap."

Julie pressed her ear to the door, eyes bright with interest. "I hear it now," she said in a conspiratorial whisper.

"Martin probably heard you squeal and is rushing to the rescue. If he wasn't such a good hand, I'd fire him." Kurt squeezed her hand, feeling absurdly happy. "Trainers should be able to ravish riders whenever they please," he added with a grin.

She rolled her eyes and turned to the door. "Martin's a good groom, and he's already learned a lot from you. He even had his hair cut like yours."

"Yeah?" Kurt tried not to look too pleased. "Well, he's a dependable kid. I want to find someone to hire him—"

He plugged himself with a mental groan. Already he'd dropped his guard, a dangerous thing he needed to watch.

"When what?" She pounced on his mistake.

"We better go," he said. "We'll talk about it later." But not much later. With any luck the case would wind up smoothly. For now, though, he planned to enjoy her company. She made him happy, and he hoped to return the favor.

Kurt pushed open the door of the tack room, almost hitting a restless Ace who stood only inches away. "Glad you got him ready, Martin," Kurt said mildly, "but next time keep him in the stall. That's why we have tie rings."

Martin nodded but didn't move, his concerned brown eyes locked on Julie. Kurt blew out an exasperated sigh. Adam, Sandra, Blue, now Martin. He couldn't fault the boy's taste, but Julie had more than her share of protectors.

"Saddle Cisco for me please, Martin," he said, as he legged Julie onto Ace. "I'm riding today."

Within minutes he joined Julie, and they guided their horses toward the track. A bushy-faced terrier darted from beneath a feed truck, yapping indignantly. Ace leaped sideways but Julie didn't move, her seat so still she seemed glued to the saddle.

"Glad you like the wild ones, Julie," a familiar voice called. "Can you take my young horse out next?"

Kurt glanced over his shoulder and saw Cody leaning by the rail, a white cup wrapped in his hand. Probably not coffee, judging by the man's too-wide grin.

"Sure, right after this guy," Julie said as they walked the horses through the gap and onto the track.

Possessiveness drove Kurt. He edged Cisco closer to Ace, so close his leg rubbed Julie's knee. "Just getting Ace used to some jostling," he said when she shot him a puzzled look. Cody could bring coffee and doughnuts every morning, but he wasn't going to touch her. No way. Not while Kurt was around.

"After we warm up, I'll put Cisco a few lengths in front," he went on, "and you and Ace can chase us down. I'll come back on the outside and run with him. What's wrong?"

"Think you can stay with us?" She shot a dubious look at Cisco who plodded along, head low and relaxed, oblivious to the racehorses pounding past.

"Don't let the spots fool you," Kurt said. "Up to four furlongs, Cisco can run Ace into the ground."

Julie laughed. "Now I admit he's smart—unusually smart— and he is pretty good on a trail." She shot the horse a look of grudging approval. "But he's just an App. With your weight and western saddle, there's no way he can keep up with a Thoroughbred."

"You just concentrate on putting Ace on the proper lead," Kurt said, grinning back. "Help him stay balanced, or he'll blow the turn. I'll worry about my poor little App."

They were both trash talking as they cantered in tandem around the track. She made one final adjustment to her goggles. "Now we'll see if Easterners can ride as well as they talk," she called over the gusting wind.

Her voice lifted in challenge, and Kurt felt a rush of adrenaline as he asked Cisco for more speed. Both horses

194

accelerated into a gallop. Ace didn't seem intimidated by Cisco's presence, and his stride was steady; he was clearly up in the bridle and eager to run. But let's see how he reacts when he feels some dirt, Kurt thought.

He shook his reins, and Cisco burst into high gear, passing Ace and kicking up a spray of dirt. Julie yelled something, but her words splintered in the wind. He glanced under his arm and saw her tap Ace on the shoulder. Her horse smoothly changed leads. Kurt stopped worrying, knowing Ace wouldn't blow the turn if he were on the left lead.

The red and white quarter pole was a blur. Ace's nose edged up; Julie slipped past on the inside, but Cisco was much too stubborn to let a horse gallop by and he fought back, inching up to Ace's shoulder. Kurt leaned forward and let him run, relishing the speed, knowing Cisco loved a good fight as much as he did.

Julie's arms pumped with determination, and it was clear she didn't like to lose either. She pushed Ace down the stretch, rising in the stirrups as they crossed the finish line, half a length in front.

Ace hauled at the bit, ears pricked, looking like a winner as he searched for another horse to challenge, but Cisco galloped steadily beside him and both horses soon slowed to a long-reaching trot. A perfect work, Kurt thought. The duel would freshen the gelding and make the horse more aggressive for his first race.

Ace had made it around the turn without any trouble too. Julie might only need to give him a shoulder tap and remind him to switch leads.

"Good job," he called, more than happy with her riding. "We'll go over to the paddock and let Ace mellow out." He stiffened when he saw her flat mouth. "What's wrong?" Maybe she thought Ace wasn't ready. Maybe the gelding hadn't handled the turn as well at it had appeared. But her solemn question surprised him.

"Could Cisco have caught us?" she asked.

Ah-ha. So that was it. "What does your horse say, Julie?"

"Well, Ace thinks he won. He's still strutting."

"And that's what we're working on today," Kurt said. "It's all about attitude."

"It'd be nice to have some speed with the attitude." Her eyes narrowed as she stared at Cisco. "We should have beaten you by a lot more. Please tell me you painted on those spots and that Cisco is really a Thoroughbred."

Kurt's lips twitched. Cisco was seven-eighths Thoroughbred, but his appearance and personality were all Appaloosa. "You'll do fine in the race," he said, keeping a straight face. "Cisco had to work hard—really hard—considering he's only an App."

"Guess I underestimated him," she said, leaning forward and giving Cisco's neck an approving pat. "He's an awesome horse. Doesn't seem to be anything he can't do." Her dimples flashed with mischief when she looked at Kurt. "So you could have beaten us but realized I'd be a sore loser?"

He reached over and tugged her ponytail but didn't deny it.

They passed the grandstand and walked into the saddling enclosure. She stopped grilling him about Cisco's bloodlines; the conversation shifted to the best places to eat. He preferred steak over sushi, but with Julie racing tomorrow he knew she'd want a lighter meal.

"Sushi would be great," he said, enjoying her open expression, the way her eyes sparkled when she spoke, the contentment he felt when she smiled. He didn't care where they went. Would have been happy with a hot dog.

"There's a Japanese restaurant in the south end. You'll be happy to know they also serve an excellent rib eye." She gave him a perceptive smile and slowed Ace. "Want me to dismount?"

He shook his head. "Just ride him around the walking ring until he's seen everything. Martin and I already schooled him in the paddock."

Julie guided Ace around the small ring while Cisco rested a hind leg, happy to relax. Kurt dragged his gaze off Julie and tried to concentrate on the two-year-old. Ace seemed braver now, making no objection when Julie rode him away from Cisco. A maintenance man clanked a garbage can, and the gelding didn't even react. So far Ace was training nicely, much better than Lazer—

"Kurt!" A sultry voice sounded behind him.

He placed a hand on Cisco's rump and swiveled in the saddle, watching as Tiffany rushed across the concrete, her spiked heels rapping a keen staccato.

"I thought that was you." She pressed against the rail, and it was apparent she favored low-cut blouses. "Is that your horse, the one you entered yesterday?"

"Yes, and that's Julie West riding him," he said.

From his vantage point in the saddle, it was impossible not to notice Tiffany's generous cleavage, but Julie shot him such a mocking smile he averted his head and cemented his eyes on Tiffany's face. Cisco had no such inhibitions, however, and shoved his head into her chest; Kurt snapped a rein and straightened his nose.

"Your horse must be male." Tiffany giggled up at Kurt, turning her back on Julie. "About your earlier dinner invitation, turns out I'm free tonight." She had a lovely dulcet voice that carried beautifully, much too beautifully.

"I'm sorry," Kurt said, "but I'm busy now."

Tiffany gave a pointed smile. "I hope you found the man who wants to buy your trailer."

He shifted uneasily in the saddle, aware he did owe her a favor but also aware Julie had halted Ace ten feet away. And she was no longer smiling.

"I'm sorry, but I already made other plans," he said. "Another time would be better. Maybe lunch tomorrow?"

"Gosh," Julie said, her eyes shooting green shards. "I just remembered I have a prior commitment. So you don't have to worry about those other plans." Her shoulders set in a rigid line, and she headed past them toward the exit.

"Hey," he called. "You can't go yet. Ace isn't finished. Walk him around a couple more times."

Her cheeks flamed at his rebuke, but she resumed circling. Tiffany gave a loud laugh, and Kurt wished he'd just let Julie leave. But, dammit, Ace had his first race tomorrow, and Julie knew the plan. She couldn't quit because she didn't like the railbirds.

Cisco's nose edged back to Tiffany's chest and Kurt tightened his rein, afraid the App might stain her blouse.

"It's okay," Tiffany said. "It can be dry cleaned." She didn't step back, although he noticed she didn't pat Cisco either. Her interest in horses was clearly from a distance.

"I'll pay for any slobber marks," Kurt said to Tiffany as Ace and Julie circled past.

"Watch out for hickeys too," Julie muttered.

"What did you say?" he asked.

She shot him a mutinous look but continued circling.

Tiffany raised an amused eyebrow. "If it turns out you're free, Kurt," she said, not bothering to lower her voice, "just give me a call. I'm in the office until four. And you already have my home number."

She turned and clicked back to the race office. Cisco swished his stubby tail in disappointment. No peppermints from her. Kurt consoled his horse with a pat and rode toward Julie. "I told her I was busy tonight."

"You won't be busy with me." She stuck her nose in the air.

He blew out a sigh. He didn't like to pussyfoot and had little patience for games, but if she needed him to grovel, he would. Just a bit. "This business with Tiffany is work. She did a big favor for me—"

"And you pretended you were selling your trailer so you could get to know her?" Julie shook her head in disgust.

He considered pulling together a trailer story—he was pretty good at on-the-spot fabrications—but didn't want to dish out any more lies. "I want to be with you. Just you and no one else." He held her gaze, hoping she'd feel his sincerity. "That's all that really matters."

"No other women." Her voice shook, and she looked spitting mad. "That's what you said, only a half-hour ago. I gather Tiffany wasn't free so you needed a stand-in. Well, now that your first choice is available, I'll do us both a favor and back out. Is this horse finished now?"

At his reluctant nod she turned and headed toward the barn, letting Ace cover the ground with his long-reaching stride. Kurt followed at Cisco's more ambulatory pace, and the distance between them widened with every step.

Dammit. He refused to trot. Didn't have the time or inclination to chase women, and he certainly wasn't going to chase after his jockey, especially in this instance when he hadn't even done anything wrong. It was ironic that whenever he tried to be honest he looked more like a liar.

However, Cisco seemed to sense his ambivalence and broke into a spirited trot, and Kurt reached the barn right behind Julie and Ace. A welcoming Martin appeared by the door with Ace's lead and a red cooling sheet draped over his arm.

"I'm not feeling well, Martin," Julie said. "Would you take care of my saddle for me?" She rushed away, not looking at Kurt, but the choke in her voice twisted his gut.

Martin looked at Kurt with accusation in his wide eyes. "She didn't even take her saddle. The special one that was her mom's. She never gallops in anything else."

"I'll take it to her," Kurt said, knowing she'd want it for her next ride.

Martin just stared with hound-like forlornness, and Kurt's gut gave another twist.

"Hey. Want to use Cisco to pony Ace?" Kurt asked. "You can ride behind the barns. Both horses need cooling."

"Oh, yeah!" Martin nodded, full of instant forgiveness. "I've never ponied a racehorse before." He snapped his mouth shut, as though afraid Kurt might change his mind.

"You'll do fine. Just keep them away from other horses."

Kurt barely had time to dismount before Martin edged in, stuck his toe in Cisco's stirrup and scrambled into the saddle, so eager to mount he didn't bother to shorten the stirrups. Just snagged Ace's lead rope, flashed Kurt a thumbs-up and vanished behind the barn.

Martin was happy again, and heck, he deserved a chance to ride. Julie and Sandra had been giving him lessons on Okie, and Cisco was savvy enough to keep them all out of trouble. But Kurt feared it wouldn't be that simple to appease Julie. He dragged a hand over his jaw and headed off to find her.

A horse pounded behind him. He stepped to the side of the path, checking over his shoulder.

"Where's Julie?" Sandra called as she slowed her horse.

He shrugged and held up Julie's saddle. "I'm looking for her. She was planning to ride a couple more, but we finished quicker than expected."

"Damn. I wanted to help her with Cody's horse. That animal's so rank he makes Otto's mare look like a puppy dog." Sandra clucked at Okie and trotted away.

Kurt circled the barns. It was nine thirty a.m.; the track closed at ten, and most serious trainers had finished for the morning. He turned and headed to the oval. Spotted Julie's vest and helmet as soon as he stepped up to the rail.

She rode a tall chestnut with a white face and four white legs. The horse had no martingale but clearly needed equipment to keep his head down. His nose was in the air, and he sidled, crablike, across the track.

He looked green, very green, and broke into an awkward canter, cross firing and clinging to the outside lead. A delivery truck rumbled around the tall grandstand, and the horse leaped sideways, then shoved his nose out and charged forward.

A horse galloped by on the inner rail; the chestnut bolted after him, his steps frenzied. Julie braced her feet, trying to stop him with a pulley rein, but the chestnut pounded into the clubhouse turn, unbalanced and clinging to the wrong lead.

Something scared the horse—oh, shit, Julie's saddle had slipped—and the chestnut veered sideways, almost clipping another horse.

"Man, those two horses nearly went down," someone said.

Kurt stared helplessly, unable to look away, his throat too tight to talk. The rider behind Julie was still swearing about the near miss even as an intrepid pickup rider galloped after her. But the outrider was thirty lengths back, gaining too slowly, and the chestnut careened around the turn, ears flattened, his fear intensified by the galloping horses.

Just keep him on the track, Julie, Kurt willed. He'll stop sometime. But the horse's eye rolled toward the barn, and it was apparent he was going to duck out.

200

"Get that rail up!" Kurt yelled to the dolts standing by the gap.

Too late. The chestnut dropped his right shoulder and scooted sideways through the opening. Julie's slim body catapulted. She smashed into the dirt, almost impaled by the tip of the jutting rail.

His stomach caved. *Please let her be all right. Please, please, please.* He dropped the saddle and rushed to her crumpled body.

He heard a ragged gasp—she was alive, at least—and dropped to his knees, crippled with fear. She'd hit the ground so hard. Her back, her neck…

"It's okay," he said, pretending a calmness he didn't feel. "Breathe in. Now out. Good girl, just like that."

Her eyes opened. She gripped two of his fingers as she fought to breathe, fought to suck air into her clogged lungs, and the frantic look on her face made him ache.

"Breathe in again. There you go." His voice sounded so level, it surprised him.

She managed a shallow breath, her panicked eyes holding his.

"In and out again," he said. "Good girl, another breath."

He heard steps and looked up, pushing the curious bystanders back with a protective glare. His expression softened when he turned around. Her breathing seemed to be steadying, and already the grip on his hand had loosened. She straightened her legs.

"Don't move yet, honey."

Still winded, Julie stared up at him, filled with despair. He was so kind. So capable. So gorgeous. Naturally he enthralled her—and every other woman around. But she couldn't compete with Barbi dolls like Tiffany. Didn't want to.

He must have seen the pain in her eyes. "Where does it hurt?"

"Everywhere," she said. *Especially my heart.* "But I don't think anything's broken. See?" She wiggled her arms, her legs, her fingers.

"Don't move yet," he said urgently. He ran his hands around her neck, over her back. "What do you feel? Any pain there? How about here?"

She just stared, murmuring short replies, her thoughts as scrambled as her body. He must have had comprehensive first-aid training. His hands were knowing and unexpectedly gentle for such a tough-looking man. But of course, she knew all about his special touch. She quivered at the memory and fought the urge to dip her head into the comfort of that hard chest.

"I'm okay," she said. She had to get away, especially now, when both her body and emotions were bruised. "I just need to sit up so I can breathe."

He helped her to a sitting position, supporting her in his arms. "You scared the shit out of me," he said, his voice close to her ear.

*Thump, thump.* The hammering of his heart surprised her. He seemed so calm, so composed.

"Scared me too." Her mouth wobbled. "I never had much control. Cody's saddle slipped, and then things really went downhill."

"We always land in trouble after our little arguments," he said.

"They don't seem so little to me." She prayed he didn't hear the catch in her voice.

"Maybe not so little," he said, "but it wasn't what you thought. Tiffany—"

"You okay, Julie? Do we need the ambulance?" Cody sidled up, followed by an outrider.

"I'm all right," she said. "Just had the wind knocked out. Is your horse okay?"

Kurt's arms tightened around her, and she sensed his frustration. He had no patience for incompetence, no doubt would complain about Cody's horse being too green for the track. True enough, the chestnut needed a lot more work. But Otto seemed to have disappeared, and she simply couldn't afford to lose another trainer.

"What happened back there?" the grim-faced outrider asked.

Julie shot Kurt a glance, pleading for his silence. "I pulled the bit through the colt's mouth, and it scared him," she said. "It won't happen again."

She stared at Kurt, holding his hooded gaze. She knew he was honest, brutally so. However, silence seemed to be his method to avoid lying, and this was just a little twist on the truth. Not even a lie. Cody had used a small ring snaffle with no chin strap. She probably *had* pulled the bit through with that first desperate yank.

Kurt only stared, the center of his eyes so dark they seemed bottomless. Finally, almost reluctantly, he spoke. "I have a stronger bit that Cody can try. An extra breastplate too. Now let's go to the hospital and get you checked out."

"No, I'm fine, thanks." She pushed his arms away, along with her despair. Jockeying was tough enough. It was impossible to cope with a relationship too, and Kurt was not an easy man.

"You can lie down in my trailer," Cody edged closer, "since I feel responsible." He offered his hand and she took it, trying not to wince as he pulled her to her feet. "After all," he added, "it was my horse."

She walked slowly, hiding her throbbing pain, as Cody escorted her off the track.

"His horse, his trailer," she heard Kurt say to the outrider. "Now isn't that fucking warped reasoning?"

The outrider only laughed.

# CHAPTER TWENTY-TWO

Kurt switched lanes, inching his truck behind a pokey green mini van that reeked of exhaust. Traffic on the one-way street was slow and snarly, just like his mood. Cyclists breezed past, unhampered, but vehicles simmered in the late-morning sun.

He cut toward the curb, ignoring indignant blaring from the white Explorer on his bumper. The driver crawled by, shaking his fist. Kurt stepped from his truck and made a rude gesture of his own.

A pedestrian edged past, giving a wide berth, careful to avoid eye contact.

Kurt didn't give a fuck. Right now Julie was with Cody, and he didn't give a fuck about that either. He stalked down the alley behind 'Pieces of Eight' and scanned the back of the shop. A steel door led to a vacant parking space, empty except for a green garbage bin with two worn wheels and a cracked lid. Paw prints crammed the muddy path that edged around the building to the front of the store.

Nothing remarkable. There was a window, although even that was barred. But as he turned to leave a chill fastened to his spine—a chill so cold and unexpected that goose bumps rose along his back. He checked over his shoulder, hit with the distinct sense someone was watching.

Houses fronted the back of the alley, but they seemed deserted. No curtains fluttered, no noses pressed against glass. Nothing to account for his uneasiness.

But he turned back, inexplicably drawn to the shop window, and at the edge of the thick mud he was hit with such an acute awareness of Connor, he stumbled.

He let out a ragged breath and pressed his damp palms against his jeans. Lingered until he regained his composure then grimly retraced his steps, circling around to the front of Friedman's store. The tinkling doorbell announced his arrival.

Betty scurried forward with a reproachful frown. "I'm glad you came back. You didn't leave your phone number, and Ted wanted to check about the chain."

"How's he making out?"

"Almost done," she said. "It'll be finished tomorrow."

"Good. Then I'll just duck back and see Ted."

"Oh, no." She clutched nervously at her throat. "Mr. Friedman is back from Antwerp. You stay here. I'll have Ted come out."

She disappeared with jerky steps, one hand still clutching her neck, but in seconds she reappeared. "Ted will be out with some samples once Mr. Friedman finishes with him."

"Mr. Friedman's here? In the shop?"

"Yes, he just walked in the back door. He's tired from his trip but did bring some new orders."

"That's good news," Kurt said, thinking of Archer's phone taps and what they might have picked up. He dragged a hand over his jaw, knowing he should remain anonymous but tempted by the chance to meet Friedman.

Caution prevailed.

"That's my drive honking." He gestured out the window. "I'll come back tomorrow. Tell Ted that one." He tapped a finger over the glass. "Second chain over. Looks strong. Pretty too."

"But we need you to sign an order form—"

He gave a dismissive wave and walked out. Called Archer as soon as he was in his truck. "Check the report on Connor's clothing," he said. "Find out if his boots were covered with mud and dog shit. We might get a match from the alley behind Friedman's shop. And have someone slip back tonight and check the garbage container. They'll have to be careful. The place is run down, but the bars and doors are new. Could be sensors or cameras."

He paused, picturing the back of the shop. "Probably not sensors," he added. "Too many paw prints. But have them dress up as street people, just in case."

"I'll look after it," Archer said. "We placed an alert at the border and will have taps and twenty-four hour surveillance on Otto. Starting tomorrow."

"Tomorrow! Why so slow?"

"Authorization takes time. You know how it works."

"And sometimes it doesn't work at all." Kurt couldn't hide the bite in his voice. "Christ, Archer. Push it through. Friedman has another shipment lined up for Antwerp. He'll need more stones. Otto could be crossing any time."

"Excellent. We need him with the goods, or a decent lawyer would get him off."

"There are no decent lawyers," Kurt snapped.

"Why are you so prickly with people," Archer asked, "but a marshmallow with animals? Don't your horses like the Alberta grass?"

"They're not here to eat. My two-year-old is running tomorrow. The other one runs on Friday. First lifetime start—"

"Good, good. Got a meeting now but hope they do well." Archer's voice carried the gruff heartiness of someone who knew nothing about a subject and didn't want to learn. Paper shuffled in the background.

"Yeah, thanks," Kurt said dryly. "I'll check in tomorrow. Send some race video. We can talk more about racing then."

He snapped his phone shut and leaned against the headrest, bored at the prospect of another monotonous night. Even Otto couldn't provide a diversion now that he had no horse at the track.

A young lady bounced by with a Jack Russell terrier strutting at her ankles. It was a fresh May morning, and the dog's lively expression marginally improved his day. The lady slowed to let her dog sniff at the lamppost.

The terrier dipped his nose and darted forward. The owner threw Kurt a rueful smile before the determined dog yanked at the leash and rushed her off to another marking spot. Kurt idly admired the woman's curves. From the back, she looked a bit like Julie. Same jaunty walk, same little hip wiggle.

He shook his head and rammed the key in the ignition. A melancholy song filled the cab, reminding him of Julie—with Cody—and he snapped off the radio. Maybe it was time to firm up that date with Tiffany. Have a little dinner companionship along with the thick steak he really wanted. Lots of information floated around a race office; he might learn something useful.

Besides, he'd already incurred Julie's wrath for seeing Tiffany. It was unlikely things could get any worse.

# CHAPTER TWENTY-THREE

The numbers on the clock radio changed, chipping away another piece of dawn. Kurt pressed a heavy arm over his eyes, trying to postpone the inevitable. It had been a late night, and he wanted more sleep. But his mouth felt like cotton, he needed to use the bathroom and as usual, he craved coffee.

With an irritable grunt he hauled himself from the bed. He showered, shaved and headed for the track.

The sky was a gunmetal gray, the sun still hidden by the ridge, when he crunched into the parking lot. He lingered in his truck, sipping his coffee while he thought about last night's dinner.

The evening hadn't been a complete waste. Tiffany was charming with a keen understanding of track politics. The dinner had been delicious, and she certainly had displayed a considerable capacity for liquor. But she'd insisted she didn't know Otto, Friedman or their connection, so he'd hit a dead end with any line of questioning.

He hadn't wanted to linger past dessert—especially not with a pair of wounded green eyes haunting him—and had returned to his motel alone and with a sense of relief.

He drained the coffee and tossed the cup on the floor. One of these mornings he'd gather up the empties but not today. Shaking off his lethargy, he locked the truck and rounded the corner of the barn, wondering if Julie would be too bruised to ride.

Oh, fuck! He jerked to a stop. The coffee he'd just enjoyed turned sour in his gut.

An ambulance, three city police cars and a track security vehicle blocked the entrance to G barn. He broke into a run, scanning the spatter of faces. There—he spotted Julie and Martin, both on their feet, both unhurt. Relief spurted through him, and his nauseous stomach settled.

"Sorry, sir." A uniformed cop stepped forward and blocked his way. "No civilians allowed under the circumstances."

"What are the circumstances?" Kurt asked, pulling his gaze off Julie and staring down at the cop.

"I can't say, sir."

"Is anyone hurt?"

The officer's eyes flickered sideways. "Yes, there's been an accident," he said.

Shit, a bad one, Kurt decided. He glanced at Julie and Martin. They looked dazed but uninjured as they spoke with a stony-eyed officer who scribbled in a coiled notebook.

"Get a blanket over those two," Kurt said. He jammed his hands in his pockets, resigned to waiting by the perimeter of yellow tape. The interrogating officer finished with Julie and turned his attention to Martin. Kurt rushed toward her. The short cop made an officious attempt to stop him but lowered his arm when he saw Kurt's expression.

Kurt swept her in his arms, absorbing the trembles that wracked her body. Someone shoved a blanket in his hand, and he tucked it around her. She stared at him, wordless. The dark centers of her eyes drowned the green.

The officer finished questioning Martin and flipped his notebook shut. A second blanket was pressed in Martin's arms but he just stared, a white face on a shivering body.

Kurt shifted Julie to his left arm, eased the blanket from Martin's hand and wrapped it around the boy's shoulders. Both Martin and Julie watched him with blank eyes, but neither said a word.

Ambulance attendants huddled in a circle, not moving, not in a hurry.

"Do you have a horse in the barn, sir?" the officer with the notebook asked. The radio clipped to his belt crackled, but he adjusted a dial and the noise subsided.

Kurt nodded warily.

"Would you step over here, please. Julie and—"

"Martin," Kurt said.

"Julie and Martin can sit in the warm car. We'll keep an eye on them." A solemn officer nodded assurance.

Kurt shepherded Julie and Martin to the police car. "Have an attendant treat them for shock," he said before following the notebook officer toward the barn entrance.

"I'm afraid there's been a fatal accident," the man said as they entered the shadowed aisle. "The victim is in a stall with a black horse. Julie and Martin were first on the scene. They think the horse belongs to a man called Otto Laing but said they've never seen the animal before.

"We need to remove the body but no one wants to go in the stall," the officer continued, his voice lowering. "If there were any chance the victim was alive, we'd have shot the horse but…" He shook his head. "Can you help?"

Kurt turned away from the man's regretful expression and walked down the aisle, automatically taking shorter breaths in an effort to block the unmistakable smell of blood, flesh and death. Horses churned in the stalls, wide-eyed and panicky. Even Cisco was affected, his nostrils pink and flaring as he stared across the aisle.

Five policemen and a track security guard watched as Kurt approached. They silently stepped back. Their eyes swung to the door directly across the aisle from Cisco—Otto's boarded-up stall.

Sorrow, guilt and regret crashed like a wave in Kurt's chest, and he struggled with his composure. Had to squeeze his eyes shut for a ragged moment before daring to peer through the knothole. He knew who was down before he saw the mangled body.

Nick's farrier tools were scattered in the aisle.

A quivering gelding pressed against the back wall. Dark bay not black, Kurt noted clinically. From the fetlocks down the horse's legs appeared crusted with mud. But it wasn't mud.

Nick's head was split. One hand, the hand with four fingers, extended toward Kurt as though in a last appeal. He sprawled face-down in the streaky straw, but Kurt imagined his eyes were reproachful. Bluebottle flies crawled over his matted hair, buzzing and lifting heavily in the air before landing again, bloated with insatiable greed.

Kurt's stomach pitched, and he squeezed his fists, hard, before turning toward the waiting officers.

"We can run some rope to that empty stall across the aisle," he muttered, "and chase the horse across."

Under his direction the men rigged up a rope chute. The stall door wasn't latched, and he avoided touching the bolt, pulling the door open from the top before stepping into the stall with the frightened horse.

The animal's ears flattened. He lashed out with both hind feet.

Someone cursed. Kurt jumped back into the aisle but left the door open, hoping the horse would choose to flee the grim stall. But the terrified bay kept his rump aimed at the door, not budging from his dark corner.

"Did anyone call the vet for a tranquilizer gun?" Kurt asked.

"I have a gun on my hip," someone muttered.

Kurt shot the speaker a scowl. "That's not necessary. Step back from the rope. Give him more room."

The men shuffled away from the makeshift chute.

Kurt grabbed a whip and entered the adjoining stall, ignoring the occupant, a chestnut gelding who snorted with suspicion. He pulled himself up the side of the wall, thrust the whip past the clump of ceiling cobwebs and through the tiny gap between the ceiling and top board. Poked Otto's horse on the rump. The animal flinched, dropped halfway to the ground, then whirled and leaped over Nick's body before bolting across the aisle to the open stall.

An alert officer slammed the door shut.

By the time Kurt stepped back into the aisle, two ambulance attendants had rushed into the vacated stall and were crouched over Nick.

"Okay. Now we can look after this situation. Your name, sir?" The officer with the coiled notebook planted himself in front of Kurt.

Kurt propped the whip against the wall and answered the man in monosyllables, his mind churning with his own questions. Why had Nick been in that stall? He was an experienced horseman and would never corner a frightened animal. He didn't even shoe for Otto.

Suspicions swept him, and a muscle ticked spasmodically in his jaw. Had Nick been curious about the shoes on Otto's horses? Too curious maybe? Maybe he'd encountered Otto.

A shovel could have caused that type of head injury. Enclose a panicky horse with a prone body, and the rest was predictable. The border check. Surveillance. What the hell had gone wrong?

"Mr. MacKinnon? Please answer the question."

The officer's irritated voice yanked Kurt back. He nodded. "Yes," he said quietly, "the horse probably belongs to Otto. That's his usual stall, the one with the boards."

"All right. Thanks for your help. We may want to talk to you again." The man's voice carried a silky threat, and he made Kurt repeat the name of his motel.

"Aren't you going to check the stall?" Kurt asked.

"What for?"

"For whatever killed Nick."

The officer slapped his notebook shut. "Look. Even an idiot can see the horse killed him." His flat stare locked with Kurt's. "And I don't consider myself an idiot."

"Maybe you should."

The officer's mouth tightened, and Kurt bit back the rest of his suggestion. It was always useless to get into a pissing contest with the local law. The RCMP and city police were working jointly on Connor's murder, although city police hadn't been advised of Kurt's presence.

Still, Nick's battered body affected him, and he'd seen plenty of bodies before. His thoughts jumped to Julie and Martin. No wonder they'd been reeling.

He rushed outside. A car edged from the parking lot—one driver, with Julie and Martin hunched in the rear seat.

He jogged alongside the car, rapping his knuckles on the hood. The car stopped; the driver's window lowered.

"Where are you taking them?" Kurt asked.

"I'm driving Martin home. His mother is there. There's no answer at Julie's house, so we're moving her to the hospital for observation."

"No need. I'll look after her."

The officer's voice rose. "Now look here."

"I'll look after her," Kurt repeated.

The man's mouth thinned with displeasure, but he turned toward the back seat. "Where do you want to go, miss?"

Julie's gaze skittered over the attendants as they removed a white-mounded stretcher. "With Kurt, please." Her voice was faint and reedy.

Kurt helped her from the car and into his truck. Started the engine, blasted on the heat, and thumbed the tear tracks from her cheeks. "Do you know if Martin fed the horses?" he asked gently.

She remained blank-faced for long seconds but finally nodded. "At first we didn't notice anything," she whispered. "There was a bad smell and the horses were restless, but we were laughing...we didn't know...we were laughing." She groaned and swung to the window.

"Stay here. I'll be right back." He grabbed his cell phone, punching in Archer's number as he loped to the barn. Wasted no time with civilities. "Goddammit, Archer. A farrier was found dead in Otto's stall this morning. City's been here and removed the body. They're calling it an accident. It's not."

"Jesus."

"What happened at the border?" Kurt struggled to keep his voice low. "I thought Otto would be searched up his fucking ass."

"Don't know." Archer's voice was unusually subdued. "But I'll find out."

"A bit fucking late now." Kurt ground his heel in the dirt as he turned and checked his truck. Julie was sitting exactly as he'd left her. "Better get some plainclothes guys out here with video and camera," he said. "There's blood. Maybe not all Nick's. And lift fingerprints off the stall door. I'll watch it here until they show."

He snapped the phone shut and rejoined Julie. Fiddled with the heater, the blanket, the radio. She seemed oblivious to his stalling.

Ten minutes later an unmarked Crown Vic swooped in front of the barn. Kurt signaled he would return and drove from the lot to his motel.

He opened the truck door and guided her into his room. "Still cold?" he asked.

She sat on the edge of the bed, pale, silent, unspeaking. Only her fingers moved, twisting and pulling at the edge of the blanket.

Kurt joined her on the sagging bed, just wishing she'd let it out. "Does Nick have a family?" he asked.

She nodded and sucked at her lip, eyelids blinking furiously.

"Oh, honey," he murmured, hating his helplessness. He stroked her cheek; the gesture seemed to penetrate her shell. A tear welled in the corner of her right eye. She looked at him then. Her face crumpled, and she buried her head in his chest.

He didn't know how long she cried. Didn't care. But by the time her shaking subsided and her sobs dwindled to weak hiccups, his shirt was damp.

"I didn't think a horse would ever do that." She rubbed at her pale cheeks. "Especially to someone like Nick. He was so good with them. Loved them all. Nick was supposed to shoe our horse last night." Her voice strengthened, turning thoughtful. "Strange he was in Otto's stall. Maybe the horse was cast, and he was trying to help him up."

"Maybe," Kurt said. Skepticism roughened the word, but he kept his hands gentle as he stroked her back.

Her eyes narrowed. "The last time Otto hauled a horse in, someone else died. So weird. Someone should ask him—"

He planted a kiss on the top of her hair, hoping to distract her. "Give it time," he murmured. But she felt so good in his arms, he lingered. Couldn't resist dragging his mouth along her jaw and nuzzling her neck.

A second later she stiffened and jerked away. Stared at him, then at the bed and her thoughtful expression turned to disgust.

214

"My God. You'll use any situation to take advantage of the ladies."

"No ladies here," he said jokingly, deciding any topic that took her mind off Nick and Otto was probably a good one.

But she winced, clearly insulted.

He mentally groaned at his poor choice of words. "I didn't mean it that way," he said quickly.

"Doesn't matter. I'm obviously not a lady. You only needed one trail ride." Her voice cracked, but she gave a dismissive shrug. "Everyone needs a little fun. However, the next time I have sex, I'll do the choosing."

"But you did choose the last time. You said 'yes', very clearly." He stretched back on the bed, pretending her words didn't hurt, but his face felt like it was carved in granite.

She jerked up and jammed her hands on her hips. "That kind of yes doesn't count. We just ran into a mother grizzly. What happened afterwards was basic relief."

"Ah, so those little noises you made were sighs of relief?" He watched as color flagged her cheeks; she wasn't a bit pale now.

"You're an unprincipled asshole who'd nail anything that moves."

"Not lately," he said.

"I'm leaving."

He propped a pillow behind his head, watching through narrowed lids. Thought she was moving stiffly but wasn't quite sure. "Walk out now and you're not riding my horse tonight," he said.

She'd already reached the door, but her hand dropped from the knob and she wheeled to face him. "Even you wouldn't do that."

"Sure I would." But he couldn't hold her gaze. "Sex is pretty important to unprincipled assholes like me," he added.

She flushed with temper. Her cheeks were still stained with tears, but the signs of shock had vanished. A little more color, and she'd look completely normal.

"Just one kiss and you can ride Ace," he said.

She shook her head in disbelief.

"A little more and you can ride Lazer," he added, reassured by her reaction. If she really thought he was a complete asshole, she wouldn't look so shocked by his ridiculous proposal. His face didn't feel so tight now; in fact, the side of his lip even started to twitch.

She stared intently, probably guessed he was joking. However, she continued to look beautifully indignant, and anger was preferable to her helpless sadness that tore at his gut.

"A little more and I can ride Lazer?" She crossed her arms. "What do you mean? How much is a little more?"

"I don't know. Whatever you feel like. Gotta hurry though." The sides of his lips quivered, and he knew his stone face was cracking. He was just so damn relieved she was back to normal. Fresh, feisty and refreshingly honest.

"Just a minute," she said. She swept into the bathroom and closed the door. The tap gurgled. Something clinked. Maybe she was brushing her teeth, always a good sign. The door inched open. "You have to close your eyes," she said.

He obligingly closed them, listening to her steps as she approached the bed. "It has to be a good kiss though, honey." He'd only been joking, but he wasn't going to let this opportunity pass. She had him balled in knots, and a kiss from her might keep him going for a week.

"Don't worry. It'll be good." Her sultry voice purred above him. "And wet."

*Splash!* A wall of cold water slammed like a gut punch, soaking his face, his shirt, the bed.

"Fuck!" He scrambled up, splattering water like a dog, rivulets streaming down his face.

"You don't look so smug now...honey." She turned, carried the ice bucket back into the bathroom then tossed him a towel.

He snagged it with one hand and blotted his face, absorbing the water, his disappointment, his shock. "You're full of surprises," he said. "How did you know I wasn't serious?"

She gave a smug smile. "That definitely isn't the way successful trainers pick their jockeys."

"Depends how badly we want them." He lunged. One squeal and he had her flat on her back, pinned to the bed. She stared, eyes incredulous, then started thrashing. "Hold still, or you'll hurt yourself," he said. "I want that shirt off. Now."

Her eyes glittered with fury as he unbuttoned her shirt. He shoved it open and softly whistled.

"Ah hell, Julie." Compassion roughened his voice when he saw why she'd flinched when he'd helped her step down from the truck. Why she'd been walking stiffly. Ugly bruises snaked from the top of her ribs to below the waistband of her jeans.

She understood now and lay still, staring up at him, vulnerable and exposed. "I'm okay to ride though. I'm really okay."

He rose and stepped back, shaking his head at the blotchy smear of color. Hated what he had to do. "No, you're not okay. Not combined with what happened this morning. I'm sorry."

"It won't affect my riding."

He reached down and probed her hip. She flinched.

He sighed and lowered himself on the bed. "I can't let you ride the two-year-old. You're in no shape for acrobatics. It could be a wild race tonight with all the first-time starters."

"Please, Kurt. Please let me ride." She tugged at his arm. She rarely touched him but did now, looking at him with her heart in her eyes. Her heart for his horse.

"No!" He set his shoulders, steeling himself against her plea. There was no way he could let her ride. "Absolutely not."

"Please. It's important to me."

He turned his head and rose, didn't want to see her disappointment. Rifled through a drawer, cursing as he fumbled for a dry shirt. Glanced over his shoulder. She slumped on the bed, looking so shattered his chest constricted.

"Goddammit, Julie," He slammed the drawer shut. "Ride him if it's so fucking important. But you might screw yourself up for Lazer. And that's a bigger race."

Her wobbly smile made his heart kick.

"Thank you so much," she said. "I'll take good care of Ace. I promise."

"It's not the horse I'm worried about." He yanked off his clammy shirt, pulled on a dry one and stalked toward the door. Couldn't believe he was going to let her ride. But she'd looked so damn devastated, and it hurt to see her sad. 'I'll drop you off at Sandra's." He dragged a hand through his hair. "Make sure she stays with you for a few hours. Ice your chest. Have a warm bath. Take care of yourself."

She just stared at him, unmoving, her beautiful face luminous with gratitude, and the last thing he wanted to do was return to a crime scene. "Come on," he said. "I've got stuff to do. And button up that shirt, you…hussy."

That made her react. She bounced off the bed, still with the radiant smile, and punched him in the shoulder then wrapped her arms around him in a grateful but far-too-brief hug.

# CHAPTER TWENTY-FOUR

By the time Kurt drove Julie to Sandra's and returned to the barn, it was midmorning. A white panel van was backed against the door behind the barrier of yellow tape. Solemn onlookers kept a respectful distance.

The man Kurt had seen in the unmarked Ford waved him into the barn.

"I'm Sergeant Hans Leaman." He passed Kurt a pair of latex gloves and shoe covers. "Assume you're MacKinnon?" At Kurt's nod, he added, "We were told to work with you but to be discreet. We have a forensic team here. They lifted prints off the dead man's tools and the door and stripped the stall for lab analysis. We've got pictures and video. Only thing left is to check the animal."

"Find anything?"

"Just some nails and a lot of blood. Nails are bagged over there."

Kurt picked up the bag, examining its contents through the plastic. All were old horseshoe nails with the heads cut off. "The horse was moved across the aisle," he said, dropping the bag back into the evidence bin. "Guess you've seen him?"

"Yeah, but we haven't dared open the door. He's cranky." Hope gleamed in Hans' eyes when he looked at Kurt. "Think you can get close enough for a blood sample?"

Kurt walked to the front of the stall, studying Otto's horse as he pulled on the gloves. The bay seemed calmer. He still stood by the back wall but at least faced them.

"Pass me the needle, but don't latch the door," Kurt said as he slipped into the stall. "I might need to get out pretty quick."

He waited a moment by the door. The horse raised his head and snorted—wary but curious. Kurt stepped closer, one foot, two, three. When the horse tensed, he stopped. Finally the animal's shoulder was inches away. He raised his arm. The gelding flinched so he lowered it and waited, repeating the process until he was finally able to stroke the horse's wet shoulder.

"You're no rogue, are you," he murmured, patting the animal's sticky neck.

*Sticky?*

He pulled his arm back and stared at the smear on his fingers. "This horse has holes poked through his neck," he said slowly. "He's all bloody. Looks like someone stuck him with a pitchfork."

"Maybe the poor guy he trampled tried to defend himself." Hans' voice was dry; he remained a prudent distance from the door.

"Then someone moved the pitchfork, because it wasn't in the stall this morning," Kurt said. "Maybe the horse was forced over the victim's body."

"So it *is* a homicide." Hans' voice lowered, and he passed Kurt a needle.

The gelding swished his tail when Kurt pushed the needle in his neck but didn't step away, seemingly happy to oblige. Blood slowly filled the vial.

"Need anything else?" Kurt asked.

"Can you scrape some dried blood off each leg?"

"Yeah, but pass me some hay."

Kurt exchanged the vial for four plastic bags and a flake of sweet-smelling alfalfa. The horse rushed forward and shoved his nose in the hay, delighted to have a meal.

"Forgiving animals, aren't they," Kurt stated as he scraped blood from the front legs into a plastic bag.

Hans just grunted but no longer stared at the gelding in raw accusation. He'd even relaxed enough to lean over the stall door.

Kurt moved to the horse's hindquarters and scraped off two more samples. He pushed the straw away from the animal's hind feet, inspecting the trail of dried blood. Christ! He rocked back on his heels, startled by the glut of nail holes. Fresh holes, just like the mare. But unlike the mare, this horse had no back shoes.

He rose stiffly, heavy with thought as he gathered the samples and left the stall.

Hans took the vials with a satisfied grunt, oblivious to Kurt's turmoil. "That's it then, buddy. Hope this doesn't compromise your role here. We were given specific instructions to avoid that." He slotted the vials in a square steel case. "Keep your head up," he added.

Kurt watched from the doorway as their vehicles crunched away, leaving him with a renewed sense of isolation. And regret. He could no longer ignore the regret. He swallowed, shoving back the sour taste in his throat. Didn't want to think about why Nick had visited Otto's horse—not now, not while his emotions bubbled like blisters.

He dropped a chair in front of Cisco's stall and sat, determined to flatten his feelings, trying to draw from years of practiced control.

Cisco leaned over the door, always non-judgmental, always happy to see him. Kurt gave the horse an absent pat while the App tilted his neck in bliss. A few people wandered past, throwing Otto's horse dark looks and asking nosy questions, but Kurt's brusque answers discouraged conversation.

An hour later, Otto finally lumbered down the aisle.

Kurt flicked the piece of straw from his mouth and stepped into the aisle, blocking Otto's path. "Friendly animal you trucked in last night."

A variety of expressions darkened Otto's face, but none looked like remorse. Kurt's hands clenched.

"Yeah, the race office called. Told me what happened." Otto sneered. "That idiot had no business fucking with my horse."

"Did you ask Nick to shoe him?"

"No, he must have gone in there by himself. After I left."

"Now why would a busy guy like Nick do that?"

"We'll never know," Otto said. "I hear he's dead. Now get the fuck out of my way."

"Not yet."

221

Otto's sneer turned gloating. "Good, because I've been waiting to do *this* again." He stepped forward and drove a fisted slab into Kurt's stomach.

Kurt twisted but the blow landed hard, hard enough to drive his air out in a whoosh. He staggered and stumbled back.

Otto charged with a maniacal laugh, and Kurt reflexively snapped his leg into Otto's groin. The man slowed but didn't stop. Kurt sidestepped, kicked Otto's face then whirled and chopped a lethal arm across the back of his neck.

Otto dropped like a sack of sand.

*Get up. Get up.* Kurt circled the man on the floor, fists clenched, his breath escaping in furious gasps.

"That won't help." Sandra's voice was distant, blurred by the roaring in Kurt's ears. He looked up. She kept talking, her mouth was moving, but he couldn't make sense of her words.

He turned back to Otto, sprawled on the floor, and edged closer, wanting to hurt him some more—needing to hurt him.

"That won't help Nick," Sandra said.

Kurt opened and closed his hands, battling for control. The thunder in his ears hurt, and he shook his head, trying to deaden the sound. Trying to deaden his feelings.

Slowly he backed away.

Otto struggled to his knees, staring at Kurt, bleary-eyed but belligerent.

"Get out of here, you asshole!" Sandra hissed, stepping between the two men. "And take that fucking horse with you."

Otto lurched to his feet, raking them both with a virulent glare. Sandra edged closer to Kurt as Otto shoved past her and out the door.

"I don't think it's wise to antagonize him," Kurt said, his ragged breathing loud in the tomblike barn.

"What were you doing? And I'm not a total idiot. I only talk tough when you're around." She shook her head. "Otto doesn't care about Nick at all, does he?"

"He definitely has sociopathic tendencies," Kurt said.

"Well, be careful. Fighting gets people suspended, and we like you around here. And it's not just because of your nice horses." She shrugged as though embarrassed by her admission.

222

"How about I pony Lazer and Ace for free today? Believe me, that's a rare offer."

"Guess it's a good thing you came along then, free ponying and all." Kurt forced a smile, but his voice turned serious. "Thank you, Sandra," he said. "I was rather...annoyed. You didn't leave Julie alone, did you?"

"No. She's fine. Gary's with her."

Kurt acknowledged a slight twinge of jealousy. "Okay. And I accept your ponying offer. But just jog Ace one lap. He's racing tonight."

"Oh, right. Ace's first lifetime start," Sandra said. "That could be exciting."

"Could be," Kurt said.

# CHAPTER TWENTY-FIVE

"Horse looks sharp, Martin." Kurt patted Ace's neck, admiring how the light reflected off the gelding's washed and polished coat. Martin's mouth inched upward in a wan smile. "You sure you want to be here?" Kurt asked gently. "You might want to take some time off. I gave your mom some numbers for people you can talk to about Nick's accident."

Martin looked down, scuffing the toe of his worn boot in the straw. "Psychiatrists." He snorted. "No way. I'm not emo."

"Actually they're psychologists," Kurt said, "and they can help. They've helped me."

"You?" Martin's eyes widened.

Kurt examined Lazer's feet, feeling Martin's avid eyes. "Everyone has stuff happen in their life. It doesn't help to bottle things up. Doesn't mean you're not tough." He ran his fingers over the shoes, checking their tightness, surprised he was even talking about this with a kid.

Martin stopped scuffing the floor. "I never thought someone like you would need help. Not like me, you know…" Martin's voice trailed off. "Maybe I'll get Mom to call." His voice strengthened. "But not tonight. Tonight is Ace's first race. And I'm definitely going to be there."

"You sure have Ace looking like he can run," Kurt said, relieved by Martin's show of excitement. "Pass me the syringe, and I'll wash his mouth."

Kurt squirted water into the horse's mouth, standing back so the green hay slime didn't splatter on his boots. "Now the Vicks."

"I didn't see any snot." Martin's eyes darkened with concern as he opened the blue jar and pressed it in Kurt's hand.

"This stuff clears breathing passages, blocks distracting smells. And washing his mouth gets rid of food particles. Everyone has a pre-race ritual. This is mine. I've done it this way since I was your age, helping my dad. Until it stops working, I'm afraid to change."

"You? Afraid? You're not superstitious, are you?"

Kurt just smiled as he flipped through his assortment of bandages. He didn't consider himself superstitious. Not really. But much of racing depended on luck, and there was no way he'd risk incurring bad karma, not if it could be avoided. "The track is a bit cuppy," he said, "so I'll wrap his front legs for support. This red looks good on a dark horse, don't you think?"

"I'm not that good with colors." Martin shoved his hands in his pockets and stepped back, clearly uncomfortable with anything resembling fashion. "Sandra always uses purple," he added helpfully.

"We'll go with red to match my silks," Kurt said. He wrapped Ace's front legs and unbuckled the halter. "Pass me the bridle you cleaned."

Kurt slipped the snaffle into Ace's mouth. "I'm going to put his tongue tie on here so we won't have to do it in the paddock. So many young horses, it might get hairy over there."

He wet the thin cloth that would keep Ace's tongue in place and looped it around the horse's lower jaw. "Let's go," he said, looking at Martin. "But stay close. I'll need your help saddling."

"You want me in the paddock? Cool! I've never done that before." Martin's exuberant air punch startled Ace, who jumped sideways. "Sorry," he mumbled sheepishly.

Kurt just yanked the brim of Martin's ball cap. At least the kid's haunted look had disappeared, pushed aside by excitement and inevitable race jitters. And some races definitely caused more jitters than others.

His hands had felt awkward when he bandaged, but he didn't want to acknowledge his own fear. Didn't want to worry about Julie. Wouldn't let himself. This was just another race, one of hundreds. He turned to Martin and forced a careless nod. "Let's go find out how fast our horse can run."

Spectators were sparse when Kurt led a wide-eyed Ace into the walking ring. The gelding shied at a curly-haired boy who'd climbed onto the rail, making rumbling noises as he pushed a toy tractor. An apologetic mother rushed over and plunked the youngster back in his stroller.

A man in a spotless white cowboy hat passed Martin the bridle number, and Kurt guided Ace into the number eight stall of the saddling enclosure. The official pulled up the gelding's lip to check his tattoo; Ace resented the familiarity and wrenched his head away. A steel gray colt jigged past, diverting Ace's attention, and the official quickly made the check and moved on.

Julie's valet appeared. Kurt placed the pad on Ace's back, layering it with the numbered saddlecloth and her tiny race saddle. The valet stood on the opposite side as they buckled the two girths. Ace's muscles bunched, but the gelding was mesmerized by the nervous gray being saddled on the move, and his wide eyes tracked the horse until the gray colt vanished in the slot beside them.

"Hold him tight, Martin, while I stretch his front legs," Kurt said.

*Crack!* Noise boomed, and the thick planks beside them quivered as the protesting gray smashed the wall. Ace flattened his ears and lunged forward, knocking Martin to one knee and dragging him alongside.

"Hang on!" Kurt yelled.

Martin's heels trenched the dirt, but he didn't release the panicked horse. By the time Kurt reached them, Martin had regained his feet, his jaw set with determination.

"Good job hanging on," Kurt said, reaching for Ace's reins. "It would have been a pain in the ass chasing him back to the barn. I'll lead him for a bit. Get Ace away from his noisy neighbor."

Martin nodded, glancing over his shoulder at the seven horse who still pounded the walls, objecting vigorously to every step of the pre-race procedure.

Kurt scanned the rest of the competition as he led Ace around the walking ring. The compact bay in front of them had nice hindquarters and would probably love the short distance. The blinkered colt ahead of the bay was not as well-muscled but had a nice hip and a businesslike attitude.

Of course in a race full of first-time starters anything could happen. His throat was dry, and he squeezed Ace's reins. Please, keep your rider safe, he thought, just as the spastic gray charged out of the enclosure and reared straight up.

The gray wavered on his hind feet with the handler trying to maneuver him back down, but the colt lost his balance and flipped. His legs waved in the air like a stuck turtle.

Everyone hushed. Seconds later someone shouted and the horse scrambled up, still bouncing. The crowd breathed again.

Ace had watched the commotion too and started to shiver. It began with his shoulder but soon his entire body trembled, burning precious energy. Kurt guided him behind the blinkered horse, hoping the bay's quiet confidence would reassure Ace.

Martin also needed to lighten up. He still looked pale after Ace's bolt and studied the quirky gray with obvious apprehension.

"There's a cute little redhead standing over there." Kurt stopped Ace in front of Martin. "And I don't think she's waving at me."

Martin flushed but glanced over. He gave the girl a jerky nod then studiously averted his head.

Kurt's attention was caught by the parade of color filing from the jockeys' room. "I need to talk to Julie," he said. "Take Ace. Keep him moving, but don't let him drag you around. He'll feel better if you're confident."

Martin sucked in a breath but squared his shoulders and gamely took the horse.

"I'll be close by," Kurt said, stepping onto the grass to await Julie. He sucked in a regretful breath when he saw her stiff walk, the way her right shoulder tilted. Goddammit, she was obviously sore, obviously shouldn't be riding. But her face glowed with such anticipation, his regret slid away. There was no way he could deny her this race.

"Good evening, sir," she said.

"Ms. West. How are you?" He probed her face, but she shrugged off his concern with an eager smile. She wore his racing silks—MacKinnon stable colors—and his sense of possession sharpened.

"Your horse looks good," she said, her attention on Ace.

"Martin has him polished. He's on the muscle. You're last to load, so he won't have long in the gate. The seven horse has been acting up. If there's a rodeo in there, jump off and get the hell out."

"Sure." She crossed her arms and grinned.

"I mean it, Julie." His fear crystallized at her blasé attitude. "And don't hurry him out of the gate. A couple of these horses might blow the turn. Don't let them push you wide. Just relax, let him find his stride. Try to avoid traffic trouble and make it fun for him."

She nodded. Uncrossed her arms and flicked her whip against her boot. Clearly eager to get going. Kurt said nothing else, waited beside her as Ace towed Martin around the ring. The horse's head was bent to his chest, ears pinned, and he looked as eager as Julie.

"It's only four furlongs," Kurt added, unable to remain silent. "Ace isn't bred for early speed. It's the experience that's important, not where he finishes. You'll probably be running at the back most of the way. Just give him a good run down the lane. I want him passing a horse or two there."

She nodded, looking so tiny that dread shivered through him. God, he hoped Ace didn't have a claustrophobic fit in the gate, or blow the turn or stumble or veer in front of another horse.

He squelched his fears and forced a smile. Nodded at someone he didn't know. "Riders up!" the paddock judge bellowed.

Martin guided Ace over, and Kurt legged Julie into the saddle. She slipped her toes in the irons and knotted the reins while he led the gelding to the group of waiting escort riders. It was a routine he'd followed hundreds of times before with countless horses and riders. But as he handed the pair off to

Sandra, he was hit with the weird compulsion to grab Ace and turn him around. Forget the damn race.

Ace needed more training. He wasn't really ready. Too many new things could scare him: the crowd, the announcer, the other horses. In a second, he would freak.

Ace walked calmly onto the track.

A trumpet salute sounded as the procession of two-year-olds paraded in front of the grandstand. Kurt tore his gaze from the tiny rider perched on Ace's back. Looked at Martin. The boy's face was bright with nervous anticipation—the feelings Kurt usually had before a race. But not today. Today his gut corkscrewed with fear.

He gestured at the middle of the grandstand. "Let's watch from up there." He scaled the steps two at a time, Martin scampering beside him, and only stopped climbing when he could see across the infield.

There'd be a straight run from the chute before the horses entered the turn and fired for home. Ace looked like a veteran, warming up calmly beside Sandra's horse. But there was a lot of pressure, and that goofy gray was breaking from Ace's inside.

"Ace is probably happy to be with Sandra's horse," Martin said. "He and Okie are good buddies now that their stalls are close."

Kurt swiped his clammy forehead and nodded. Ace would be fine. Julie would be fine. But maybe he should have walked over to the starting gate so he could watch them load. So he'd be close by if anything happened.

"Ace looks great," Martin said.

Kurt nodded again but shifted sideways, wishing Martin would shut up. He stuffed his program in his hip pocket, surprised to see it tightly rolled, like a kid's telescope. He didn't usually mutilate his programs. Couldn't remember ever doing that.

The starter called the horses. Kurt's fists balled as the group turned for the chute, and Julie's red helmet approached the gate.

One by one, the horses disappeared. He kept his gaze fixed on the splash of red as Julie circled Ace, waiting their turn to load. There were only two back now, the seven horse and Ace.

The seven horse balked.

Blue silks flickered from within the gate as a horse reared, protesting the delay. Julie had better be ready. The starter wouldn't make this young bunch stand around long. The doors would open as soon as Ace walked in.

The seven horse was kicking up a commotion, and his panic was spreading. Horses' heads jostled; colors moved behind the bars.

"Good thing Ace isn't loaded yet. Some of the horses are really freaking out." Martin's sharp eyes were glued to the gate. "Man, did you see that horse go up in the air! Looks like the rider's off."

Kurt groped in his back pocket. Dammit, he'd forgotten his binoculars.

"The seven horse is scratched," the announcer said, his voice cutting through the crowd's grumble.

*Good.* Kurt felt too tense to be charitable. Now Julie wouldn't have that bronco on her inside. The seven horse was led to the far end of the chute, and Julie's helmet disappeared in the gate.

The last horse was in. Oh, Christ. He stopped breathing.

"They're off!" the announcer said.

A horse bobbled, one of the runners close to the rail. The horse stayed on his feet, but the jockey was down. There was a collective sigh of relief when the rider picked himself out of the dirt. Kurt started breathing again. The riderless horse galloped after the pack, running in the middle of the track, with flapping reins and a carefree attitude.

Kurt's attention swung to the horses galloping down the backstretch. Ace ran five wide. Julie's helmet bobbed along in a maze of churning bodies. Bobbing way too much. Ace was running ragged. *He'll blow the turn if he goes in like that.* Steady him, Kurt willed.

By the three eighth pole, the horses had strung out. Ace was fifth, four lengths behind the leader, but running awkwardly.

"Boy, that chestnut is really smoking," said a white-haired man in front of them. "He'll go gate to wire. Look how easy he's moving."

Kurt blocked the comments, his breathing lightening when Ace finally settled into his smooth ground-eating gallop. "Good girl!" he yelled with such intensity the white-haired man turned and raised an eyebrow. Ace'll run the hook okay now, Kurt thought, as the gelding entered the turn on his left lead.

The crowd moaned as the betting favorite, a blinkered bay running second, drifted across the track and bumped the horse on his outside.

"Did you see that hit?" Martin shouted gleefully. "This is better than a hockey game!"

Kurt couldn't watch anyone but Julie. His heart pounded with every beat of Ace's hooves. By elimination, there were only two horses in front of her, and Ace was running the turn beautifully. As the horses straightened down the stretch, the chestnut was still four lengths in front, a white-faced bay was second and Ace strained to catch them both.

The crowd roared, anticipating a big payoff. The chestnut flicked his ears in front of the grandstand, faltering at the unfamiliar wall of noise. Bixton waved his whip, reminding him it was a race. The chestnut dug back in.

But Ace blitzed down the lane, his stride long and effortless. He charged past the bay and swept across the finish line in second place, confident and full of run.

Kurt sagged with relief. Martin cheered and jabbed a jubilant elbow in Kurt's ribs. Kurt barely felt it; he was too drained. Julie's riding was aging him faster than any police work.

"Thank God that's over," he muttered as the last runner straggled across the finish line, and an outrider nabbed the loose horse. "I'll go pick him up." He wiped his brow, trudged down the stairs and stepped over the rail.

Julie looked ecstatic as she trotted Ace back. Fine for her, Kurt thought sourly. He felt like he'd been kicked in the stomach.

"Beautiful ride," he heard himself say. "Just what I wanted." He groped for something else, but his mind was numb. "How did he feel?" he asked lamely.

"Super!" Her teeth gleamed against her dirty face, her silks were filthy and three sets of muddy goggles draped her neck.

231

She'd never looked more beautiful. "He was wonderful once he settled," she added. "Ran the turn like a train."

Kurt just stared, his relief so sharp it was bewildering. He fumbled to unbuckle the girth but his gaze drifted back to her fragile chest, watching as it rose and fell beneath his silks. He'd have to check on the type of protective vest she wore. Some weren't as good as others. And her saddle looked so worn. One equipment failure, one stumble, and she'd be crushed.

He felt cold. She still jabbered on about Ace and he forced another nod, another inane comment. "You rode him perfectly," he mumbled.

Ace held his head high, staring imperiously over the crowd as she whipped off her saddle. "He thinks he's a big racehorse now." She laughed and gave Ace a grateful pat before turning back to Kurt. "Thanks for giving me the ride, in spite of everything. I really appreciate it." She clutched the saddle in front of her, her face so earnest. So precious.

"No problem. You two clicked." I'm the one with a problem here, he realized. His legs felt heavy, and he was reluctant to lead Ace back to the barn, reluctant to let her go. He took a hard swallow. "Are you going to the pub tonight?" he asked.

"Yes."

"Good. Maybe I'll see you there?"

"Ah…Cody's coming too. We're sort of going there together."

"Sort of?" He thought regret flickered over her face but wasn't sure. She was finally learning to hide her feelings, and a poignant sadness swept him.

She squared her shoulders, staring at him through the barrier of swirling, suffocating dust, but her enunciation was very clear. "Cody and I are going out tonight."

"Okay." He swallowed convulsively—the dust made it impossible to breathe, but he seemed to be the only trainer with a problem. "Some other time then," he managed.

He turned Ace on his haunches, passing Martin, who was high-fiving a group of raucous teenagers. The red-haired girl stretched so far over the rail it seemed she would topple into Martin's arms. At least the kid was having some luck.

Kurt led a strutting Ace back to the barn, wishing he could share the horse's exuberance, wishing he didn't feel quite so empty.

By the time Martin appeared, he was hosing Ace and weighing alternate plans for the evening. He gave Martin an absent nod as he considered calling Tiffany. They could pick up right where they'd left off. No reason not to call her—except that the idea had zero appeal.

"Still smiling over that cute redhead?" Kurt asked as he pulled his gaze from the water puddling around Ace's hooves.

"No way." Martin shook his head, but a telltale flush stained his cheeks. "I'm just happy about how well Ace ran. But I'm going back to the grandstand after I feed. Catch up with my friends. They all want to hear about my job."

The kid looked happy. Kurt shoved aside his own disappointment. "I'll do the feeding tonight," he said. "Just hold Ace while I grab a sweat scraper. Then you can scram."

Martin's grin widened, and Kurt was even smiling when he entered the barn. Maybe he'd hang out with the horses tonight. Stick around and clean some tack. He slowed when he saw an open door, a door that was usually locked—Otto's tack room.

He quickly checked Otto's horse. The gelding stuck his head over the door and nickered, seeming to consider Kurt an old friend.

Obviously Otto hadn't been around for a while. The stall was filthy, filled with soiled straw that even a starving horse wouldn't eat. A cracked water bucket was overturned in the far corner.

"Did he quit feeding you?"

The gelding gave Kurt's arm a hopeful nudge.

Kurt shook his head and slipped into Otto's tack room. It didn't look promising for the hungry horse. The room was empty of hay, empty of grain, empty of almost everything. Even the hobbles were gone, along with Otto's bits and bridles. The metal box was still there though, its contents a secret.

A murder weapon maybe?

No, Otto wouldn't be stupid enough to leave anything there. Then again…

Kurt left the tack room, so preoccupied he almost forgot to grab the sweat scraper before rejoining Martin. "Looks like Otto's horse isn't getting fed." He pasted on a bland expression as he scraped the dripping water off Ace's belly. "Were you here when Otto packed up?"

"Yeah," Martin said. "He threw a lot of garbage in the dumpster. Loaded the rest in his truck. He was talking on his phone a lot."

"Maybe arranging for feed?" Kurt forced his voice to remain neutral.

"No. Sounded like he was talking to someone from a bank." Martin ducked his head, looking sheepish. "I wasn't trying to listen or anything, but I was brushing Ace. Couldn't help overhearing."

"It's okay," Kurt said. "People don't expect privacy if they're talking in a barn aisle. Maybe he's selling the horse because of the…accident."

Martin nodded earnestly. "Otto said he'd come by Saturday afternoon and get his money. He didn't even swear. Not one word. That's why I thought he was talking to the bank. My mom's always polite then too."

"Probably a good policy," Kurt said, digging in his pocket. "By the way, I give staff a bonus when my horses finish in the money. You deserve it."

Martin's eyes widened as he stared at the bills in Kurt's outstretched hand. "A hundred bucks! Oh man, thanks. Thanks, man." He pocketed the money and slanted his Flames cap to a more rakish angle. "You know, I really like this racing business. My girl—I mean, my friend, thought it was pretty cool in the paddock when I stopped Ace from running away."

"It was cool, Martin. You were a big help. Ace was the best-looking horse in the race. Have fun with your friends."

He watched Martin saunter toward the grandstand. The boy's shoulders seemed squarer, and it looked like he'd grown a couple inches. Funny how horses had that effect.

Ace jerked at the lead, insisting on his share of attention, and Kurt led him around another twenty minutes before putting him in his stall. He wrapped the horse's legs and stepped outside.

234

The sky was dark, but the walkway that led to the grandstand was well lit. Several horses and their attendants walked toward the track, although none of the shapes were bulky enough to be Otto's.

Kurt walked to his truck and called Archer. "Can you tell me where Otto is?" he asked. "I assume you've got someone on him by now."

If Acher didn't like Kurt's tone, he didn't show it. "Yes, he's covered," Archer said. "What's happening at your end?"

"It's quiet. But it would help if I knew Otto's location. The teenager who works for me overheard a phone conversation. Seems Otto has a payday on Saturday. He might have been talking to Friedman."

"Or any number of people."

"No, Friedman seems to be the only one Otto doesn't curse around."

"Okay. I'll see what the phone tap picked up." Archer cleared his throat. "About the death this morning, the autopsy report will be available in a few weeks. The Calgary Police reported no sign of foul play, but we're playing everything tight at this point. Wait a minute and I'll check on Laing."

Kurt cradled the phone between his head and shoulder, pushed aside an old coffee cup and a collapsible shovel, and hauled a cardboard box out from beneath the seat.

"Kurt."

At Archer's voice, he straightened and repositioned the phone.

"Your boy is standing at a betting window," Archer said. "We have someone in the line next to him."

"Good. Call me if he heads back to the barn. Has the surveillance guy got a backside pass?"

"The surveillance guy is a female and no, she doesn't. We're afraid of leaks from the racing office. But the exits are covered so Otto can't leave without us picking him up. There's also a tracking device on his truck." Archer cleared his throat again. "I'm sorry about the victim. The request for the border check wasn't circulated in a timely fashion."

"You mean someone fucked up."

Archer waited a beat. "Yes," he finally said.

Kurt balanced the phone against his ear as he rummaged through the box, pushing aside duct tape, plastic, tweezers and a stuffed teddy bear. Finally found his lockset. "Just be sure to call if Otto heads back."

He closed the phone before Archer could ask any questions, pulled a blanket over the box and walked back to the barn and into Otto's tack room.

He closed the door behind him, switched on his penlight and crouched beside the metal box. The padlock was a good one. He tried several picks before finding one that fit. A heavy-footed horse clomped by; he stopped, listening, before resuming his delicate probing.

Ah, there it was. A click, and the lock released. He yanked the padlock off and tipped back the lid.

Tightened his mouth in disappointment. Only farrier tools, a motley collection of used horseshoes and two strips of thick black rubber. The shoes clinked as he shoved them aside. A stained paperback, *How to Be Your Own Farrier*, was curled at the bottom.

He shook the book but nothing fell from the pages so he turned his attention to the shoes. Four were aluminum race plates, but the others were traditional steel. Average shoes, average thickness.

He snapped some pictures and replaced the padlock then listened by the door before stepping into the aisle. A few people worked at the far end of the barn, but they were immersed in race buzz. No one looked his way.

He returned to Otto's stall. The gelding sifted through his manure but nickered and rushed to the door, lipping off a piece of hay that clung to the front of Kurt's shirt.

"You're friendly today. Hoping for some food?" He opened the door and rubbed the horse's neck. The horse obligingly stretched his head, turning sideways so Kurt could scratch all his hard-to-reach places. They both jumped when the phone rang.

Kurt stepped from the stall and flipped open his phone. "Yeah."

236

"Your horse pal is heading over to the barn, reportedly in a foul mood. He has a fresh bruise on his left cheek. Know anything about it?"

"Part of an earlier discussion," Kurt said.

"Ease up. Your kind of discussion lands us in legal trouble."

"You knew what you were getting when you called me." Resentment hardened Kurt's voice. Archer was probably taping the call, protecting his ass. "Did you get the horse's blood results back?"

"Preliminary. So far, no illegal substances were found, and all the blood came from the victim. By the way, Laing passed the security booth three minutes ago."

"Gotta go. I'll call tomorrow."

He stuck the phone in his pocket and sat in front of Cisco's stall. Didn't wait long. Otto's horse jammed his flaring nostrils over the door, stared down the aisle then edged back and stood motionless in the darkest corner of his stall.

Otto swaggered in from the shadows.

"Why, I wonder, are your horses always happy to see you?" Kurt asked.

Otto walked past.

"Gee, you're quiet." Kurt rose from the chair. "Tough night at the windows?"

Otto disappeared in his tack room. Kurt stiffened, then remembered all the shovels and pitchforks were gone and relaxed his fists.

Otto reappeared. Didn't look at Kurt, just locked his tack room, trudged down the aisle and out the door.

"Don't forget to feed your horse!" Kurt called.

But the man was gone.

Kurt sat down, rubbing his jaw. Otto's restraint was unexpected and creepy. Someone must have cautioned him, someone very persuasive if they had realigned him so quickly. Someone damn dangerous.

Otto's horse shuffled back to the front of his stall. His head stretched over the door, and he stared at Kurt with soulful brown eyes. Kurt rose, knowing he couldn't let the animal starve.

He found an extra bucket, gave the horse hay and water and lingered by the door, watching the gelding devour the hay.

A familiar horse clopped down the aisle.

"There's the big trainer," Sandra called from beside a sweat-streaked Okie. "You should have told me to bet your two-year-old. I missed that one."

"I missed it too," Kurt said. "Didn't think Ace would get up in such a short race. His pedigree says he can't sprint."

"And Appaloosas can't run. Ace got along well with Julie, just like Cody's planning to." Her voice was muffled as she tugged at her cinch.

"What did you say?"

Sandra seemed to be having unusual difficulties with her saddle and struggled to loosen her latigo. "Pedigrees don't mean shit," she said.

"No, what did you say about Cody?"

"Oh, that." She shrugged but didn't turn around. "I heard that Cody stocked up on bacon and eggs and hopes to have a guest for breakfast tomorrow."

"That's Julie's business." Kurt crossed his arms. "And I'm sure she has better taste in men."

"Cody's a good-looking guy."

"His looks might be okay. But he almost killed her with his horse," Kurt snapped. "It's a brain he lacks."

"His looks are more than okay. He's also easygoing and has enough of a brain to know the timing is right." Sandra pulled the heavy saddle off, and Okie grunted with relief. "Julie finally unloaded her guilt and is ready for some fun. And Cody's more than happy to provide it."

Sandra adjusted the saddle against her hip and headed to her tack room, whistling cheerfully.

Kurt dragged a hand through his hair, knowing a setup when he heard one. He also knew he'd hurt Julie badly. She completely misunderstood his relationship with Tiffany, and he should have tried harder to explain.

He rose and folded up his chair. "Is everyone going to the same pub as last week? I'll give you a ride over. Guess I'll head that way after all."

# CHAPTER TWENTY-SIX

Kurt held the door open, his anticipation rising as he followed Sandra inside. Champs wasn't as busy as last Saturday night. Conversation flowed but it was relaxed, almost hushed. No country music either. A chalkboard advertised tunes from the sixties and seventies; the mood was a mid-week mellow.

Julie, Cody and Gary Bixton sat at a large table ringed with empty chairs. Sandra walked over and plunked herself between Cody and a grinning Bixton. Kurt rounded the table and nabbed the chair on the other side of Julie.

"Hi," she said. Her face was solemn, but he thought there was some warmth in her voice. "Did Ace come back okay?"

"Yeah," Kurt said. "He seems fine. Did you ride any other races tonight?"

"No, but Red Jollymore is giving me two rides next week." She smiled then with a mixture of speculation and gratitude. "Do you know Red very well? He's one of the biggest trainers here and really respects your opinion."

"We've talked a bit. He has the nice bay, Sweating Bullet, in Lazer's race tomorrow." Kurt glanced over Julie's head, grateful Sandra had distracted Cody. It was doubtful Cody would check on Julie in the next few minutes, not while Sandra was listening to him with such rapt attention.

"How's your dad doing?" Kurt lowered his voice. "I gather he and Nick were good friends."

"He's upset. Can't believe Nick was trampled by a horse. Wishes Otto would leave and take that crazy gelding with him."

"I think Otto will be gone soon," Kurt said. "Until then, you and Sandra need to stay away from him."

She shrugged. "We try not to be alone when he's around. He didn't even ask me to gallop. Maybe he's using someone else." The wistfulness in her voice was unmistakable, and it was clear she had no intention of avoiding Otto. Was eager for any ride—whatever the cost.

"Stay away from him." Kurt's voice hardened. "He's unpredictable. Please," he added.

She hesitated but must have noticed something in his expression. "Okay," she finally said. "I'll stay away."

He nodded, but Cody shot him a suspicious look so he studied the wall, pretending interest in the race pictures. Cody's attention swung back to Sandra.

Julie scraped at the label of her beer bottle and Kurt reached over, stilling her hand. "I'd still like to have dinner with you," he whispered. "Whenever you're free. Just let me know…maybe tomorrow?"

She searched his face, her gaze steady. "I assumed you'd be meeting someone tonight. Tiffany, maybe?"

"No." He shook his head, emphatic.

"Okay then," she said. "Dinner after Lazer's race tomorrow. That would be great."

Her acceptance stirred a bittersweet mix of relief and frustration. Too bad she wouldn't dump Cody right now. Obviously she was only with that asshole because of their earlier misunderstanding.

"Dinner tomorrow," Kurt said. "And if you're not riding on Sunday, let's head back to that mountain. Did you ever tell anyone about the grizzly?"

"Just the warden so he could post a warning. Certainly not Dad—he'd have been horrified with me—surprising a sow like that."

More likely he'd be horrified with me, Kurt thought, sucking in a regretful breath. "Listen, Julie." He wet his mouth. "I really need to talk to you."

But already her attention had shifted; she'd turned to Cody, her official date for the evening.

He considered his next move then leaned forward, deciding Lazer was his best hook. "Are you looking forward to the race tomorrow?"

She glanced back at him, face alight. "Oh, yes," she breathed. "Dreaming about it. Lazer and I win, but that's the best thing about dreams. The ending is always perfect."

His own uncertainties about Lazer mushroomed, and he regretted not shipping out a more reliable horse. He had so many good ones. It would have been easy to give Julie her first win. She'd been working hard. Deserved a break.

"Don't be disappointed if Lazer doesn't fire," Kurt said. "He should run okay with that group but winning is probably out—"

Kurt stopped talking as Cody stretched a possessive arm along the back of Julie's chair. "How you doing, beautiful?" Cody asked. "Need another beer?" He leaned closer and whispered something in her ear.

Kurt leaned back, amused by how hard the man was trying. Fawning over a woman never worked, and it certainly wouldn't impress someone as smart as Julie. But whatever Cody whispered made her laugh, a spontaneous sound that flattened Kurt's smile—that fucking guy was such an asshole.

No one else seemed to mind the jerk. Bixton just grinned and sipped his drink; Sandra picked up the laminated menu and complained about a price increase on the Caesar salad.

Cody's head moved closer, almost touching Julie's now. More low laughter. The guy was all over her, monopolizing her attention, pouring her beer, making her dimples flash. Kurt rubbed his knuckles. He glanced away, then back. Wondered if she'd had supper. Since it was a race day, she probably hadn't eaten much.

He touched her shoulder, somewhat mollified when she quickly turned from Cody. "You hungry?" Kurt asked. "I'm going up to order a hamburger. Want one?"

"Oh, yes. I'm starving." She smiled hopefully. "Fries too?"

"Of course. Fries too. Be right back." He held Cody's resentful glare with a challenging stare of his own, rose and walked to the bar.

Screw etiquette. Cody was a lousy date, not worth worrying about. Certainly not worth stepping aside for. Kurt didn't usually compete for women—there was always another perched at the next bar stool—but Julie was different.

"Kurt!" Tiffany's delighted voice echoed through the sleepy room. She rat-tat-tatted across the floor in her sexy heels and wrapped her arms around him in an intimate hug.

He glanced over the top of her head. Everyone at the bar seemed to be watching. Sandra scowled, Bixton appeared envious and Julie looked...stricken.

"Hi, Tiffany." He quickly disentangled himself and stepped back. "Let me buy you a drink before I return to my table."

She stuck out her lower lip and pouted. "I just wanted to say congratulations. Your young horse ran well tonight. Oh, by the way, this is Nate." She grabbed a man in red suspenders and a tailored suit, tugging him to her side.

"Hello," Nate said, shaking Kurt's hand. "Tiffany insisted we use your entry in our exactor, so we had a good return on our investment."

"Good. Seems I was the only one who didn't bet my horse." Kurt signaled the waiter and ordered two hamburger specials.

Tiffany stepped closer. "Nate is just a banking friend," she whispered. "I really had a good time last night."

"Yeah, me too." But he fought the urge to check over his shoulder even as he made polite conversation.

By the time he returned to his seat all he could see of Julie was her rigid back. Even Sandra shot him a glare before continuing her conversation with a grinning Bixton. The table, however, had brightened considerably and now was crammed with a colorful display of shooters.

"Another one down the hatch," Cody said. He clinked his glass against Julie's, and they simultaneously chugged. "Nothing to it, beautiful," Cody said. "You're getting the hang of it. Almost beat me that time. Now we chase with beer."

Julie swigged her beer then accepted the next shooter Cody passed her.

Kurt folded his arms and tried to look bored. If Julie and Cody wanted to get blitzed drinking the shooter menu, that was their business. He didn't give a shit. But he was definitely going to leave after he ate. No way would he sit and watch them giggle and drink and giggle some more.

It was a relief when the food waiter arrived, balancing a tray of steaming plates. "The one with the fries is hers." Kurt gestured at Julie.

Julie didn't look at Kurt but gave the waiter a polite smile. "I'm not hungry anymore, thanks." She reached out and drained another shooter, surprising even Cody.

"Wow, babe, you're one up on me." Cody set his glass down and rose with a smirk. "Be right back. I'm going to play our song."

Kurt bit into his hamburger, watching Cody weave toward the bar. Julie grabbed another shooter, not seeming to care she was chugging alone.

Cody strutted back, and the words to 'Julie, Do Ya Love Me' filled the room. The food stuck in Kurt's throat as he recognized the tune Sandra had been whistling. He pushed the plate away, his appetite replaced with full-blown frustration.

Julie was already reaching for another shooter. He grabbed her hand. "Better slow down. I don't want a hung-over jockey riding my horse tomorrow."

She tilted her nose, haughty as a drunk can be. "I don't care if I ride Lazy."

"Lazer," he snapped. "And you do care. Have some food or coffee instead."

"I prefer these delicious shooters." She slurred the last two words, dismissing him with a swish of her hair.

"We should find a spot that's a tad quieter." Cody's reddened eyes flickered over Kurt then back to Julie. "My place is only twenty minutes away. I'll call a cab."

"Okay, but first I want to drink the pretty green one." She tried to pick up the glass but sloshed most of it on her hand.

"You can drink mine too, beautiful. I gotta pick something up." Cody tossed some coins in the air, leered at Kurt and headed crookedly toward the men's bathroom.

A muscle ticked in Kurt's jaw and the side of his forehead throbbed. Drunk or sober, Cody was an asshole. And Kurt had pushed Julie into his arms. He couldn't just stand back and let her leave with the prick, not while she was so wasted.

He rose so fast his chair toppled. Stalked around the table to Sandra. "Don't worry about Julie," he said. "I'm taking her home now."

"Give your head a shake," Sandra said. "She won't go with you. Not after seeing that snob from the office plastered against your chest. And I don't blame her."

"Just don't worry about her," Kurt said. His gaze swung to Bixton who stared with an expression that resembled approval.

Kurt rounded the table. He winced as the glass clinked loudly against Julie's teeth. "Phone call for you," he said. "Some trainer looking for a rider."

She looked up, her eyes glassy. "What?"

"You'll have to go outside so you can hear. Come on." He put his arm around her waist, grabbed her purse and propelled her outside.

She stumbled on the doorstep, blinking owlishly as she peered around. "What phone?"

"Over here." He guided her to his truck, buckled her in the seat and pressed his cell phone in her hand. Slammed the door and slid behind the wheel.

Cody burst from the bar as the truck rumbled past the door. He looked furious, even more so when Kurt honked and waved.

"I can't hear anyone. How do I work this?" Julie asked, oblivious to Cody's hollers behind them. Her nose wrinkled as she peered at the display and pressed random buttons.

"Let me see." He reached over and studied the phone. Shit, Archer's number was displayed. She'd probably hit redial. He turned the power off and dropped the phone on the seat. "Ah, too bad," he said. "Looks like your caller hung up."

"I wonder who it was...where are we going?" She fidgeted in her seat, twisting and staring in confusion.

"You wanted a drive home, remember?"

"I did?" She wrinkled her forehead and hiccupped, then settled against the headrest. "I guess I am tired. And my stomach hurts. Oh, look at all the pretty lights!"

She stared out the window, fascinated by the cars streaming in the opposite direction.

He drove south for twenty minutes. She was drunker than he'd thought but explanations couldn't be postponed, so he veered into the parking lot of a deserted strip mall, unclipped both their seatbelts and lifted her onto his lap.

"We need to straighten out some things. Remember Tiffany? The girl in the paddock yesterday, the one at the bar tonight?"

"Yes. She's the one who always sticks Sandra and Dad in the oldest barn. She's only nice to the big shots...or to the really nice guys." Julie glared up at him before mumbling into his chest. "Guess you're a big shot."

He felt his mouth twitch. "She's just part of my job, Julie."

"That's what Gary says, that all the girls he sees are part of his job."

"And that's all Tiffany is. Or ever was."

"Why do men always have those kind of jobs?" She shook her head and hiccupped.

"We'll talk about it another time when you're not so...when it's not so late. But you're the one who matters. If you see me with someone else, or I act...in a different way, just remember it's only because of the job."

"The job? Training?" She blinked, her expression a mixture of confusion and grain alcohol.

"Never mind. Let's get you home, honey. You need your sleep." He lowered his head, intending only a quick kiss, but somehow it deepened. Her arms wrapped around his neck, filling him with longing.

He'd been so afraid he'd wouldn't be able to touch her again, and such gratitude filled him he felt almost giddy. He tugged her shirt loose, his hand found her breast and she felt so damn good—she gave another hiccup.

He swallowed and lowered his hand. Tucked her shirt back in. "Let's just sit for a minute, honey. Then I'll take you home."

"What's wrong?" She linked her fingers behind his head and pressed closer.

"Not a thing." He shifted her rear a little further from his groin. "But we can talk tomorrow."

"I don't want to talk." She giggled and tried to kiss him but landed off target and hit his left ear.

"You're really drunk, Julie."

"I am not!" She straightened, so aghast he grinned.

He knew better than to try to reason with a drunk, but the chance to probe was irresistible. "You almost went home with Cody." His stomach kicked at the thought. "Would you really have done that?"

"Maybe." Her voice lowered to a mumble, and she didn't look at him. "Did you sleep with Tiffany?"

"Not even close."

"Cody and I weren't close either." She sniffed. "And there's no way I would have gone home with him. Besides, Gary would never let it happen."

"What are you talking about? Does Gary look out for you like that?"

"Yup." She gave a rueful smile but it trailed off to a yawn, and she covered her mouth. "He's a combination of Sandra and Blue. I just don't understand how I walked out the door with you." She frowned and glanced around, as though expecting to see Gary's face plastered against the window.

"You know," Kurt said, "I've always had an extremely high opinion of Mr. Bixton."

"Yeah, Gary's great." Her eyelids flickered. "Let's not talk for a minute. Just be quiet and watch the lights." She snuggled into his chest and was instantly asleep.

He held her for a moment, reluctant to let go. But after a few minutes, he straightened her shirt, smoothed her hair, rearranged her in the seat. When he clipped the seatbelt she mumbled something about ketchup with her fries but didn't open her eyes.

He turned the radio on and continued south, feeling more optimistic than he had in years. They'd driven less than a mile before her breathing deepened, and another sound mingled with the music. Snoring.

His woman snored. *His woman*—he liked the sound of that. Contentment warmed him as he drove, her soft sounds intermingling with the Top Twenty Country Countdown. The truck's headlights panned a square sign announcing Turner

Valley, and after a slight hesitation at the intersection he chose a wide gravel road that looked vaguely familiar.

"Stop!" She jerked upright, arms flailing as she fumbled for the door handle. "Let me out!" Her left hand pressed against her mouth, muffling her words.

He pulled over in a spray of gravel, released her belt, leaned over and flipped open her door. It swung open. She thudded into the dark.

*Oops.* He leaped from the driver's seat and rushed around the truck. She lay where she'd fallen, propped on her elbows, one knee under the running board, and retched forcefully.

He helped her to a crouching position and tucked her hair behind her ears. There wasn't any food coming up, he noted clinically, just liquid. He slipped off his jacket and wrapped it around her trembling shoulders. "You'll feel better soon," he said.

"Just go away, please," she managed.

He walked back to the side of the truck and rummaged behind his seat. Found a squashed box of Kleenex and a wrinkled sweatshirt. Gave the shirt a cautious sniff. A bit of diesel and horse, but otherwise it seemed clean.

When the gagging sounds slowed, he ventured back.

She was crouched on the ground, shivering, arms wrapped around her chest. He gently wiped her damp face.

"I'm sorry," she mumbled, not looking at him.

"Everyone gets sick when they mix drinks like that," he said. "Good thing you woke up. I wasn't sure if this was the right road."

She managed a feeble smile.

Her teeth were clicking as he helped her back into the truck. He turned the heat up and unbuttoned her soiled shirt. She made a garbled protest—not understanding—but he eased her shirt off and replaced it with his rumpled sweatshirt. "I rolled the sleeves up. There you go. Let me know if you need to stop again."

"I just want to go home." Her face was pinched and white, her earlier gaiety replaced with misery, and he cursed Cody even as he blamed himself.

Forty minutes later they drove into the West's driveway. "Better be quiet. Looks like your dad is asleep." He switched off the ignition, silencing the loud engine. "Sleep in. Don't come to the track until the races. If I see you galloping in the morning, you're off my horse."

"Your horse?"

"My three-year-old. The gray." He used the patient tone he reserved for preschoolers and drunks.

"Okay, Cody."

He jerked his head around just in time to catch her smile. "You're such a smartass," he said. He reached over and helped her with the door handle. "Don't fall out this time. Wait and I'll help you."

She rolled her eyes, huffy at the memory, and, of course, didn't wait. She stumbled to the ground and had to grab the door to regain her balance. He grinned, stepped out and helped her to the house.

An ominous growl leaked through the front door.

"Quiet, Blue. Don't be so loud," she muttered as she struggled to insert her key.

"Not so loud yourself," Kurt whispered, prying the key from her hand and unlocking the door. He stepped back and edged the door open with his foot. "Don't let the dog—"

But she swept the door wide open, and Blue charged out. He gave her hand a quick lick as he passed then jerked to a stop in front of Kurt. She flounced into the dark house without a backward glance.

"Wait, Julie," he said but she was gone and he was alone with her tough-ass dog. "Good dog," he said cautiously.

Something thumped from inside. Blue looked back, cocking his ears.

Kurt swallowed. "I better go check on her."

However, the dog growled so he remained motionless, trying not to flinch as Blue sniffed his pants, his big muzzle lingering by the front of his zipper. *Jesus.* After an endless moment, Blue turned and trotted into the house, and Kurt's breath escaped in a whoosh.

Another thump. He shot a longing glance at his truck before following Blue inside.

It was difficult to see anything in the inky darkness. Julie hadn't bothered to turn on any lights or perhaps couldn't find them. He almost stepped on her. She said something about her feet. He bent down, groping in the darkness until he felt the bootjack stuck to her heel.

"That thing isn't working," she mumbled.

"I'm surprised Blue doesn't do this for you." Kurt tugged her boots off and helped her stand.

"He's only a dog," she snapped. "Good night."

She lurched down the hall, bounced off a wall and vanished around the corner. The sound of a slamming door boomeranged through the house.

Blue whined, sounding so puzzled Kurt felt for his head and patted him in empathy. The dog wasn't as scary when he couldn't be seen.

Steps creaked in the hall, and the sudden light made Kurt blink. Adam materialized, squinting and bleary with sleep. A gray t-shirt hung halfway down his hairy legs.

"Kurt? That you?" He rubbed his eyes and yawned. "I thought Julie was staying at Sandra's."

"Her plans changed. Sorry to wake you."

"No sense driving back this late." Adam scratched his head. "I'll rustle up a sleeping bag. Surprised she didn't think of that."

He opened a closet door and thrust a green bag in Kurt's arms. "Couch is in there. Make yourself at home. I'm going back to bed." He shuffled down the hall.

Kurt opened the sleeping bag and gratefully stretched out on the couch. Blue whined. His claws clicked as he circled twice then thumped down on the wooden floor, a barrier between the stranger and the rest of the house.

# CHAPTER TWENTY-SEVEN

An unfamiliar ceiling stretched above Kurt's head. Light seeped through the curtains. He raised himself on an elbow. A massive rack of elk antlers and an antique rifle loomed over the fireplace but horse pictures crammed the remainder of the walls, pictures of the same jockey winning, over and over again.

Must be Julie's mother, he thought, relaxing on the sofa. Clearly she'd been an accomplished rider.

A screen door slammed, and boots thudded against the floor. Blue trotted into the room, tongue lolling, and dropped to the mat to lick his paws. Seconds later Adam poked his head in.

"You and Julie must have had quite a night? It's six-thirty and she's still asleep."

"What time does she usually get up?" Kurt asked.

"Four. In time for the morning feeding. Then she drives to the track."

Kurt winced. She worked both ends of the clock, making herself available to any trainer for morning gallops and hanging around the track at night, trying to snag a jock ride. No wonder she always fell asleep in his truck.

"Come and have a coffee," Adam said, "before I run over to the Farmers' Market."

Kurt yawned, not feeling too lively, but Blue stared at Adam's retreating back then looked at Kurt and whined. A command appearance then. Kurt rose to his feet, hauled on his shirt and walked to the kitchen.

"Do you have any sort of chance tonight?" Adam asked as he poured Kurt a cup of coffee.

Kurt dropped into a worn kitchen chair. "My horse can run a little." He sipped some coffee and ran a hand over his stubbled chin, trying to wake up. This brew was stronger than the stuff Adam made last week. Different smell too. He took in several more gulps, savoring the caffeine, feeling himself recharge. "Yeah, Lazer can run if he wants," he added.

"But will he want to?" Adam asked. "Here let me top up your coffee."

A robin flew by the window, its shadow flitting across the table. Looked like it was going to be another nice day. The track would be dry and fast.

"I really don't know what Lazer will do." Kurt stretched out his legs. "He had excuses for most of his losses. I do know he's fit, impeccably bred and gets along well with your daughter."

Adam dropped a spoon in the sink with a sharp clink. "The handicapper only has him at twelve to one. There are some tough Alberta-breds in the race. They may not have the fancy bloodlines but around here 'good bred' only matters in a sandwich. A lot of the eastern runners are wimps." Adam gave a disdainful snort. "A little bumping, a little dirt. Those pretty horses want to give up and go home."

"That sounds like Lazer." Kurt straightened in the chair. Adam seemed uptight, and he sensed it wasn't about betting strategy.

"I'm just razzing you," Adam said without a hint of humor. "No one can guess what will happen in a race. Or at a track." His eyes hardened, boring into Kurt's. "Nick was a good man, a careful man. What happened to him was tragic. And strange. There was an earlier incident, a cop who'd been at the same barn. Looking for Otto."

Kurt studied the image on his mug: cattle and three penners. One rider had her arm thrust in the air, and he studiously traced the picture with his index finger. "Julie did mention something about that," he said slowly.

"I figure the track hired a private investigator to come and look around," Adam said. "Having two people shot and kicked to death isn't good for business."

"No," Kurt said. "I don't suppose it is."

251

"Now I'm not one to poke my nose where it shouldn't be," Adam's voice hardened, "but I don't want my daughter hurt. She's had a tough time getting over her mother's death. She's honest with her feelings and expects the same of her...associates. Dishonesty is something we won't tolerate."

"I don't think you need to worry."

"Good." Adam set his mug down, but his green eyes were wary. "I have to go. You relax and finish that coffee before driving back. Good luck tonight."

Kurt waited until the screen door slammed then moved to the kitchen window and watched the dust follow Adam's truck down the road. He definitely had received his walking orders—it would be much easier if Julie didn't live at home.

He rinsed his cup, placed it in the sink and glanced under the table. "Okay, Blue, can you find Julie for me?"

The dog scrambled to his feet, and his nails clacked an eager trail down the hall. He shoved his nose against the second door on the right, whining softly. Kurt turned the knob, and Blue barged past and ran to the bed.

His pink tongue slopped over Julie's cheek, but she only muttered and burrowed under the blanket.

Kurt stepped over the sweatshirt and jeans scattered on the floor. The mattress squeaked as he sat down and tugged back the covers. He lifted her hair and pressed a light kiss against the back of her neck. She grumbled. He tugged the sheet further down and tickled the graceful curve of her bare back.

"Quit it, Blue," she said.

Kurt stilled, had actually forgotten about the dog. He glanced over his shoulder but Blue wasn't protesting—not yet—only watched expectantly as though confident she'd rise soon.

"Blue?" She rolled over. Stared at Kurt in dismay then abruptly yanked the sheet over her head. "I thought it was a nightmare." Her voice was muffled by the pink sheet.

"I'll see you later." He pried the covers from her face. "Just make sure you get lots of rest."

Her eyes widened. "Is Dad out there?" she whispered.

"He left about five minutes ago. Do you have a drive in tonight?"

She nodded.

"Are you angry I dragged you out of the bar?" he asked. "Is that the nightmare part?"

She frowned at him through a tangle of hair. "What do you mean?"

"Never mind." She was obviously exhausted. He patted her head, rumpling her hair even more. "I'll lock the door on the way out. Go back to sleep."

"Okay." She made no argument, only settled on the pillow, closed her eyes, and did exactly what he asked. Amazing.

Blue cocked his head and whined, looking just as surprised as Kurt.

## CHAPTER TWENTY-EIGHT

"Good morning, Kurt," Sandra said. "Did Julie get home okay?" She lingered outside the stall, watching as he unwrapped Ace's bandages.

"She did," he said. "Do you have time to pony this fellow? Easy walk around the track?"

"Sure." But Sandra wasn't easily distracted. She edged closer, her voice bubbling with mischief. "Cody dropped by a while ago. He wasn't very happy when you and Julie disappeared. Did you two go right home?"

Kurt simmered at the mention of Cody but only hunkered down to examine Ace's legs.

"Guess I'll have to ask Julie," Sandra said. "But she'll just clam up. Even Gary can't get much out of her, even when they lie awake talking all night." She winked. "You should know my spare room has double beds."

Kurt fumbled with the bandage, knowing he'd been too quick to judge, too quick to grab what he wanted. Julie had said she didn't date but he'd brushed that aside, had considered her fair game because he thought she was sleeping with Bixton.

He walked past Sandra and over to Otto's new stall, gripping the rolled bandage as he tried to settle the churning in his gut. He was just as big a prick as Cody.

Otto's gelding had been chewing on the wood but rushed to the door with a hopeful nicker.

"Is this fellow getting fed?" Kurt asked quietly.

"No," Sandra said. "I think you're the only one not afraid of him. Honestly, who would want to go in his stall?"

The horse stared over the door, his eyes calm and accepting.

"Damn. Otto should be shot." Kurt crossed the aisle, grabbed a water bucket and three flakes of hay. "Has he ever packed up and abandoned a horse like this?"

"Nope, but I heard there were so many complaints this week the race office finally suspended him. Doubt he'll be back. He's not the type to worry about a horse." She shrugged. "I'm going to grab a coffee. Be back in about fifteen minutes for Ace."

Kurt nodded and opened the stall door. The horse stuck his nose in the water bucket, drank deeply then lifted his dripping muzzle and grabbed at the hay. Kurt ran his hand along the gelding's warm back but felt only a single welt. This fellow wasn't as scraped up as Otto's mare—except for the pitchfork injury, Kurt amended, as his fingers touched the scabbed holes.

It might be possible to check his feet. The horse munched happily, unaware he was considered a killer and unfairly blamed for a popular man's death. Kurt slid his hand around the horse's fetlock, and the gelding obediently lifted his leg.

When Kurt pressed on his boggy sole, he flinched. Kurt sighed and lowered the leg. Same reaction as the mare. Two horses, both tender-soled, both with an unusual number of nail holes. The smugglers had to be using horseshoes to move the diamonds, yet according to Julie, the shoes had been normal.

He rubbed his forehead and left the stall, jarred by a sense of inadequacy. Connor had always been more stubborn, more observant. Obviously he'd spotted something—but Kurt couldn't even figure out what had drawn him to Otto's trailer.

A grim figure burst into the barn. "You fucker. Where's Julie?" Cody rushed down the aisle and planted himself in front of Kurt, fists clenched in white-knuckled balls. "Where's Julie? Answer me, asshole!"

"You can't be talking to me," Kurt said, turning away.

"Where is she?"

"Let's just say she's not having breakfast with either of us and leave it at that."

Cody shadowed Kurt down the aisle, his voice quivering with rage. "Is that the only way you can get laid? By hijacking someone else's date. I paid a lot of money for those shooters—"

"So you were trying to get her drunk?" Kurt's mouth tightened.

"We were just having fun until you came along."

"She's not used to drinking like that," Kurt snapped. "Stay away from her."

"Is that a threat?"

Kurt stopped. "Yes," he said.

"You prick!" Cody's face contorted. He abruptly rammed his booted heel at Kurt's thigh.

Kurt tried to dodge, but the kick was too quick, the pain agonizing. He reeled back, struggling to remain on his feet. Straightened and let his anger override the pain. "Cheap shot, Cody. But all right. Let's do this."

Cody didn't hesitate. He darted forward, feinting high, then jabbed his fist at Kurt's stomach. Kurt blocked the punch, shooting out with a left hook that snapped the man's sneering head back. His satisfaction flared, but Cody recovered quickly and slipped under his fists, knocking his legs out with some sneaky footwork.

Kurt hit the concrete. Saw Cody's boot aimed at his head, rolled and grabbed him by the ankle. Twisted and sent the man sprawling.

Kurt scrambled up, adrenaline surging now, watching as Cody rose with lithe grace. The man must have some kind of martial arts training. He was quick and strong, able to use both fists and feet. It would be a fun fight, Kurt decided, with a rush of eagerness. He'd have to watch the man's left foot though. Cody had already landed it twice. Best to take him down quickly.

They eyed each other, both wary, both silent. The air was punctuated with their breathing, and the sound of rattled horses circling in the straw.

Cody edged to the left. Kurt snapped a kick at his chest, but Cody just grinned and dodged then danced forward, driving his left boot into Kurt's stomach. Fuck. Kurt managed to block the quick fist that followed, countering with an uppercut that tilted Cody on his heels.

He tracked Cody across the aisle and kicked his left knee. When he stumbled, Kurt launched forward. He straddled his back, using his weight to pin the man to the floor.

"Finished?" Kurt growled.

Silence.

He jerked Cody's arms higher.

"Fuck," Cody said.

Kurt ruthlessly raised his arms another notch.

"Fuck, yes."

Kurt stood up and stepped back.

"Guess I ate the most dirt today, you fucker," Cody muttered as he brushed the straw off his shirt. "You should drop by the gym some time. Have a little rematch. I want another shot."

Kurt inclined his head in grudging respect. "You got enough shots in today."

"Yeah. Entertaining fight," Sandra called from the doorway. "Bet you weren't arguing about who had the fastest horse."

"No horse is worth that." Cody grimaced, studying his knuckles. "No girl either."

Kurt said nothing. His leg throbbed, but he felt much better; he'd always loved a good fight.

Sandra tossed her cup in the garbage bin. "Is Ace ready now that you burned off some of that frustration?"

Kurt shot her a scowl. Sandra was too uppity, too mouthy, too perceptive.

Cody saw Kurt's expression and shook his head. "Dude, you need to lighten up. Glad I'm not stuck in this barn." He walked by Sandra, shaking his head and inspecting his knuckles.

Kurt hurt too, but waited until Cody was gone before rubbing the top of his thigh. Damn. The guy kicked like a mule. His leg felt like it had been stabbed with a hot poker.

He bridled Ace and led him outside to where Sandra waited on an ever-patient Okie.

"Just jog Ace around and loosen him up," Kurt said. "I want to see how he moves. His shins might be a bit sore."

"Yes, boss." Sandra winked and led Ace to the track.

Kurt headed to the rail at a more sedate pace, trying to hide his aching leg, watching as Ace moved into an even trot. The gelding obviously suffered no ill effects from yesterday's race. He gestured at Sandra to continue then pulled out his phone and walked slowly toward the privacy of his truck.

Archer sounded relieved. "Been trying to reach you," he said. "My private line rang last night. Showed your number."

"I must have sat on my phone," Kurt said.

"Keep it turned on. Now here's what we got. Nothing was found in Friedman's garbage. But we have the lab analysis, and the material on Connor's shoes matches the fecal samples we picked up behind his store."

So Connor had been in that alley. Kurt rubbed his neck, recalling the eerie feeling when he walked behind the shop.

"Kurt?"

"Yeah, I'm here," Kurt said, his voice so low he had to force himself to speak up. "Otto hasn't been around the track today. What's he doing?"

"Packing up his apartment," Archer said. "He had a few phone calls. One from Friedman, two about some gambling debts, and the last from a horse buyer. He made a deal to sell an eleven-hundred pound Thoroughbred to the local meat man."

"That horse doesn't weigh eleven," Kurt said. "And he'll weigh a lot less if they don't pick him up soon. Maybe we should buy him. We might need him, you know, for evidence. He's not a bad fellow. Be a shame if he went for meat."

"Absolutely not. The last animal we bought wasn't any use."

"But maybe—"

"Forget the horse. Our phone tap confirms a payoff tomorrow afternoon, so we'll pick up both men then. We'll have full search warrants. If Friedman has diamonds in his possession, we'll be okay. Maybe we'll find the murder weapon or something that shows how they smuggled the rocks."

"They had to come up in the shoes." Kurt rubbed his jaw. "The second horse had his hind shoes pulled the moment he arrived at the track, same as the mare. Had to be a reason, but damn, it's a puzzle. Julie saw the first set of shoes, said they were normal."

"Julie, that jockey? Can you trust her?"

"With my life," Kurt said.

258

Silence. Uncomfortable silence and it was clear they both remembered the time he'd trusted Anne Marie. But she'd been working him too; her loyalties were with the gang and when he'd confided he was undercover, an informant had been hurt. However that was years ago, before he'd learned to play it cool. Before he'd learned to stop feeling.

"Well, your instincts are good," Archer finally said. "I know you don't need the money, but I hope you'll consider coming back to work for us."

"This kind of work isn't good for me," Kurt said, rubbing his thigh.

Archer laughed but not unkindly. "It's good for us though. You've one of our highest success rates."

"Just let me know when Otto's on the move," Kurt said.

"Don't spook him. And what's this Friedman like? Will he give us any trouble?"

"Don't know," Kurt said. "But his employees are scared. And he keeps Otto in line."

"Can you check him out? Get a read. His file is thin—I don't want any surprises tomorrow."

"All right. I'm picking up something from his store. I'll try to talk to him then."

Kurt parked four blocks south of 'Pieces of Eight' hoping the walk might help, but his thigh still throbbed from Cody's boot. He approached from the back of the store and scanned the alley. The fender of a silver Mercedes protruded from the lone parking space. Marcus Friedman was in.

"Good morning," Betty said, putting away her rag and spray bottle when Kurt walked into the shop. "Ted finished your piece. I have it right here." Beaming, she centered a silver pendant on a blue velvet tray.

"Nice," he said. "I like the way the mountain is feathered. And that stone at the bottom looks real." He watched her face when he mentioned the stone, but her expression didn't change.

"Even jewelers have mistaken zircons for diamonds," she said.

"What's the difference?"

"I think it's the hardness." Her shrug was quick and apologetic. "I don't know much about them, but zircons are more sensitive to knocks. And the price, of course. This necklace is six hundred and eighty-five dollars. A real diamond would be much more expensive."

He waved his credit card for effect then paused, holding it slightly out of reach. "I really would like to know more about this stone. May I talk to Mr. Friedman?"

Her eyes widened; she shook her head. "That's not a good idea. He wants to finish his own work. In fact, Teddy and I have the weekend off. Monday as well." She shook her head again, her expression imploring. "We really shouldn't bother him. He doesn't like interruptions and now…well, he's very busy."

"I'm very busy myself. And I expect he'd want to help a customer." Kurt palmed his card, feeling like a bully as he leveled her with his relentless stare.

"Yes, well…maybe." She pursed her lips, slowly backed away, turned and retreated into the back room.

Ten minutes later Marcus Friedman emerged, carrying the subtle smell of expensive cologne and a more obvious air of displeasure. He straightened the collar of his silk shirt, swept Kurt's casual clothes with a look of disdain and sniffed. "You require some assistance?"

Bingo. A satisfied smile curved Kurt's face. It was the voice. The voice from the barn—Otto's late-night visitor.

"Yeah." Kurt smoothed his expression, struggling to look like a confused shopper. "I'm buying this zircon pendant for my girlfriend. I need to know if she'll believe it's a real diamond," he gave Friedman a man-to-man wink, "and what the difference is."

"Of course, she'll think it's a diamond." Friedman's lip curled. "I've spent twenty years working with these stones. The absorption spectra is the difference, but you wouldn't understand that."

"Try me," Kurt said.

Friedman's lips thinned as he stared over the showcase.

"You're probably right," Kurt added, struggling for a little more humility. "I probably won't understand, but I'd like to know. My girlfriend's pretty smart."

"The diamond measures ten on the hardness scale," Friedman snapped, "the zircon only seven and a half. The zircon has double refraction so, of course, has inferior hardness. Typically the crystal system is tetragonal with indistinct cleavage. Specific gravity is four point six to four point seven." He stared at Kurt, his voice slightly malicious as he recited. "Crystals are transparent to translucent."

"I thought most zircons were colored." Kurt's humble smile hurt his face.

"This zircon has been heat treated to obtain its lack of color." Friedman made a disparaging gesture at the necklace. "The stones occur in igneous rocks as browns and greens. In the Middle Ages, zircons were thought to bring wisdom, honor and riches. That they would drive away evil spirits."

"Price seems pretty high for a fake rock," Kurt said.

"You're not listening." Friedman's voice rose, and his pronunciation became more clipped. "It is not a fake. Don't confuse it with cubic zirconia, a cheap, artificial material."

"All right, I won't. Gotta admit, the silver design is nice." Kurt gave a meek nod. "Thank you for your time."

Friedman didn't bother to reply. "No more interruptions," he snapped at Betty before returning to the workshop. The door slammed behind him.

Betty's cheeks flagged with pink, and she stared down at her thick-soled shoes.

"Thank you, Betty." Kurt passed over his credit card, trying to hide his sympathy. "I imagine he's tired, from his trip and all."

Betty's head bobbed. "Yes, he always likes to be alone after his travel. Usually he closes the shop for a few days. The break is nice except Ted works on commissions, and we need more sales."

"Maybe Ted should take his best pieces home," Kurt said. "Sell the stuff somewhere else, a place where there's more traffic." He scrawled his name on the credit card slip and pocketed the blue box. "He could always put aside Mr. Friedman's share of the money."

"Yes, maybe we should do that." Betty tilted her head. "There's a craft fair at the mall tomorrow. It's a very busy spot."

261

Kurt nodded in solemn agreement. By tomorrow evening, this place would be crawling with cops, and the jewelry in legal limbo. "I think you should take as much stock as you can," he said.

# CHAPTER TWENTY-NINE

Kurt tilted his chair against Cisco's stall and flipped *The Racing Form* open to the eighth race. A mottled nose reached over his shoulder and snorted against the page.

"Yeah, Lazer's not very impressive." Kurt gave Cisco's jaw an absent scratch. "He's the only horse in the race who's never finished in the money."

He studied the form of the other runners. Frostbite and Brenna's Hitter were the two speed horses, and both would want to be on the front.

Bixton was riding the favorite, Sweating Bullet, a horse with an explosive closing kick. The unbeaten colt had won all his starts from off the pace. Kurt remembered the horse's morning gallops, and it was apparent he was training well. Bullet would be the one to beat, and the race would set up well for his running style. Frostbite and Brenna's Hitter would battle early, but both of them looked incapable of rating—leaving it ripe for a late runner.

He couldn't discount Brenna's Hitter though. She was a game little filly and had beaten the boys before. If early fractions weren't too fast, she was capable of wiring it, especially if the track favored speed. She had a win and a third but in her last start had hooked up with another speed horse and faded badly in the stretch.

Frostbite had one win but appeared to stop cold unless the pace was dawdling. Kurt circled that horse's name. He didn't want Lazer behind Frostbite after the quarter pole.

TerryJoh was a stalker and always a factor. In his last start he'd finished second to Sweating Bullet and had never run worse than fourth. Aussie Cal was a late runner and would be motoring at the quarter pole. He was coming off a win, but the time was leisurely. Probably a lightweight. Kurt drew a line through Aussie Cal.

He also crossed out the two remaining horses, Fort Point and Norvik. They were moving up in class and, unless they had great racing luck, would be well back.

And then there was the enigmatic Lazer.

Lazer had morning odds of twelve to one, based largely on his breeding and the fact that he'd raced at Woodbine. Kurt doubted the bettors would be as generous as the track handicapper. He added a heavy question mark by Lazer's name.

It was possible the colt would run big. He loved the Calgary surface and was adept at the tight bullring turns. Kurt penciled a line through Lazer's last race. That was in the cold rain, and Lazer had hated the weather. He drew another line through the first race. A horse could be forgiven anything their first start.

The second race was troubling though and not so easy to excuse. The jockey had checked Lazer to keep from clipping another horse, and the colt had simply stopped trying. The remaining races were just as mystifying. Maybe the colt lacked courage. Or maybe, as Julie believed, the loafing really was related to some sort of focus problem.

Kurt wasn't certain but it was best to be optimistic, so he drew a heavy black line through the remaining three races. Now Lazer had a clean slate and looked damn good. He'd bet Lazer to win, Sweating Bullet second and the game little filly, Brenna's Hitter, to hang on for third. Conditions were setting up for a nice payday. It was almost a sure thing.

Behind him Cisco gave a derisive snort, scattering water spots across the page.

For the second time that day, a warm mouth woke Julie. She pushed Blue away, stretched in contentment then dropped her arms in horror.

*Shit, shit, shit.* She covered her face with her hands as her brain spit out memories, every one of them bad.

She'd been sick. Had she thrown up in Kurt's truck? She scrunched her face, trying to remember. No, probably not. She had a vague recollection of sitting in the ditch. The shooters! Just the thought of them made her stomach lurch. She'd guzzled way too many of those silly drinks trying to forget her feelings for Kurt. And she had a huge race tonight.

Gingerly she lowered her hands and propped herself up. Everything worked. Her stomach and head hurt, but she'd ridden with much worse pain. It wasn't such a disaster.

Not such a disaster! Oh, God!

She dropped her head in her hands, appalled at her behavior. The night before the biggest race of her fledging career, and she had drunk like an idiot, to the extent that the trainer himself had to drive her home. It was surprising he was still letting her ride Lazer.

She was hazy as to how she'd ended up in his truck. Hopefully she hadn't begged him for a drive. Embarrassment surged, and her face hammered hot against her hands. Lucky she hadn't been with Cody; she guessed he wouldn't have been so mannerly. And Kurt had been a gentleman. He didn't have to ply his women with liquor—quite the opposite.

She pressed the pillow over her face remembering that in the truck he'd been the one to push her away, literally. No doubt he'd be in one of his frosty moods today. And who could blame him?

*Thump, thump.* Blue rested his head on the edge of the bed, his tail knocking the floor, his brown eyes shining with approval. He thought everything she did was perfect. She patted his head, marginally cheered by his devotion.

Besides, Kurt had been kind this morning. He must like her a little. Maybe with time his feelings would turn into a lot more. She was used to fighting for what she wanted, and it was a long season. She just had to make sure Lazer ran well so Kurt would stick around. And that he'd keep using her as his jockey.

Energized, she tossed the covers aside and scrambled from the bed. Rushed to the bathroom scales. One hundred and seven pounds. Great, she could use her three-pound saddle and hit her weight. She dashed into the shower, already focused on the race.

Lazer had better be ready to run tonight, because she was going to insist he make a big effort.

# CHAPTER THIRTY

Lazer swung his head, jarring Martin's arm. The brush ricocheted off the wall and clattered to the floor.

"I tied him but he won't stand still," Martin complained as he bent down and scooped the brush from the straw. "He keeps pawing and jumping around."

"He's excited. Knows he's going to race." Kurt stepped into the stall and jerked on the rope. "Quit."

Lazer stopped his gyrations. He still shimmered with energy, but Martin was able to brush his mane. "How does he know he's racing?" Martin asked.

"Mostly from us. He senses our excitement. Plus he was only jogged this morning so there's been a schedule change. He knows something's up."

Kurt watched as Martin brushed Lazer with proprietary pride. The kid was a good groom but kept such a low profile other trainers didn't notice. It would be a shame to leave him without a job when he was clearly flourishing in the track environment. "Can you help me in the paddock?" Kurt asked.

Martin whipped around, eyes incredulous. "You mean tonight? In the race where everyone will be dressed up? Lazer's race?"

"Yeah, that one." Kurt grinned.

"Oh, man! Wicked! I gotta run home and change. And tell my mom too. She's even coming to watch."

"Think your red-headed friend will be there?"

Martin pumped his head. "Oh yeah. She'll be there. Girls sure like horses, don't they?"

"They sure do," Kurt said but his pleasure at Martin's reaction dimmed as his thoughts jumped to Julie. She might be peeved at how he'd shanghaied her into his truck, and if she really did like Cody he'd scuttled that for her.

He didn't want to think about it. Passed a mane comb to Martin, and tried to concentrate on nothing but the best way to tame Lazer's stubborn mane.

Julie slipped into the barn. Her pulse pounded, and every sense seemed to have sharpened. She recognized Martin's voice and Kurt's deeper timbre. Her stomach kicked, but she squared her shoulders and walked toward Lazer's stall. She had to face him sometime. It would be much easier now than in the saddling enclosure before the race.

"Hi, Julie." Martin careened past, arms and legs pumping, his teeth a line of white. "I'm helping saddle tonight!" he yelled.

"Super!" she called back. That was quite a coup. She knew more experienced people who would have been delighted to help Kurt. Everyone wanted to be connected with the quality horses. The other runners would all have huge entourages, but Lazer only had the three of them.

Kurt stepped from Lazer's stall, his expression inscrutable, and the butterflies in her stomach morphed into giant moths. Was he disgusted with her drinking last night? Maybe he'd even decided to use another jockey.

"How do you feel?" he asked.

"Fine." She spoke in a rush. "Thanks for taking me home. I'm really sorry about drinking like that. And about getting sick."

"Let's take a look at Lazer's race," he said.

She followed him toward the tack room, her emotions jumbled. He always kept his emotions walled, but apparently she was still riding his horse. She gave him a grateful smile. He opened the door and smiled back—such a deep smile her toes curled.

Relief loosened her chest, weakening her legs and she sank down on the squeaky cot.

"What do you know about these horses?" He flipped open *The Racing Form* and sat down beside her.

She pointed to Brenna's Hitter, determined to act professional, despite the blast of heat that radiated from him. "This filly is fast but hard to rate." She moistened her lips. "She and the one horse, Frostbite, will probably set the pace. But if she gets an easy lead and relaxes, she could be tough."

"What about Bixton's mount?"

"So far the horse is unbeaten, but his regular rider from Seattle broke his leg. This will be Gary's first time up. But Gary dropped Brenna's Hitter for Sweating Bullet, so he must think Bullet's the best."

The sagging cot made it impossible to keep any distance between them. She didn't want to scoot away and look like a prude, but heat pulsated from his leg, making her skin tingle, and there didn't seem to be nearly enough oxygen in the tiny room.

"I don't think the jockey change is going to hurt the horse," she added, her voice breathless. "Gary's very good."

Kurt nodded, but his attention was on *The Form*. "You're coming out of the two hole," he said thoughtfully, "so there'll be a wait. Lazer is never quick leaving the gate, so you'll be shuffled back. A lot of dirt will fly. I'm running him in full cup blinkers. They might keep him focused and at least will cut down on the dirt. Don't be afraid to go around traffic. He's plenty fit and can handle the turns. And don't get stuck behind that Frostbite horse. He'll run out of gas and when he shuts down, he'll be taking horses with him."

She nodded—her stomach churning not only from Kurt's proximity but also from the looming race. Tonight she'd be matching wits with top riders, competing against quality horses. Lazer lacked early speed, had focus issues and habitually gave up when dirt smacked him. But she was finally riding in a huge race. Her mother would be proud.

She wiped her warm forehead then clutched her hands. At least having other horses in front would let her see how the race was setting up. She wished she were better prepared, wished she'd spent more time watching Lazer's replays. Usually she was very diligent, but her totally unprofessional feelings for the man sitting beside her had been too distracting.

She stared out the tiny window, watching as a fly struggled to free itself from a web. Warm fingers on her neck made her jump.

"Relax," he said. "It's just a race."

She opened her mouth to argue. It wasn't just a race. Not to her. But his hands felt incredibly good, so she closed her mouth and let him knead her stiff neck.

"You're so tight, I should give you a full body massage," he said.

"Yes." She sighed. "That'd be nice."

He tilted her chin, studying her intently. "I do give good massages," he said.

"I'm sure you do." She remembered how good his hands could feel. Her cheeks warmed, but he kept holding her chin, studying her face as though searching for something.

"Then you're not upset about last night?" He blew out a breath, and the angles of his jaw softened. "Thank God," he said.

She blinked, puzzled, but he'd already stretched out on the cot and pulled her down beside him, covering her mouth with a deep kiss, and it was apparent he still wanted her—physically at least. His tongue stroked her mouth, making her senses hum, and his big hands trailed along her back, molding her against him.

When he finally raised his head an inch, his breath was ragged. "Let's go directly to that massage and forget the damn race." He nuzzled her neck, his mouth warm and insistent.

His body crackled with so much sexual energy, she suspected he was serious. "We have a few minutes before I have to weigh in," she jerked upright, "but I'm not missing this race. Lazer and Martin don't want to miss it either."

His hot gaze lingered on her mouth. "If we continue like this, sweetie, you won't make the weigh-in."

She scrambled to her feet, afraid he spoke the truth. A little kissing and she tingled all over, and when he looked at her with those hot eyes, she just wanted to slide her hands beneath his shirt and explore that hard body.

"I'm not missing this race," she said. "Don't even joke about it." She crossed her arms and backed further from the cot. "And don't look at me like that," she added.

He still eyed her through narrowed lids so she stayed out of reach, waiting until they were a safer gray, not that dark color they turned when he was thinking of sex. My God, he was gorgeous, sprawled on the cot, all big surly male, looking as disappointed as Dude when a mare was led past the breeding pen.

His dark hair was slightly rumpled, his collar crooked. She caught a glimpse of chest hair, knew there was a scar about an inch to the right, close to the spot where his chest muscles bunched. Her eyes drifted lower, lingering on the bulge in his jeans. Maybe there was enough time, maybe—

"We have twenty-five minutes before you need to report in." He sat up and checked his watch. "Are you going to be overweight? Lazer's only assigned a hundred and fifteen pounds, and with your apprentice bug, we can shave it down to a hundred and ten."

She made a non-committal sound deep in her throat, hiding her disappointment at the abrupt subject change. Nothing mattered to him very long. Certainly not her. He was all trainer now, composed and businesslike, while she couldn't quite pull her thoughts off his body and masterful kissing.

"So? What do you weigh?" he asked.

"One hundred and seven pounds," she said. "I'll use my light saddle and hit the weight dead on."

"Don't use that word. That's bad luck."

"What word? What's bad luck?" She took a curious step forward. He really looked worried, had even winced.

"That phrase, the one you just said."

"Dead on? Are you superstitious?"

"Not a bit." But he spoke way too quickly.

She stared at him, such a big, tough hunk of a man—cool, composed, always in control. It didn't seem possible he'd be ruled by a superstition. A giggle slipped out, then another until she was outright laughing.

It seemed she laughed for minutes and when she finally sobered, all her emotions had drained, and she felt more relaxed than she had in weeks.

The room was ominously quiet though. Firming her mouth, she wiped her wet eyes and peeked at Kurt. He'd lain back on the cot, muscled arms looped beneath his head as he stared at the ceiling.

Oh, no. He had that reserved expression he often wore. Of course, all guys hated to be laughed at. But this was totally unexpected.

She tried to be solemn but her words carried a little bounce that was impossible to hide. "Sorry, but you're the last person I'd ever expect to be superstitious." Her dad called it *super-stupid*, but she definitely wouldn't mention that. "It's just that I'm nervous about the race and everything. I think I have a touch of the giggles."

"No problem. Laugh away," he said. "But tell me when ten minutes is up. I have to keep my arms crossed, in total silence, so that any bad karma is blocked. Or there's no way I can run Lazer tonight. It'd be much too risky. That's not a superstition either," he added, his voice flat, "but an absolute rule."

Her mouth dropped, and she stared in disbelief. This was no longer funny. He would actually scratch his horse because his jockey had used an unfortunate phrase? She'd suspected Kurt was too good to be true, guessed he must have a flaw. Well, she'd just found it.

God, it must get complicated, especially at a track where racing luck was so critical. Her empathy welled, and she walked over and sat beside him on the cot, holding his hand and squeezing it in understanding but she remained silent—just as he'd requested. She definitely didn't want him to scratch Lazer, and if it meant shutting up for ten minutes, she could do that too. She'd also remember to never say 'dead on.'

A radio blared from the aisle. Someone dropped a shovel, but it was quiet in his tack room, quiet except for his ragged breathing. Ragged? Puzzled, she looked down, scanning his expression.

His lips twitched. A chuckle burst out of him, and he tugged her into his chest.

She stared in disbelief as he laughed—laughed at her.

"You're not superstitious." She knocked his arm in exasperation. My God, would she ever understand him? "You're just a jerk," she said.

"Sometimes I am." He sobered then slipped his hand around the back of her neck. "But this jerk adores you."

Then he kissed her, barely touching her mouth. But so tender and lingering the impact was every bit as powerful as his earlier kisses. Even more so because he'd said he adored her. Her heart tilted as she absorbed his words. He adored her. From a man like Kurt, that was huge.

"I believe I could forget the race after all," she admitted.

"Just ride safe, Julie," he said, his voice husky. "I have something for you." He sat up, leaning her against him as he pulled a blue box from his pocket and flipped it open. "The stone is a zircon set below our mountain. It's supposed to ward off evil spirits."

A lump balled in her throat. She stared at the beautiful pendant. *Our mountain.* The stone gleamed, seeming to mark the spot where they'd made love. So that afternoon had been important to him too. He'd obviously gone to a lot of trouble to find the necklace. He didn't seem like a man who enjoyed shopping, and his thoughtfulness moved her as much as the gift.

She had to swallow before she could speak. "This wards off evil spirits?"

He lifted her hair and placed the chain around her neck. "You never know what lurks around a track," he said. His warm fingers brushed her skin as he fastened the clasp, sending familiar shivers down her spine.

"Thanks," she said, her voice husky. She looked down, pretending to admire the silver and the way it contrasted against her tan. She didn't usually wear jewelry when she rode, but she was definitely not taking this off.

He rose, effortlessly lifting her and setting her on her feet. "Come on. I'll walk over with you and drop off my spare silks."

She glanced at his owner silks hanging next to a race bridle. "Is that red plaid the MacKinnon tartan?"

"Yeah, the clan that's credited for Drambuie and the haggis masher."

She wrinkled her nose, not keen to taste either but not yet ready to leave. She still had to bring up the subject of Sandra's magnets. "Is this the bridle Lazer will be using?" She picked the gleaming leather off the hook and fingered its crownpiece. The magnet would fit right on top, right over Lazer's brain, if only Kurt would agree. "I brought you something too." She slid a hand in her pocket and passed him a flat disc, handling it reverently. "Just tape the magnet on the crownpiece. The side with 'Nikken' faces up."

He held it in his palm for inspection and actually chuckled. "This tiny little thing is what you said would help?"

"It helps children and adults focus, so why not horses?" She knew she sounded defensive but prayed he'd try it. Lazer needed all the help he could get. And so did she.

Still grinning, he slipped it into his left pocket. "I'll think about it. Better get you over to the weigh-in. It's almost ninety minutes before post."

She blew out a sigh, turned and opened the door. At least she'd tried. However, the dismissive way he'd pocketed the magnet didn't bode well.

They walked along the pathway. As they neared the jockeys' room, disappointment in his casual reaction to the magnet switched to a jittery buzz. The palms of her hands were moist. Already people drifted around the mezzanine, showing up early for the big race, a race she'd be riding.

"See you in the paddock," he said.

She forced a nonchalant wave, knowing he wouldn't want a fearful jockey on his horse. Yet nausea churned in the pit of her stomach because four weeks ago, she'd only dreamed of riding in a race this big. It was the opportunity of a lifetime, and she had the horrible feeling she was going to mess up.

Kurt sat in his truck, listening to Archer's update.

"Otto hasn't left the apartment, and we picked up another call confirming a two o'clock meeting with Friedman tomorrow. Three quick-response teams are on alert. It'll be a joint forces op with Calgary, but I'm flying out from Ottawa." Archer paused a beat. "Our legal people are praying we find something. Evidence is sketchy, but we can't let Friedman leave the country."

"Yeah." Kurt's mouth tightened. "If only I could figure out how they're using those horses."

"Maybe forensics will help. Or maybe Otto or Friedman will cave."

"Not Friedman," Kurt said. "He's a cold bastard, right down to his manicured nails. Bet he's the fucker who did Connor. A gun is his style."

"Will he give us any trouble tomorrow?"

"Not sure," Kurt said slowly.

"Well," Archer said with a grunt. "An unmarked car will come by your motel at noon. You should be home by next week. You were quick with this one."

"Not quick enough." Frustration clipped Kurt's words. Both Connor and Nick had found something he couldn't. And both were dead because of it.

He shoved the phone in his pocket and returned to the barn. Stopped in front of Otto's boarded-up stall and pushed open the door.

The stall was stripped to the floor, but dark streaks marked the side boards. He swallowed, studying the blood spatter as he reconstructed the events of that grim night.

The track's security log showed Otto and his new horse had arrived late, shipping in when few people were around. But Nick had been working long hours, dealing with an influx of horses. And obviously Kurt had sparked his curiosity when he'd asked the farrier to check Country Girl's feet.

Kurt squeezed his eyes shut, fighting his remorse. No doubt about it, he'd set Nick up. The farrier had no idea he was poking around a snake pit. Maybe Nick had asked Otto a question about the gelding's feet. Or maybe Nick had spotted the diamonds when Otto removed the back shoes.

Otto was violent and hot tempered. He would have panicked. The man was strong enough to have bludgeoned Nick and dragged him into the stall. Otto's presence would have upset the gelding. A few jabs with a pitchfork, and the terrified horse would have trampled anything in the straw.

275

Then what? Kurt's hands tightened around the stall door as he pictured the grim scene.

Otto had a dead man in the stall and a pocketful of stolen rocks. He would have been afraid someone else might wander by. The normal urge would be to dump the evidence and run.

Kurt reached in his pocket, pulled out a pair of latex gloves and stalked to the garbage can by the door. Rifled through it but found no horse shoes, only coffee cups and the ubiquitous baler twine.

He stepped outside and scanned the parking lot. Otto's trailer was still tucked in the left corner; a metal garbage bin sat a scant thirty feet from the end of the lot. Faded white letters on the front read 'No Manure.'

He stalked to the bin and raised the cumbersome lid. Hinges squeaked and flies buzzed around his face, followed by an overwhelming stench. He sifted through an assortment of beer cans, tip sheets and pizza boxes but found no horseshoes, no blunt instruments.

Only the end of a black rubber pad.

He yanked it out, studying the pad with narrowed eyes. It was the same thickness as the rubber sheet he'd seen in Otto's lockbox but with a crucial difference. After another minute of rummaging he discovered a second pad. A bleak smile creased his face.

Nick had been right. Otto's horses had been wearing pads—thick black pads with hollowed-out centers. Otto must have placed the jewels in the hollow pad, sandwiched it with another flat rubber and nailed them on the horses. He'd probably chosen animals that kicked, realizing no border inspector would be keen to get close. Or perhaps Otto had roughed up the horses until they did kick.

Once he'd established himself as a legitimate trainer, he would have been able to cross into Canada with barely a nod. And if a vet pulled out his animals for a border check, it would have been cursory.

Julie hadn't noticed anything odd about the shoes because they'd been normal. But to Nick, thick pads were notable.

Especially since Kurt had triggered his interest by asking him to inspect the mare.

Kurt trudged back to his truck with heavy steps. He rummaged in his box for a plastic bag and pressed redial on the phone. "Archer, the smugglers used hollowed-out pads to move the stones. I found a couple in the garbage bin. Otto always pulled the hind shoes as soon as he arrived. When he hauled in late Wednesday, the victim was working in the barn. Otto probably cracked him with a shovel or something. Used the horse to cover it up."

"Excellent." Archer's voice oozed satisfaction. "Now we have the method. And forensics will have a field day with those pads."

"Let's pick Otto up now."

"No. We can't spook Friedman. The FBI are moving on the smugglers in Montana. A woman was killed in the last home invasion." Archer's voice turned rueful. "And naturally we're taking heat about our porous borders."

"But Otto's too unstable to be running around." The hair on the back of Kurt's neck rose, and he gripped the phone. "He could hurt someone else."

"It's out of my control. See you tomorrow," Archer said, and the line went dead.

# CHAPTER THIRTY-ONE

Julie chewed her nails and stared at the screen in the common area of the jock room. Ten riders crammed around the monitor, all intent on the first race. Some, like her, only had one mount. Others had five or six.

Gary Bixton was riding in every race.

Right now Gary wasn't thinking about anything except urging his mount down the stretch. She watched him on the screen, arms pumping as he fought to hold off the chestnut filly surging on the outside. Gary's bay floundered on the rail, and the chestnut gained speed with every stride.

She leaped to her feet as the horses battled across the wire. Around her, voices rose as jockeys argued about the winner.

"Gary got it on the nod," someone said.

"Nah, no way."

Numbers flashed—a photo for first. She waited, silent and edgy. If Gary had the win, he'd be generous with information. If he lost a close one, he wouldn't be very talkative. She exhaled with relief when his number appeared on top, and the race was declared official.

"Man, Bixton's hot this year," Allan, a wiry rider in his mid-forties, proclaimed. "He could win on a mule."

"Helps to get the good horses." Liam Anderson's voice was spiked with envy. "He'll take the big race tonight on Sweating Bullet. My horse can't handle that distance."

Julie had memorized the horses, the riders, the color of their silks. Liam was on Frostbite, the other gray in her race, the horse Kurt feared would cause a traffic jam.

"Who's on the Woodbine colt? I heard he's had some fast fractions." Liam glanced at Julie. "You've been exercising him. Is he any good?"

"She's riding him, you fool," a voice sniped behind her.

Julie nodded. "He's talented."

"You're riding him? Really? How'd you pull that off?" Liam stared with blatant disbelief.

A flush heated her cheeks. All the guys looked at her now with expressions that ranged from shock to envy. Little wonder. Until Kurt had arrived, she'd only ridden cheap claimers. And not very many of those.

Liam whipped out his program, running his finger down the entries. "Trainer must be going for the weight allowance or something." His beady eyes narrowed. "How did you get that horse?"

"I jump out of bed early and gallop horses," she snapped.

Liam sniggered. "More likely you jump into bed."

"Shut up." Allan punched Liam's arm and turned to her. "Ignore the twerp. I talked to MacKinnon about riding. He said he likes the way you handle him."

Someone chortled at Allan's choice of words.

Julie crossed her arms and glared at Liam, pissed at his ugly innuendoes. Kurt had given her the mount before they'd ridden in the mountains. There'd been no ulterior motive.

The jockeys from the first race burst in, dirty and disheveled, and attention swung to the returning riders.

"Man, I got stuck on the rail," someone complained.

Gary swept in several minutes later, wearing a victor's grin.

"Congratulations, Gary," Allen called.

"Thanks, boys. That was one of those races!" He raised his hair theatrically with his left hand and walked across the room, still grinning. "What a dog I'm on in the second, Jules. Think I should pack a lunch?"

She forced a smile. He probably guessed she was nervous, probably knew her stomach felt like she'd swallowed a bucket of nails, that it hurt even more as the big race loomed closer. Six races to go. She swallowed, debating about running to the bathroom again.

"Relax." Gary's voice lowered, and he stepped closer. "You're in the catbird seat. If your big gray fires, you'll win. If not, he'll be at the back, but that's where he's been running. Just like you."

She rolled her eyes and gave a choke of laughter. "Are you trying to make me feel better or worse?"

"My point is, nobody will blame a loss on you. But Sweating Bullet is the favorite. If he loses, it will be my fault."

He looked so disgusted, some of her tension eased. "You sure have it tough," she said. "Always stuck riding the favorites."

"Don't get saucy, darling. Just remember to stay away from Liam the Lump. When Frostbite stops, it's like someone pulled the emergency brake. Have to run, gotta switch silks. Oh, and Jules, avoid the rail if you can."

He gave her shoulder a squeeze and turned, pulling off his shirt as he rushed away. The door to the male quarters slammed. She felt oddly bereft. She scanned the remaining jockeys, checking to see who else was sitting out. Allan had a mount but Liam was still there, his thin upper lip curved in a perpetual sneer.

Liam the Lump. She hadn't heard that nickname before, but it was perfect. Liam was a rough rider with a bad seat, but it was his constant petulance that repelled her the most.

"Must be nice," he said as he wound a black tensor wrap around his wrist. "I've been riding here for five years, and guys like Bixton still ignore me."

"Try smiling," she said, adjusting the headphones of her iPod, careful not to tangle them with her new necklace.

"Yeah," he said, "and maybe if I was female, I could try spreading my legs too."

She flipped him a finger then turned her music up and fingered the lucky pendant. It felt warm, seemed to pulse with Kurt's confident vibes. Feeling inexplicably fierce, she narrowed her eyes, holding Liam's glare.

He was the first to look away.

Lazer snorted with indignation as Kurt rinsed his mouth. Water globules splattered the stall, dotting Martin's chest.

"Shit!" Martin leaped away from the spray of water. "This is my good shirt."

"At least the water's not green," Kurt said. "Pass me the bridle." He slipped the bit in Lazer's mouth.

The track announcer called, "They're off!"

Lazer trembled in eagerness, his ears flicking as he tracked the sounds of the seventh race.

"Keep a tight hold in the paddock, Martin. Don't let him get too close to the others. Especially the filly."

"I won't let go, no matter what."

"I know," Kurt said. "The odds are juicy, so I placed a couple bets. I'll have to cash in for you, but you can hold the tickets for luck."

Martin's eyes widened when he saw the betting tickets Kurt passed him. "Fifty dollars to win and a ten dollar triactor." He turned and earnestly patted Lazer's neck. "Please, fellow. You run hard, and I promise to take you for grass every morning."

"Let's go."

At Kurt's command, the three exited the barn and headed over to the paddock for the eighth and feature race.

The grounds pulsed with energy. Spectators rimmed the paddock, eager to see the local racing sensation, Sweating Bullet, an Alberta-bred and the crowd favorite. Kurt led Lazer into the walking ring and joined three horses already parading in a circle. Lazer sidestepped, swishing his tail and staring suspiciously at the crowd.

The stocky bay ahead of them kicked out, smashing his hind legs against the rail, and the crowd folded then surged forward again. Their murmurs swelled when Sweating Bullet stalked into the enclosure. The blood bay's arrogant gaze swept the other horses; his figure eight noseband only enhanced his regal bearing. The horse simply bristled with confidence.

Lazer raised his head and snorted a challenge.

At least, Kurt hoped it was a challenge. With Lazer, it might have been a friendly hello. He saw Julie's valet waiting beside Martin and led Lazer into the saddling enclosure.

Martin held the horse, jiggling with the bit as Kurt laid the pad and saddlecloth over Lazer's back. The valet passed Kurt the saddle but as he reached around to buckle the overgirth, Lazer's muscles bunched. The horse plunged forward, almost striking Martin with his foreleg.

Martin held on and backed Lazer up, mouth set in a determined line.

"Well done." Kurt nodded with approval and they were able to finish saddling. "Now lead him around while I wait for Julie."

Martin guided Lazer around the walking ring. The kid's mother beamed from the rail as her capable son led the prancing horse. He'll be all right, Kurt thought, with a flare of satisfaction. Martin was at least a decade younger than anyone else in the paddock, but he acted like a veteran, and his cool poise was helping Lazer.

Kurt remained on the grass, savoring the intoxicating moments before a race, the shared hopes of the other trainers and nervous excitement of the owners. There were no losers yet, just a race full of possibilities.

Color caught his eye as riders filed from the jockeys' room, their faces a study in contrast as they coped with the pressure. Some grinned, although the smiles were usually tight and forced. Others were solemn, like Gary Bixton. Even thirty feet away Kurt could see Bixton wore his game face—sober, focused, confident.

Kurt finally spotted Julie, and his forehead broke into a cold sweat. Not good. She looked scared, mouth pinched, walking like a robot. And there wasn't much time to loosen her up.

"Hi, Julie," he said as she approached. "How about a kiss for luck?"

"No jokes." She frowned and glanced at the scowling jockey behind her as though afraid he were listening. "Rider instructions only."

It was a relief to see some animation return to her face, even if it was only a frown. "All right, riding instructions only," Kurt said. "Turn left. Go fast. And ride him like you're on the best horse in the race because...with the bridle adjustment, he is."

"You actually put the magnet on him?"

282

"I did," he said.

She smiled then, a beautiful smile that connected to something in his chest. He wanted to wrap his arms around her and never let go. But he jammed his hands in his pockets and watched Lazer.

The colt strutted beside Martin and the kid walked just as cocky, as though certain he was leading the best horse in the paddock. If confidence won a race, this one was in the bag. Kurt turned to Julie. "Your horse is ready to run."

But there was no longer any need to pump her up. Intensity radiated from her; she was in her own zone now, focused on her mount, focused on her job.

"Riders up!" the paddock judge hollered. Kurt stepped sideways and legged her into the saddle. She placed her booted toes in the irons and knotted her reins. He took Lazer from Martin and led her to the walkway where Sandra waited.

Julie tipped her stick at Kurt, and she and Sandra joined the column of horses filing onto the track. He swallowed away the dryness in his throat and turned away. Nothing more he could do. It was all up to her now. And luck—ever-fickle racing luck.

Julie stared over Lazer's arched neck as they stepped onto the track. The colt felt so ready. He coiled beneath her, alert and aggressive, and her confidence soared as she absorbed his boldness.

Spectators crammed against the rail, making comments, yelling encouragement. She recognized her dad's holler but blocked most of the clamor, only vaguely aware of the trumpet call. Her senses focused on Lazer as he arched his neck and strutted past the crowd.

"That horse is such a showoff," Sandra said as she and Okie escorted Lazer in front of the buzzing grandstand. Her voice lowered, and she studied the top of Lazer's bridle. "Is he wearing it?"

Julie nodded. They both grinned and galloped toward the backside.

When the starter called them, Lazer's neck was warm but not washy. Not like Frostbite. The other gray was coated with white

283

foam, creamy even between his hind legs. Liam's horse definitely won't make the distance today, Julie thought, before turning and scanning the other riders. They all looked serious; even Gary was—

*Oh shit, what am I doing?* Panicky, she tried to redirect her thoughts. She didn't want to lose her focus, not now, not at the worst possible moment. And then the assistant starter was beside them, reaching up to take Lazer's line. The colt tried to jerk away but was guided toward the gate.

He rammed in, crooked, slamming her knee against the metal bar. She cursed at the searing pain. He charged forward, bumping his nose against the grill, but the gate clanged shut behind them, and now there was no way out but straight ahead.

She pulled her goggles down, drawing in even breaths as she tried to reconnect with her edgy horse. On the right, bars rattled. A rider yelled. She glanced sideways as an attendant struggled to untwist the three horse. Please get him straight, she thought. That horse might broadside us, standing crooked like that. He's right next to us—

"Stop it," she muttered to herself. Lazer's right ear flicked.

"Two to load," a voice hollered.

Oh, Christ. She grabbed a piece of mane and adjusted her reins, lengthening them so she wouldn't jerk her horse on that first leap.

"One back!"

That would be Brenna's Hitter. The speedy filly was in the outside hole and would be charging over, trying to grab the rail before the first turn. A lot of dirt would be thrown up as the frontrunners pulled clear. She'd be pushed back and could take Lazer a little to the outside. Keep him clear of the kickback and see what's happening. She stared through the grilled door. Ready.

"No, no. Not yet!" someone called.

Yells jangled with the clink of steel as a horse fought the gate. She kept her eyes straight ahead, staring at the expanse of dirt, imagining the feel of Lazer as he burst out straight and fast. The assistant starter adjusted Lazer's nose in the vee. The colt's ears flattened.

*Clang!* The gates sprang open, the noise mingling with riders' shouts.

Lazer launched forward. The three horse veered to the left, smacking them with his shoulder. But Lazer muscled back like a diesel truck and the three horse disappeared, left to jostle for position behind them. Atta boy!

Liam had grabbed the rail, and Frostbite's distinctive white tail streamed in front of them. A streak of red flashed on their outside as the filly, Brenna's Hitter, gunned for the lead.

Lazer had been quick from the gate too. A wall of runners loomed on her right, but the colt wasn't slowing down. His nose was shoved in Frostbite's blowing tail as they entered the first turn.

Shit! This wasn't where they were supposed to be. She and Kurt hadn't even discussed this scenario. The possibility of running up front hadn't occurred to either of them. But Lazer ran effortlessly, and they were close enough to the two frontrunners that dirt didn't bombard them. The pace didn't feel brutally fast either.

She adjusted her grip on the reins and decided to let Lazer run. Better than arguing with him. And Kurt had said to ride like he was the best horse in the race.

So she coasted along, third on the rail, tucked in behind Liam's mount and Brenna's Hitter with the rest of the field pounding behind them. A horse's white bridle shoved up by Lazer's shoulder, and suddenly she was boxed in on the rail. The soft cuppy rail.

As they rounded the first turn the white-bridled horse drifted wide. She grabbed the space and moved Lazer several paths out. The speed horses pulled away, swept out of the turn and galloped by the grandstand for the first time. Clods of dirt hit Lazer in the face. He faltered.

*Come on!* She shook her stick but Lazer was backing off from the stinging dirt. She checked under her right arm and saw enough room to swing wider still, and when she guided him further from the rail, he dug back in. But two runners had grabbed the space on her inside, and now she was shoved back to fifth.

*And we're way too wide!* She fought a mind-numbing panic. They charged into the clubhouse turn with Lazer covering more ground but still holding his position. The half-mile pole was a blur as the horses thundered around the turn and down the backstretch.

She kept Lazer under a careful hold. Struggled to regain her composure. His ears were pinned on Brenna's Hitter, and he seemed to be narrowing the gap even though he ran three wide. His power was incredible, but could he hang on?

Yet they seemed to be gaining on one of the leaders. Or was Frostbite fading? She saw Liam's arm rise and fall, but the jockey's whip was useless. Frostbite had simply quit running.

The rider caught behind the gray bellowed. White silks, had to be Allan. She glimpsed the jock rise in the stirrups, frantically checking his mount in a last-ditch effort to keep from clipping heels.

Then Frostbite disappeared, replaced with a blur of red and white. The quarter pole. Only Brenna's Hitter was in front of them, and Lazer was locked on the filly.

Movement flashed on her inside. A blazed face nudged up, a horse with a distinctive figure eight noseband. *Oh no, it's Gary, and Lazer doesn't even see him.* Sweating Bullet would be strong too, tracking the speed and benefiting from Gary's smart ride.

Lazer wasn't even aware of the new challenge until the favorite had edged past. They rounded the final turn with Brenna's Hitter clinging to the lead, Sweating Bullet a charging second, and Lazer third and running near the center of the track.

This is it, fellow. No dirt and lots of running room. Show me what you're made of. She dropped a dirty set of goggles, switched her stick to the right hand and pleaded for another gear.

Lazer exploded.

They blew by Bixton on Sweating Bullet, past the gutsy Brenna's Hitter. Julie glimpsed a startled face. And then they were alone on the lead with nothing in sight but an expanse of brown. Whistles and yells, the crack of a whip, the straining of other horses—sounds faded as Lazer stormed past the sixteenth pole. No one was going to catch him, not today.

His ears pricked as the crowd roared in approval. With an unflagging stride he cruised under the wire, six lengths in front of the favorite and drawing away.

Julie rose in the stirrups, bursting with elation. They had won, convincingly. "Thank you," she whispered, raising her arm to the sky.

She tried to slow Lazer, but he wanted to run another mile. Midway down the backside, she was able to ease him up and turn around.

"What the hell did you do to that horse?" Gary hollered as he cantered alongside, touching her shoulder in an eloquent salute.

She just grinned. "Did you get up for second?" she asked.

"Yeah and I think the filly hung on for third. But you were alone up there. That was some kick. Haven't seen a move like that in a long time. Wonder what the time was."

Julie didn't care about the time of the race or Lazer's explosive last quarter. He'd run his heart out, and she gratefully stroked his wet neck "You wonderful, wonderful horse," she whispered, her praise garbled by her ragged breathing.

Choking with joy, she whispered another string of endearments. Lazer arched his neck and preened as they trotted to the pick-up area where Kurt waited, tall and distinct among the cluster of trainers.

He looked so cool, so composed. She didn't know how he did it because her joy bubbled, and she knew her entire face glowed. She couldn't hide it. Didn't want to.

She grinned and saluted the stewards before leaping off beside Kurt.

"Stay on, hotshot," he said. "Tonight you make that special trip to the winner's circle. Congratulations."

"I forgot about that part!" She pumped his hand. "Congratulations to you too."

He legged her back into the saddle. "You sure had this fellow moving. How did you get out of the gate so quick?"

She leaned over Lazer's shoulder. "It must have been the magnet," she said. "He was focused from start to finish."

Kurt unbuckled the blinkers and gave a slow nod, as though settling an argument with himself. At that moment she didn't care what combination of factors had helped Lazer. It was all wonderful, and she intended to savor every fleeting second.

Shimmering with happiness, she watched through a haze—the perfect dream—as Kurt led them into the winner's circle. He gestured, and Sandra, Martin and her dad twisted through the crowd, hustling to join them. The photographer framed the horse with his lens as they crammed around Lazer. A cooler, plaque, handshakes. The camera clicked, and the presentation was made.

"There's a nice picture for your wall," Kurt said, looking at her as though he knew exactly where she'd hang it. Right next to her mom's. A weight lifted, and she grinned, so deliriously grateful she wanted to hug him, wanted to hug Lazer, wanted to hug anyone within reach.

"Tell me about the race," he said, his calm voice grounding her.

"Lazer was focused. Had a good jump from the gate. The dirt bothered him down the backstretch, but he dug in when we swung wide. And I had a ton of horse heading for home."

"You stayed cool. You were in a tight spot for a second."

She wiped the wetness off her cheeks. Kept grinning. "I had a lot more options because Lazer is such a good horse. And you're such a good trainer."

She squeezed his arm and leaped off, clicking her heels in the air, weightless with euphoria. Behind them the crowd roared, pulling their attention to the tote board.

Kurt gave a low whistle. "Look at those payouts. We'll have money to celebrate with tonight."

"Two hundred and sixty eight bucks for the trifecta! Did you bet it?"

"A few times. You and Martin did too. Sandra has your tickets."

Julie pulled off her saddle. Her mouth seemed to stretch from ear to ear. "Sandra will be over the moon. Thanks for all you've done. And for the ride. I think Lazer will go on to much bigger things."

"This is all he ever has to do for me," Kurt said. He stared down at her. Something soul deep sparked between them, and

288

for a moment it seemed they were the only two people at the track. But an official was calling, and she gulped back her bubbling emotions and turned to the scales.

Right after weigh out, a melee of raucous jockeys, led by Gary Bixton, swarmed her. From the tops of their shoulders she saw a group of teenagers celebrating in front of the tote board. Martin was the hero in the middle, holding hands with a laughing redhead and jubilantly brandishing a fistful of betting stubs.

The last race was long over by the time Lazer relaxed and passed his urine. The colt left the test barn, an automatic stop for race winners, and walked eagerly into G barn, his head swinging as Julie, Martin and Sandra saluted him with their beer cans.

Kurt led the colt into his stall, noticed someone had placed a carrot and two peppermints in his feed bin, and the hay net bulged with alfalfa. He wrapped Lazer's legs, giving him a thorough rubdown before joining the festivities in the aisle.

"Any beer left?" he asked, pretending dismay at their sheepish expressions.

"You were too long at the test barn," Sandra said as she gathered the empties, "but the bets you placed will pay my rent for months. So if you drive us to Champs, I'll buy you all the beer you can drink."

"Thanks." He inclined his head. "But you all had a hand in Lazer's win, and I'm definitely buying tonight. By the way, whose magnet is this, and how do I get my own?"

"Keep it," Julie said. "We're only glad you were open enough to try something different."

He pocketed the shiny disc with a wry smile, reluctant to admit he hadn't been all that open. He'd attached it to Lazer's bridle only because the throbbing pain in his thigh had vanished fifteen minutes after he'd stuck the magnet in his left pocket.

# CHAPTER THIRTY-TWO

The bar bustled in celebration but Kurt felt isolated, like being the only sober person at a party. He sipped his beer while Julie and Gary rehashed every stride of race eight—for the third time. Usually when one of his horses ran big, he enjoyed the replays.

Not tonight.

"That filly's tough," Gary said. "Under a mile no one can beat her. She looked my horse in the eye and didn't give an inch."

Kurt checked his watch, wondering when the place would close. He didn't want to rob Julie of her celebration, but he was filled with a raw urgency to explain. There wasn't much time either. In less than twenty-four hours, the entire investigation would be exposed.

He stretched his arm over the back of her chair as Gary continued to laud Brenna's Hitter.

"No need to ride the broncs either, Jules," Gary added in that familiar drawl Kurt was learning to like. "You can ease up and stop racing like a starving apprentice too. It's embarrassing for us old guys to get dusted like that."

"It'll be wonderful not to ride for Otto any more." Julie's face was so radiant, the anxiety gnawing at Kurt's gut was temporarily soothed. Just seeing her expression gave him a lift.

"Otto won't be around anyway," Sandra called from across the table where she was stacking fat piles of bills. "Heard he sold his horse for meat and is pulling out tomorrow."

Kurt leaned forward. "Was he at the barn tonight?"

"Yeah, ranting to someone about their trailer blocking his, and how it better be gone by tomorrow afternoon or else. Otto's such a jerk."

Kurt stretched back in his chair and tried to relax. Sounded like everything would shake down as expected. He'd have all night and morning to be with Julie. She'd have a lot of questions and deserved honest answers. Still…he had the nagging sense he was missing something and peeked at his watch again.

Heavy footsteps sounded behind him.

"Congratulations on the win, Kurt," Cody said, posing by the table. "Guess you're buying tonight?"

Julie looked up, her eyes widening with sympathy. "What happened to your face?" she asked.

"Nothing much. Just a little misunderstanding." Cody sidled around Kurt's chair, edging closer to Julie. "No shooters tonight? I can get some if you want."

She shuddered. "No, thanks."

Cody leaned down, planting a hand on the table between Julie and Kurt. "It didn't hurt your riding though. Maybe I did you a favor, getting you to relax before the race. Maybe we should do that again?"

"Maybe there's an empty seat at another table," Kurt said.

Cody chuckled, unabashed. "Yeah, okay. See you both around. Congratulations on the win. Really," he added before walking away.

"We want new Directors for the Jockey's Association," Gary said. "There's a bylaw pending. Ten of us are here tonight, and we need to vote for the insurance coverage."

Kurt sighed as he heard Gary lobbying. Better coverage for riders was a critical issue, and he was a strong supporter. But if they started discussions now, Julie could be here all night.

"Let's go dancing after this," Sandra said, jubilantly waving her wad of cash.

Kurt's head throbbed as the commotion swelled, and he didn't know what bothered him most. Anticipation about the arrests tomorrow or fear of Julie's reaction tonight. But he simply couldn't wait any longer. He shoved his beer to the side and leaned toward her. "I know it's a sweet night, but I need to talk to you. Alone."

"Oh, but…" Her smiling protest faded as she studied his face.

"It's important," he said softly.

She stared at him for a moment then seemed to sense his urgency because she rose, scooped up her purse and said a firm goodbye to her protesting friends.

Kurt eased his truck in front of the motel door and reached behind the seat to grab his briefcase. Julie was silent although the glow from the lighted walkway outlined her pensive expression. She slid from the truck but looked so reluctant, uncertainty made him nervous.

He unlocked the door, following her into the stiff silence. The bed seemed tauntingly big, the centerpiece of a tawdry room. She jerked her head away, staring instead at the cheap picture above the desk.

Clearly she thought he was dragging her here in hopes of some quick sex.

"We won't stay long," he said quickly. "I'll take you back to celebrate with your friends. I just want to explain some things, things that affect you and me."

If anything, her expression turned more remote. He propped a nonchalant shoulder against the door and fought to look relaxed. Christ, he'd faced mob bosses with less fear, but she looked so wooden. It didn't seem the ideal time to admit he was a cop on a case; her entire body language was unreceptive, so different from in the tack room before the race.

Before the race—when she wanted to ride his horse.

Well, maybe she'd been playing him too. He knew how people could pretend. Nothing surprised him anymore. "So you hit the Calgary big times. Guess you'll be riding ten thousand dollar claimers now, instead of two." He tried to joke but his gut knotted so tightly, his words sounded mocking.

She flinched but raised her head, facing him, and he knew then he was wrong. She had the heart of a lion but, unlike him, wasn't a fake.

"I love what I do," she said with quiet dignity, "and I'll always be happy to ride a claimer. Those horses are more level than some trainers I know. And they're certainly much easier to understand."

"That's actually what I wanted to explain," he said. Her bleak expression scared him and he paused, rubbing a hand over his jaw. It was easier to deal with naked women, easier to show feelings with actions not words, but she didn't seem like she wanted to get very close. In fact, she was eyeing him as though he were a sex offender.

"Are you that reluctant to be here with me?" He raised an eyebrow, trying to keep the guilt from his voice, trying to pretend her answer wasn't even very important.

She stared at him, much braver than he, not attempting to hide the vulnerability in her eyes. "Of course I want to be with you," she said. "That's why I'm here. But it's afterwards. You always seem to have regrets. You turn mean. Even now, that nasty crack about claimers—"

"Oh, honey." He crossed the room in three strides and wrapped his arms around her, his heart beating in double time when she didn't push him away. "You're the last person I'd want to hurt. But there's other stuff going on. It makes me cranky, and I gotta tell you about it."

"The truth is," her voice wobbled," I want to be with you, even if it *is* just for sex. And it doesn't really matter how cranky you get."

"Julie." He breathed her name in a shuddering sigh. Found her mouth, unable to talk, unable to do anything but cover her with a grateful kiss. He didn't intend anything more, but her taste, her feel, her smell, the way she pressed into him...

"It's definitely not just sex, honey," he managed, his voice thick. "And we need to talk." But he was strung too tight, couldn't bear to let her go, and when she tugged his head back down and slid her hands beneath his shirt, he forgot everything but the quickest way to peel off their clothes.

Soon nothing was between them, and he was able to reacquaint himself with her sweet little body. Couldn't get enough. He wanted to go slow, had always considered himself a decent lover—a little selfish maybe but who wasn't. Still, if sex were a drawing card, he'd play it. He lingered over her sensitive spots until sweat beaded his forehead, and she nipped his shoulder in frustration.

He finally eased into her velvety warmth, watching her expression, savoring her complete trust. He intended to linger, make it last, but when she raised her hips and wiggled, he began thrusting, no longer able to pace himself.

The noises in her throat made him quicken, and he drove deeper until her shuddering climax wrapped around him. Oh, Christ. He jerked with a last surge of pleasure and collapsed, rolled to his side and pulled her with him.

"You're going to kill me," he muttered, breathless. She snuggled against him, languid as a cat while he massaged her back, finding each ache, moving gentler around the bruises and rubbing each knot until he was certain there was no tightness left.

Her necklace had slipped over her shoulder and he straightened it, then tucked the sheet around them. Drew in a fortifying breath. "I want to tell you why I'm here. Why I brought Lazer. Why we met." He leaned over, needing to watch her expression, hoping she'd see his sincerity.

Her breathing was relaxed, her soft lips curved and her long eyelashes flattened against her cheeks. Serene, untroubled, asleep. Still smiling too, at least for now.

He brushed back a strand of silky hair and cradled her in his arms, accepting that sleep wouldn't come to him quite that easily.

# CHAPTER THIRTY-THREE

"Quit it, Blue," Julie mumbled. Morning light filtered thought the curtains, along with his insistent nose, nudging her awake. She jammed her face in the pillow and yanked the sheet up. Her legs felt unusually heavy, her entire body lethargic. She needed more sleep, and she definitely needed Blue to stop kissing her neck.

Her eyes jerked open.

"It's rather disturbing how you always confuse me with your dog, special though he is," Kurt whispered, his eyes glinting with amusement. His warm mouth drifted down her neck, lingering at her throat, made her skin tingle as it dragged over her sensitive collarbone. Dropped lower.

Her breathing turned ragged as his lips trailed across her stomach to her thighs and then... She bucked in shock but he held her in place with his hand, working on her, scattering her resistance. When he finally thrust inside, she welcomed him, wrapping her legs around his hips. They explored each other again, filling the room with breathy whispers and hot kisses until she gripped his back and arched into him.

He stiffened. One last thrust. She clung to him, wanting him to stay, but he rolled over with a satisfied groan. His chest was warm and safe, and she snuggled into it, loving his feel, his smell, the reassuring thud of his heart and how his damp chest hair tickled her nose.

"Let's stay here all day," she said.

His magical hand rubbed her back, so slow, so caring, and she stopped talking and closed her eyes in contentment. No wonder his horses loved him.

"How about I check on the horses and then we'll go for a quiet breakfast?" He sounded resigned. "Some place away from the track."

"Sure." She really wished he'd keep massaging her back, but the chance for more sleep was tempting too. The mattress shifted as he rose, and she cracked open her eyes, admiring him as he padded toward the bathroom. His muscular legs and tight butt looked good in jeans but even better naked.

The bathroom door closed. She adjusted a pillow and burrowed under the covers. Her skin felt tender against the sheets, and it was likely she had whisker burns in several places, but she couldn't remember ever feeling so damn happy. She rolled to his side of the bed, found the warm spot he'd just left, sighed in contentment and fell asleep.

The sound of a drawer woke her. She caught a whiff of soap and opened her eyes. He stood by the bed, tucking in his shirt, and the tender expression on his face made her heart skip a beat.

"I'm getting up. Soon," she said. Her voice sounded oddly husky, sexy even, but that probably happened to any girl after spending a night with Kurt.

"You're not galloping this morning," he said.

"Really?" She raised an eyebrow. She'd have to work on his bossiness though. Other than that, and his regrettable tendency to moodiness, he was absolutely perfect.

"Please, Julie," he said. "Don't gallop for anyone this morning. I'll be back soon. We really need to talk."

He asked so sweetly she relented with barely any hesitation. "Okay, no riding. But I have to drop by the barns sometime this morning." She kept her face perfectly serious. "I haven't seen everyone yet, and they'll all want to congratulate me on my magnificent ride."

He moved like a panther, flipping her over and swatting her rear, chuckling at her indignant squeal. "Don't let it go to your head, honey. You're only as good as your last race. Tomorrow you might be a bum, although you do have a beautiful one." He pulled the covers back up then covered her mouth with a toe-curling kiss, a wicked glint darkening his eyes. "If you're still in bed when I get back, we'll skip breakfast."

"No way. I'm starving. I'll be ready." She stroked the stubble on his chin. "Aren't you going to shave? You look mean, and we all know you're actually a very sweet guy."

"Shush," he said with an enigmatic smile. "Don't forget to lock the door."

She heard his diesel truck roar to a start, the crunch of gravel, and then it blended with early morning traffic. Oh, wow. She yawned and stretched in utter contentment.

There was some soreness in her knee where she'd hit the gate and her left side still ached from the earlier fall, but overall she felt super. It had been a perfect evening from beginning to end. Absolutely perfect.

But a kernel of uneasiness nipped at her, making it impossible to fall back to sleep. He'd made her feel cherished last night. She still tingled, remembering the things he'd whispered, his hard body, his knowing touch. However, just last week he'd only wanted a temporary relationship.

What was temporary anyway? Six weeks, six months?

She tugged at her bottom lip. He must care for her. Every day he seemed a bit softer, more open. He'd even given her that beautiful necklace. And he definitely had been more concerned about her safety than winning the race on Lazer.

Lazer and Kurt—holy shit, what a package. Maybe he wanted to enter the colt in the Alberta Derby. The race was less than a month away. Yes. That's probably one of the things he was so keen to talk about.

No longer sleepy, she threw back the covers and skipped into the bathroom, determined to be ready when he returned. Happiness always stoked her appetite, and this morning she was starving.

# CHAPTER THIRTY-FOUR

Sandra whistled a jaunty tune, dropped the wheelbarrow with a clang and stared over the stall door, watching Kurt unwrap Lazer's leg bandages. "Where's Julie?" she asked. "The way you ditched us last night, we figured you wanted to celebrate alone."

"We did."

"I see." She nodded but leaned over the door, not trying to hide her nosiness. "Is she galloping today? Two trainers already dropped by wanting to talk. One of them has twelve horses."

"They'll have to come back tomorrow," he said, "or talk to her agent." But his hands stalled over the wrap. Julie probably didn't have an agent, but there was no doubt she'd want to take advantage of her career-boosting win. "She'll be over after we eat," he added, removing the wraps. "She can talk then."

He skimmed his hands over Lazer's legs. Tendons tight, no heat or swelling. He patted the colt, relieved he had come out of the race in good shape. He sensed Sandra's lingering presence and glanced up.

"You seem preoccupied," she said, arching her eyebrow. "If you and Julie are so wrapped up with breakfast and stuff, I can pony your horses. After all, you two did win me a ton of money."

"Thanks," he said. "Julie's quite tired today."

Sandra giggled. He tried to scowl, tried to hide his idiotic grin but it poked through anyway. He didn't want to encourage Sandra, so scooped up the rolled bandages and strode from the stall, eager to lock up his tack room and return to the motel. He already missed Julie, and it was time to tell her the truth.

Sandra shook her head and picked up the wheelbarrow. "Better shave before you see her dad. It looks like you rolled out of bed, and he's pretty protective. And tell Julie her picture's in *The Herald.* They sponsored the race, so it's on the front page. Even Otto saw it."

"Otto?" Kurt jerked around. "Otto was here? Already?"

"Yup, he and another guy."

"Did the other guy have a German accent?"

"How the hell would I know? Otto's not one for small talk. It might have been the meat man. Soon the only running that horse will be doing is from a can—"

Kurt tossed his bandages in the aisle and brushed past. "Thanks for looking after my horses," he said.

He rushed outside and checked the parking lot, squinting against the rising sun. Otto's trailer was still there. He felt in his pocket for sunglasses but found only his phone. Shading his eyes with his hand, he peered through the mesh fence separating the lot from the road.

A beige sedan with a buggy whip antenna was parked by the curb. Coffee cups spotted the dashboard, and two heads poked out from behind raised newspapers. Obviously the surveillance team.

He pulled out his cell, pressing Archer's number. A recorded voice requested he leave a message. No doubt Archer was already on the plane and out of reach. He turned his phone from vibrate to ring and sent a text message: *Call me.* Slipped his phone back in his pocket.

Apprehension twisted his gut as he scanned the parking lot. It was odd Otto had come to the track early, and he didn't like oddities.

Still, everything appeared normal. Otto's trailer was hooked to his truck, ready to haul his ill-fated horse to the meat yard, something Kurt didn't intend to let happen. The surveillance people had slapped a tracking device on the pickup, so there wasn't any danger of losing him.

But was his companion really the meat buyer? And why were they at the track so early?

Kurt rushed through every barn, accepting the smattering of congratulations as he tried to shake off his worry. Otto wasn't in any of the barns. Nor was he slouched by the rail or lazing in the track kitchen.

He skirted the oval, following the walkway to the race office.

Tiffany's sleek head was bent over her desk, but when she looked up her mouth curved in a warm greeting. "I heard about the race last night. Congratulations again," she said. "You going to Champs tonight?"

"Not sure what Julie and I are doing," he said. "Did Otto Laing stop by and pick up his horse's papers?"

Her smile turned to a pout. She swiveled her chair, crossing her legs. "I told you before, I don't know that man."

"Did you issue any visitor passes this morning?" Kurt asked.

"Sounds like you want special favors again." She leaned back, her thin blouse tightening in an attractive poise he was sure she'd practiced.

"Tiffany, please. Did you issue any passes?"

Her eyes widened at the snap in his voice and she turned, tight-lipped, to the computer. "Otto Laing picked up his horse's papers this morning." She didn't look up, and her painted nails clicked over the keyboard with brusque finality. "But he didn't request a pass."

"Anyone with him?"

"No, just him."

"Thank you."

She inclined her head in a regal nod, but clearly he'd used up all his favors from the race office.

"Thanks, Tiffany," he repeated as he wheeled away.

He stalked across the walkway, weighing scenarios. No pass had been issued so Otto's companion must have his own credentials. Probably Friedman then, not the stock buyer. But the two men weren't supposed to meet until this afternoon.

He checked his phone. Some mundane text messages, one e-mail about an allowance win at Gulfstream, but nothing from Archer. And surely Archer would know of any change in Otto's schedule. The surveillance people had looked unconcerned, but if Otto had met Friedman on the backside they might not even be aware the two men were together.

Kurt rubbed the back of his neck, chilled at the idea of Friedman and Otto skulking around. His instincts clamored, and he itched for his Sig. From this side of the track, it'd be a short walk to his motel. He could pick up his gun and be back in less than ten minutes. Breakfast with Julie would have to wait, at least until he'd checked on Otto's activity.

He jogged out the grandstand entrance and cut across the meridian, weaving through the blaring horns and exhaust from impatient commuters. Traffic sounds dulled as he followed the walkway to his motel room. The air turned quiet, almost subdued.

Julie hadn't locked the door, had even left it slightly ajar. He smiled as he glimpsed her erect in a chair, hair still damp from the shower. Tendrils framed her beautiful face, but her expression was odd. She looked lifeless, blank as a store mannequin.

He charged in.

"Close the door," an accented voice said behind him.

The 'Do Not Disturb' sign swayed on the inner knob as Kurt's hand jerked in shock. He turned and pushed the door shut, trying to breathe, trying to control that first jolt of fear.

Marcus Friedman studied him from the corner chair. In an elegant charcoal suit, Friedman could have been on his way to a business meeting. The thin leather gloves were out of place though.

So was the gun.

Kurt stared down the barrel. Looked like a Walther with a business-like silencer. A gloating Otto leaned by the corner of the door, but Kurt centered his attention on Friedman.

"What the hell?" He strained to inject the appropriate amount of bewilderment.

"Interesting picture." Friedman gestured at the newspaper spread on the bed. The winner's circle was grainy, but Kurt's face was clear enough, smiling beside Lazer, Julie and the rest.

"Nice picture. Kind of you to drop it off." Kurt raised an eyebrow at the gun. "What's the problem? Did you think we wouldn't like it?"

Friedman's expression darkened. "No jokes," he hissed.

Kurt shrugged, as nonchalant as he could be with that dark barrel leveled on his chest. "I don't understand."

"Neither do I." Friedman's words were squeezed through pinched lips. "But when a trainer moves. And claims my cheap horse. And visits my shop. And when a car starts following Otto—" His voice roughened. "Are you with the police?"

"I'm a private trainer," Kurt said, "and I work for whoever pays me. And that girl needs to get back to the barn. Everyone's looking for her. Go on, Julie." He motioned at the door.

"Not yet," Friedman snapped. "Is she your girlfriend?"

Kurt's chest kicked in raw fear. "No." He shook his head emphatically, his mind scrambling. "We won a race, celebrated together, a one-night thing. Nothing important."

He ignored her gasp.

Friedman sneered. "She stays until we check your briefcase. Unlock it."

"That's not mine." Kurt tilted his watch and made a show of checking the time. "One of my owners left it. He's dropping by soon to pick it up."

Friedman's smile turned ugly. "Open it," he said.

"Maybe Jollymore left it unlocked." Kurt masked his eagerness as he stepped toward the briefcase. And his gun.

"Stop." Friedman, no fool, waved him back and nodded at Otto. "You open it."

Otto thumped forward. His beefy fingers rammed at the catch, jarring the room with futile clicking. "It's locked," Otto said. "We'll have to bust it open."

"Doubt that's necessary." Friedman's narrowed eyes settled on Kurt, the gun steady in his gloved hand. "You can visit with the girl now," Friedman said.

Otto dropped the briefcase. The tip of his thick tongue protruded between his lips, shiny with saliva and eagerness. He lumbered across the room. The air clotted with the smell of tobacco, sweat and Julie's fear.

She cringed as Otto hauled her from the chair. He hooked a big hand over the front of her shirt and ripped. Buttons scattered, Friedman laughed and Kurt's breath shredded.

He jerked his head away, opening and closing his mouth, but his chest was caught in a vise, and simple breathing hurt. A button careened across the floor, a white, pristine button stark against the stained carpet. He tried to swallow his bile, tried to play the bluff.

Clothing tore. A scream. Silence.

His chest twisted in agony, and he couldn't not look.

One of Otto's hands plugged her mouth while the other mauled her breast. Her bra dangled in strips, and a piece of tattered lace drifted to the floor.

Otto turned Julie toward Friedman, showing her like a prize. "I always wanted to get my hands on these tits."

She bit at his hand, but Otto only sniggered and yanked at her pants, jerking until the snap ripped. The tearing sound was louder than her muffled whimpers.

"Can I fuck her now?"

"That's up to our friend." Friedman brushed a languid hand over the knee of his pants, but his perceptive stare locked on Kurt.

"4-6-11-22-12," Kurt said.

Friedman's mouth curved in satisfaction. "I knew you wouldn't be able to take it. You're not the type. Enough, Otto. Come open the case."

Otto shot Kurt a glare but reluctantly dropped Julie back in the chair. He dragged an insolent hand over her breasts before swaggering across the room. She yanked her arms and knees to her chest, wheezing in shock, but couldn't cover her nudity or the ugly handprints that blotched her skin.

Spots jumbled Kurt's vision. He jerked his head away, knowing he had to control his rage if there were any chance of getting her out. He steadied his breathing and worked on unclenching every rigid muscle in his body while Otto fumbled with the combination.

A familiar click.

"Open the case, Otto. Put it on the bed beside me." Friedman's thin nostrils flared as he shuffled through the contents. "Unusual items for a horse trainer," he said. "A gun, handcuffs." He pulled out Kurt's laptop and dumped some papers on the bed. A moment later he sighed with discovery. "Otto," he said, "move our *cop* friend to the chair. Cuff him beside the girl."

Kurt stiffened. Otto was strong but slow. This was his chance. Friedman stared then turned and deliberately pointed his gun at Julie. Goddammit!

Kurt walked across the room and sat.

Otto yanked his arms behind the chair and snapped the cuffs together. The man's fist blurred, and Kurt's head smashed against the wall.

Pain ripped through his jaw, scalding the back of his head. His vision blurred, but he heard Julie's gasp, Otto's triumphant grunt, Friedman's chuckle.

He straightened the chair, corralling his pain, and Julie slowly came back into focus. He tried to give her a reassuring smile, but it burned the bottom of his face and felt more like a snarl.

She managed a shaky smile through a mouth framed with finger-shaped bruises, and his teeth clenched as he fought his primal need to kick Otto's head in. Yet clearly Friedman and the gun were the real danger.

Kurt turned to him, forcing his jaw to move. "Let her go. She isn't involved in this."

"She is now," Friedman said, not looking up. He bent over Kurt's laptop, pressed a button and the computer whirred to life. "What's your password?"

Kurt's hopes plunged. Pretending he didn't care about Julie hadn't gained a thing. Friedman didn't intend to let her go, and now his hands were cuffed.

"Password?" Friedman's eyes were flat as a shark's as they flickered over Julie. "We can always watch. Otto does give enthusiastic service."

Otto's belt clinked. He jerked down his zipper, his eyes glazing as he cupped his bulging crotch. Julie shrank with revulsion, her body trembling as she pressed against Kurt.

"2-9-4-rebel," Kurt said.

"Wise choice." Friedman's fingers swooped over the keys, and the laptop beeped in acceptance. "Not much here except horse files." He shot Kurt a look of consternation.

A muscle pulsed in Kurt's jaw, a sliver of hope. But Friedman bent over the laptop and continued his search. "Ah, but this is interesting," he said.

Sweat tickled Kurt's forehead. His shirt stuck to the back of the wooden chair yet he was oddly cold, every nerve chilled. Friedman wouldn't do it here. Connor had been found in his car. There'd be another chance. Had to be.

Friedman's voice lowered with satisfaction as he recited from the screen. "Julie West and Otto Laing are persons of interest in the death of Corporal Connor O'Neil." He looked at Kurt and shrugged. "It couldn't be avoided. The man was kind enough to help Otto with a flat tire. Unfortunately he noticed a loose shoe and spotted the diamonds. I had to...dispose of him." His voice hardened. "He shouldn't have followed Otto to my shop. He shouldn't have been sneaking around my alley."

His tone turned malicious as he looked at Julie. "My dear, did you know you're a murder suspect?" His dispassionate gaze flickered over her broken necklace, one end now twisted around the lace of her bra. "That necklace was made in my shop but the stone's a fake, just like Mr. MacKinnon. How convenient he can claim *all* your services as expenses."

Kurt ignored her choke. Friedman's ominous confessions chilled him. He had to get her out.

"You're right. She's an expense," Kurt said. "Means nothing, knows nothing. Let her go. No need to make things worse."

"There's no mention of my involvement," Friedman said. His gaze swung to Otto whose belt dangled around his open jeans as he stroked himself and stared, slack jawed, at Julie.

"I've been reporting over the phone," Kurt said. "We know the diamonds are hidden in the shoes. That they're shipped into Canada so they're harder to trace. That you're sending them to Antwerp as costume jewelry."

"But there's no proof." Friedman leaned over the computer and scanned the files again. Muttered in German.

305

Kurt groped at the cuffs linked through the back of the chair. Tight. And fifteen endless feet to the gun.

*Ring. Ring.* The mundane sound of his cell sounded odd in the taut room. Julie straightened, staring hopefully at the bump in his pocket, and a rush of optimism flooded him. Clearly she hadn't given up.

Kurt looked at Friedman; their eyes clamped. No one spoke or seemed to breathe except for Otto, who panted like a rutting bull.

Six rings, and the phone silenced.

Friedman tightened his lips and rose. Adjusted his gloves, picked up a remote and pointed it at the television. A cooking show bubbled to life. Plump tomatoes were lined on a cutting board, and two men bantered about the sharpness of their knives.

He turned the volume up.

Jesus Christ! Kurt glanced at Julie, trying to grab her attention, but she stared, wide-eyed, at Friedman. He fought a rush of despair. Her courage was unquestionable, but this was asking a lot. She looked almost comatose and no wonder. He jabbed her with his foot.

"Sit, Otto." Friedman nodded at the desk. "Let's make a note for Mr. MacKinnon to copy."

"But when can I fuck the girl? You said I could—"

"After," Friedman said, his voice strangely gentle.

Otto squeezed in the chair by the desk. He picked up a pen, the tip barely visible in his hammy fist.

"Write, 'I am sorry. Everything went wrong and I killed them all.' You misspelled 'killed.' No, never mind," Friedman said. "Actually that's perfect. Don't change it." His voice hardened as he watched Otto struggle to copy the words. "Now sign your name."

Comprehension jerked Kurt upright. The chair clunked behind him. "No, Otto!"

Friedman pressed the barrel above Otto's eyes. The gun coughed, and Otto slumped back. A neat hole, blue around the edges, stained the middle of his forehead.

Julie gagged.

Friedman jerked the gun around, stopping Kurt's rush. "Get back," he snapped, motioning with the gun.

Kurt's jaw twitched spasmodically. He backed the chair up and sat.

"Move to the bed, girl, and take off the rest of your clothes," Friedman snapped. "Quickly now."

Julie stared, disbelieving, a cold numbness settling into her limbs. Otto looked smaller. His head lolled back like he was asleep but there was an acrid odor: urine, feces and the coppery smell of blood. Her gaze scrabbled around the room. This couldn't be real. Friedman's mouth moved. He was looking at her, but his voice was an incomprehensible drone.

Kurt elbowed her in the ribs. Someone in the room whimpered. Oh, God, had that helpless sound come from her?

"Take some deep breaths. It'll be okay," Kurt said as he watched her suck in uneven breaths. He turned to Friedman, grimacing and rolling his eyes. "Typical female. She always falls apart. We ran into a bear, and she reacted this same way. Utterly useless. Give her a minute, and she'll do whatever you tell her."

Julie felt Kurt's elbow dig in her ribs. Something hard squashed the top of her foot. His words made no sense, no sense at all. But his jabs were sharp, the pain an anchor in her fog.

"It's going to be okay." His gaze bored into her. "Remember the bear—same situation."

She stared at him, trying to understand, but her mind and body seemed paralyzed. She wiggled her fingers, watching as they twitched in bizarre directions, as though controlled by someone else.

Yet Kurt just sat there, so calm, so unruffled, and her fear hardened with resentment. He was probably used to this kind of stuff. She shook her head, struggling to understand. He was a cop? Friedman and Otto were killers? He had been so interested in the dead cop. In Otto's horse. In Otto, too. Now it made sense.

Her gaze drifted over Otto's body, back to Kurt. Bile clogged her throat.

"I love you, honey," he said softly.

She averted her head, sickened by his handsome, lying face, swept with a growing fury. Now she understood why he'd come to Calgary. Everything had been a lie. Rage gutted her fear.

"Take off your clothes, girl," Friedman snapped, "and move to the bed. Now!"

She grabbed her resolve and rose. Her legs felt like concrete slabs but she didn't want to be shot like Otto, unresisting, sitting in a chair. It took fifteen pounding heartbeats to struggle out of her ripped shirt, and she fumbled even longer with the torn waistband of her jeans. At Friedman's impatient jerk of the gun, she pushed the pants over her hips and stepped out.

Kurt saw the stubborn tilt to her chin, the battle set of her shoulders and marveled at her courage. He jerked his gaze away, desperate to draw Friedman's attention.

"This isn't necessary, you know," he said. "They'll pick you up at the airport." He tilted forward a fraction. Braced his feet. There'd only be one chance.

"Won't matter. No witnesses, no proof." Friedman's eyes flickered over Otto's body and settled on Kurt. He barely looked at Julie. "Come on, girl." He gestured.

She edged around the desk, balling her shirt and jeans in front of her, avoiding Otto's sad, ruined head. "Please let me go," she whimpered, pausing in front of Friedman, fumbling with her clothes.

He didn't deign to answer. Just smiled, gleaming with unholy anticipation as he turned and leveled the gun at Kurt.

She dropped her clothes, straightened her arm and pressed. The pepper spray smacked Friedman square in the face. His hands flew to his eyes, his screech drowning the pop of the gun.

Kurt charged across the room, ignoring the burn in his neck. Kicked the gun from Friedman's hand then kicked again and again and again, until Friedman stopped moving and curled, helpless and groaning, on the floor.

Kurt booted the gun across the room. "Call 911, then get out and wait in the office. Jesus, Julie, you were wonderful," he added thickly. He didn't look away from Friedman but heard her vomiting in the bathroom, heard her stumbling voice as she spoke on the phone, but it was distant, apart from him, and his rage darkened as he waited for Friedman to move, waited for a reason to hurt him again. For Connor, for Nick, for her.

"You're bleeding," she said as she hung up the phone.

"It's only a graze. Just get out of this hellhole. I'm so sorry. Jesus, I'm sorry."

She tugged on her jeans and one of his too-big shirts, averting her eyes from the body slumped at the desk.

"So it's true?" She struggled with the buttons and the enormity of his deception. "You really are a cop?"

"RCMP. I'll explain everything once the police arrive."

"I think that man with the gun explained things perfectly." Her voice wobbled, and she dropped her arms, apparently giving up on trying to force the buttons into the holes. Clasping the front of the shirt, she opened the door and walked out.

Her shattered expression ripped at him. What a fuck-up. He jerked helplessly at his hands, still cuffed behind his back. Wanted to wipe his eyes. Goddammit, it stung, and the blaring television hurt his ears. A man with protruding white teeth smiled stupidly from the screen as he demonstrated the best way to chop an onion.

Fuck! Kurt slammed his boot into the television screen. Glass shattered but now the room was silent except for Friedman's moans, and he felt marginally better.

Minutes dragged. Where the hell were the police? Friedman had put a nasty slant on everything and the longer she agonized over his deception, the worse it would be.

He stared at the man on the floor, willing Friedman to move, to twitch, to do something. He even encouraged him, prodding with the toe of his boot, but the chair cuffed to his back unbalanced him, and he staggered. Something tickled his neck. He glanced down, surprised at the blood that drenched his shirt.

A wailing siren grew louder then cut to abrupt silence. Car doors slammed. Seconds later two policemen with anxious eyes and flak jackets edged through the doorway. Their guns were drawn.

"RCMP," Kurt said. "ID's on the hidden pocket of the briefcase. Turn the panel to the right."

"Don't move," the first officer warned. He retrieved Kurt's identification, his wary gaze darting from the ID to Kurt's face. "Okay, uncuff him," he finally said. He pulled the key from the panel of Kurt's briefcase, tossing it to his partner before moving to Friedman.

"What a stink." The second officer swiped his watering eyes and stepped behind Kurt, struggling with the key.

At the click, Kurt shook the cuffs off. The chair toppled to the floor. He knocked it aside and lurched toward the door. "I'll be right back," he said. "Call this man." He called out Archer's number and rushed from the room, ignoring their protests.

He barged into the motel office. A wide-eyed clerk was taking pictures through the window but immediately backed away.

"Was a blond lady in here?" Kurt asked.

The clerk nodded, cringing behind the counter.

"Well, dammit, where is she?"

"She left when the cop car showed up," the clerk squeaked. "Please…we don't keep any money here."

Kurt shook his head, trying to focus, but the rushing in his head disrupted his vision and the clerk's face blurred. "Which way she'd go?" His thickened tongue balled the words, and the clerk just shook his head.

A figure materialized in the doorway, and his hope spiked. But it wasn't Julie, only another police officer. The man looked familiar though and Kurt stared, fighting his dizziness.

The man rushed closer. Kurt recognized the notebook officer from the barn. But he didn't have a notebook now, and he didn't ask any stupid questions.

He just hollered for an ambulance as Kurt's legs buckled.

310

# CHAPTER THIRTY-FIVE

The nurse swiped Kurt's skin with a chilly antiseptic, and a needle pricked. "Doctor says you can leave tomorrow. Your neck will be sore, but you're lucky. If that bullet had been a shade to the left, you wouldn't have made it."

She straightened his hospital gown, fussed over the sheets and sashayed from the room.

Archer chuckled. "Strange how all the women love your hairy ass. Hey, don't give me that scowl. I'm one of the good guys." His voice turned serious. "This didn't go down the way we planned. Too bad about Otto, but at least we got Friedman."

His smug tone grated. "What the hell went wrong?" Kurt asked.

Archer shook his balding head and stretched out in the corner chair. "We picked up a call. Friedman told Otto to meet him at the track. They drove in the backside but walked out the side exit to your motel. Our guys had their vehicles covered, but the track was your territory. You weren't supposed to win races." He frowned over the top of steepled fingers.

"I had an excellent jockey." Lethargy thickened Kurt's words. He twisted his head against the pillow, using the pain to stay alert. "Surveillance must have been sloppy if Otto made it. Prick was dumber than a codfish." His stomach wrenched at the memory of Julie's face when Otto manhandled her. "Fucker deserved to be shot," he muttered.

Archer leaned forward and clicked off the recorder. "You don't usually take things personally but considering the situation..." He shrugged and rose. "We got it done and appreciate you stepping in. There will be an internal review, of course, but the girl's account matches yours. I do wonder what she was doing in your room though," he added with a smile.

"Just keep wondering," Kurt said. "God, what a mess for her."

"She really was cool, quite the little champ." Archer moved to the rail of the bed. "And she wasn't hurt." His perceptive face was much too close.

"Not hurt? Nearly raped and murdered!" Kurt twisted his head away. "I dragged her into the sewer. She had no idea I was a cop...she saved my life."

"Guess it was a good thing she stayed the night," Archer said.

Kurt squeezed his eyes shut, fighting his remorse. A trolley rumbled down the hall, and voices tittered from the nursing station. "Friedman told her the truth, not me." His throat tightened as he recalled her horrified look of betrayal.

"Deception is necessary for undercover agents," Archer said. "And you're one of our best."

"Great. That should make her feel better. Pass me my phone. You'll have my report later." His tongue felt thick and clumsy. "Need to call her." He fumbled at the metal table, knocking the IV stand. "Where's my damn phone?"

"You won't be calling today. And don't beat yourself up so much."

Kurt's eyelids drooped. He forced them open, fighting their weight. Archer leaned over the bed, still talking, but it was Julie's anguished face he saw long after a drug-induced sleep claimed him.

# CHAPTER THIRTY-SIX

Sandra galloped down the track, stirring up a flurry of dust and waving her arm in excitement. "Still riding? The media's clamoring to talk to our local hero."

Julie blew out a sigh, slowing Skippy along the outside rail.

"It's not so bad," Sandra continued. "They just interviewed me. Martin too. They wrote down everything we said, word for word. One reporter asked if all jockeys were as brave as you. It was so much fun." She gave a rueful shrug. "Hard to believe Otto's dead, but I never liked him anyway."

Julie stared across the track, numb to Sandra's excitement. Otto was gone, and it was horrible to have seen him die. But it was Kurt's betrayal that ripped at her gut.

She didn't remember walking back to the barn, didn't remember asking Sandra to drive her home. But the ruthless look on his face as he kicked Friedman was seared in her soul. She didn't know him at all. Little wonder he didn't show his feelings. He had none.

She'd been calm when the grim-faced Mounties converged with their pens and pads. But she couldn't remember their questions or her stumbling answers. All she remembered was lying on the cold bathroom tiles, shaking and vomiting. Too shattered to even cry.

She'd been a murder suspect. A key to an investigation. *His job.* Physical intimacy had been his method to get her talking. And, boy, it had worked.

She stiffened in the saddle, fresh bile climbing her throat. His questions about Otto, his compliments about her riding, his tender kisses. She'd swallowed every lie. Now she understood why he'd asked her—an unknown apprentice—to ride for him. She was an idiot. Even Liam had it figured.

She choked back her humiliation and stared down at her white knuckles squeezing the reins, aware that Sandra's glee had faded to silence.

"Sorry," Sandra said softly. "It's just that you're so calm. I sometimes forget what you've been through."

"He was such a l-liar." Julie's voice cracked.

"Kurt?"

Julie winced at his name.

"Oh, yeah. He was a real prick." Sandra reached over and clumsily patted Julie's knee. "But one of the other cops said Kurt used to go undercover for months at a time. Elite jobs, scary stuff. Guess you can't be totally honest in that line of work."

"Totally honest! How about totally dishonest! I understand the secrecy about his job, but I thought he liked me. And my riding. He would have put me on his horses if I rode like a monkey. As for the other—" Thinking of it made her stomach heave, but she forced out the tormenting question. "How could he sleep with a murder suspect? How could he even want to?"

"Honey," Sandra said, "Kurt's just a man, God love 'em. They have a brain and a penis but unfortunately can only use one at a time."

Julie choked, torn between a giggle and a sob. "He said he loved me when he thought we might die." Her voice trailed off. She hated its hint of wistfulness.

"Probably so you'd try harder to save his ass." Sandra grinned. "But meeting him wasn't all bad. You did get your first win."

"Yes. He does have nice horses." Julie reached down and smoothed Skippy's mane. "Does Skippy's mane look better to the left or right?"

"The left," Sandra said.

Julie flipped the mane. They walked their horses side by side, analyzing the weather, tomorrow's race entries and Martin's new girlfriend.

Sandra said nothing more about 'The Horseshoe Homicides,' as one radio station had dubbed it. Julie knew Sandra craved more details, but she didn't want to talk about Otto and Friedman. Couldn't. She'd shoved that nightmare into a dark corner of her mind and didn't want to let it out...ever.

"There is good news," Sandra said as they approached the gap. "One paper ran a story about how badly Otto treated his horses. The police confiscated his gelding as he was being loaded onto the meat truck. Now there's a bunch of people lined up to adopt him."

"Great," Julie said. "Maybe the media will leave now." The prospect of facing their pointed questions made her stomach churn. "I don't want to talk to anyone. Not yet. Think I'll stay out here for a while. Will you let me know when they're gone?"

"Sure. They can't get to you here. Oh no..." Sandra scowled, staring past Julie. "The infamous cowboy cop is finally making an appearance."

The morning sun silhouetted a horse and rider as they trotted onto the track. Their imposing outline was unmistakable—Kurt and Cisco.

Julie's heart wrenched, even as her brain scrabbled for escape. Turn Skippy and gallop in the opposite direction? But then Kurt would really guess how devastated she was, and unfortunately that damn Cisco was quick enough to run them down.

"I can't wait to hear what the cocky sonofabitch has to say," Sandra said, bristling as Kurt trotted up, fast and full of purpose.

"Hello, Sergeant," Sandra said. "Still hiding your Stetson?"

Kurt ignored her, filling his senses with Julie. The bruises around her mouth had faded but her face was pale, her eyes shadowed. She'd suffered from Otto's hands but even more from his, and now she looked at him with such expressionless eyes. His chest wrenched. "Julie—"

Sandra abruptly pushed her horse forward, blocking his gaze. "Why don't you just go home? No need to hang around our cow town now that Julie's off your Ten Most Wanted."

Kurt grit his teeth. He liked Sandra, but emotion had rubbed his tolerance razor thin. "Julie, I'd like to talk to you."

"Well she doesn't want to talk to you. Not anymore," Sandra replied. "Not unless you have a subpoena."

He sighed. The redhead was bothering him and so were the onlookers flocking like vultures to the rail. Julie looked so fragile. He ached to hold her, to comfort her. To explain.

"Excuse me." He squeezed his legs. Cisco flattened his ears and charged forward. Sandra's horse immediately shuffled sideways, intimidated by the aggressive App. Kurt hooked his arm around Julie and scooped her from the saddle.

"Look after Julie's horse, please." He tossed Skippy's reins to Sandra and trotted off, with Julie flailing in front of him.

"Let me down," she said.

"Let her down," Sandra echoed as she cantered Okie after them with a surprised-looking Skippy in tow. "You asshole. Let her go. You...you...you're not allowed to ride double on the track!"

Kurt tucked Julie's arms beneath his, slightly lightheaded now that he was finally holding her. "Sorry, but you wouldn't answer your phone."

Sandra stormed behind him, hollering and attracting everybody's attention. "This is high-handed, even for a damn cop!" she yelled. "Here comes an outrider now. He'll fix you."

Hooves pounded, and a furious outrider galloped up.

Kurt whipped out his badge. "Police business. Murder investigation. Please clear the track of that lady."

The outrider studied Kurt's badge then nodded respectfully. "I heard about Nick's killer. Glad you got him." He motioned at Sandra. "You'll have to leave the track, Sandra." But his eyes narrowed on Julie, who was still struggling and clearly an unwilling passenger. "How much time do you need, sir?"

"I'll let you know when I'm finished," Kurt said. He ignored Sandra's sputters and trotted Cisco off before the watchful outrider could ask any more questions.

Julie pulled a fist loose and rammed it in his stomach. He let her whack a few times, hoping it would shake his mountain of guilt, but she was surprisingly strong, so he tucked her arm back beneath his and simply absorbed her presence. For a moment, he squeezed his eyes shut, overwhelmed with relief. She was okay.

"I see Otto gave you lessons on how to handle women." Her voice was muffled by his arm.

*Oh, God.* He loosened his grip, instantly shamed. She pulled free and slid to the ground. However, Cisco obligingly stopped, and he was able to snag her up again. He lifted her back in the saddle, but his arms felt heavier than her. "Promise you won't jump off," he pleaded. "Give me five minutes."

She hesitated.

"Please, Julie," he said.

Her nod was almost imperceptible but still a nod, so he repositioned her, making sure the saddle horn wouldn't dig in her back.

He sucked in a breath. "I'm sorry you were dragged into this mess. I never dreamed you'd be exposed to danger. You were so damn brave. Otto…"

She averted her head, but he persisted.

"Otto almost raped you. Friedman—" He stopped, unable to continue as he remembered the murderous intent in Friedman's eyes when he leveled the gun. "Just let it out." He swallowed, could feel her shivering now, and it pulled at his very core. "Your dad said you won't talk about it, but you can't wish this stuff away." His voice cracked, and he wet his mouth. "I've tried to do that, honey. It doesn't work."

Julie fought the urge to burrow into his chest. The thud of his heart, the calm timbre of his voice, even the steadiness of Cisco's walk made her feel insulated.

His voice rumbled on as he spoke about the first murder he'd witnessed. Spoke about how his misplaced trust in a mob girlfriend named Anne Marie had resulted in a shooting. Spoke of the things he did when undercover, the lies he'd told. Admitted his difficulties dealing with it all and why he'd eventually quit. Told her everything.

And finally her defenses crumbled. Kurt had been in that motel room. He knew the fear, the horror, the sordidness that seemed to cling to her skin.

Emotions ambushed her. The quakes started behind her eyelids and spread through her entire body. When the tears finally spurted, she turned to him. She cried long after his shirt was soaked, cried until she'd rinsed herself of the horror, the helplessness, the terror. Finally only hiccups remained, and she was limp in his arms.

At some point he'd removed her helmet. It dangled from the horn, bumping against Cisco's muscled shoulder. His fingers stroked her head, lulling her with the rhythm. She couldn't guess how many laps Cisco had walked but knew the tough horse would keep going until Kurt told him to stop.

"How could you think I was part of that?" she finally whispered, her voice hoarse.

"You weren't a suspect for long. Not after my second day here."

She thought she was drained of emotion, but his words stirred relief. Not after the second day. Some consolation at least. "Was I a suspect when you gave me the mount on Ace?"

He tried to thumb away a tear, but she turned from his touch. He seemed to wince, and Cisco walked another ten yards before he spoke again.

"No, you weren't a suspect then." His voice was gruff. "I watched you ride and knew you would suit. It had nothing to do with the case. Not much anyway."

She glanced up, shocked by the odd sheen in his eyes. They could turn so many shades of gray, but right now he looked like he was in pain. Maybe she shouldn't have hit him so hard. After all, his jaw was badly bruised, and there was a square bandage on his neck.

"They told me you were okay," she said. "But that you had to spend a couple days in the hospital?"

"Yeah, it was just a scratch. I wanted to call and…thank you, but I fell asleep."

*He was grateful.* She ducked her head, shriveling with despair. His hand splayed around her hip, the lighter hairs stark against his tanned skin. So casual, so composed. She wished he felt a fraction of what she did, wished she could shake the feelings from him, wished she could ask if he'd lied in that motel room

Instead she muttered, "Consider me thanked."

His arms stiffened. "I couldn't tell you what I was doing. We were after a cop killer. The man you met, Connor, he was my partner, my friend."

"I understand the secrecy. And I'm very sorry about Connor. But you shouldn't have had sex with me. It's not right to use people like that." Her voice tailed off to a miserable squeak.

"It wasn't just sex."

His words marginally unclogged her throat, and she was able to swallow. She looked at the sky, watched as a fluffy cloud was pushed along by the Chinook breeze. "So many lies. Like buying land. What else did you lie about?"

"I never lied about my feelings for you," he said. "Never."

A lightness unfurled in her chest, and her breathing seemed a tad easier. She struggled to square her concept of honesty with the moral ambiguity of his job. He was just so inscrutable, always hiding his feelings, saying whatever was necessary at the time.

Cisco kept walking.

"How did you feel when you lied?" she finally asked.

"Hated it." His voice was unusually rough and she glanced up, but he was staring straight ahead. She couldn't see his eyes.

"Guess it doesn't matter anyway. I hear you're leaving." She toyed with a strand of Cisco's thin mane and fought a rush of despair.

"But it does matter." His voice thickened. "You matter. And I'm not leaving until you feel the same way."

"And then you leave?" She forced a laugh. "After I care."

"No." His arms tightened as though frustrated. "We can work something out. It'd be tough if you rode here when I'm training halfway across the country. Most of my horses are at Woodbine or Belmont. A few are still in Florida. But none would fit here."

What was he saying? Her heart thumped so loud she feared even the intrepid Cisco might shy at the noise.

"We can try moving them around though," he said quickly. "I'll talk to the owners, see what works."

"How many horses do you have?"

"Lots. Most, I train for others. Some are real quality horses. You could do real well on them." His throat convulsed. "I don't want to rush you, Julie. You're young. You might not feel like I do yet but with time—"

He sucked in a breath, closed his eyes and dipped his head over hers. "God, I love you."

She couldn't speak, stunned by what he was saying, what he was showing. He wasn't hiding anything now, not his tormented eyes, not his raw feelings, not his heart. Joy blazed through her, leaving her so dizzy she gripped his arm.

He thought she needed more time? "Actually," she said, "I've had plenty of time."

He jerked his eyes open. She smiled up at him, her lower lip tremulous with emotion. "Julie." He breathed her name, groaned and covered her mouth in a searing kiss. Both were oblivious to the crowd, the cameras and the grinning redhead who whistled an old Bobby Sherman tune.

Cisco noticed. His ears flicked but he continued his resolute trudge around the track, perhaps sensing they didn't want to stop, not quite yet.

\* \* \*

Read Chapter One of BEV PETTERSEN's next novel

# COLOR MY HORSE

The racetrack's scenic infield was usually deserted, but today the police cars and body bag had drawn a hushed crowd. Mark sucked in a deep breath and stared over the heads of solemn onlookers.

"Who'd they pull from the pond?" Dino asked in a voice a shade too loud. "Heard old Lefty didn't show for work."

No one answered. Attention was riveted on the grim-faced officials clustered around a pitiful corpse. A police officer with a long stick waded into the murky water and snagged a dripping hat. Lefty's hat.

Mark blew out a ragged sigh. Lefty: gruff, single and a confirmed alcoholic. Awful, but at least it wasn't a child who had drowned. The Belmont track had two infield ponds, and the backstretch kids sometimes snuck over the rail, lured by the quacking ducks.

He dragged a regretful hand over his jaw then tilted his head, signaling to Dino. Nothing they could do to help, and gawking seemed disrespectful and rude. He trudged away from the ring of watchers and followed the flattened path back to the barns. Later the dirt would be harrowed, groomed for fragile Thoroughbred legs, but it was difficult to worry about horses when a man was dead.

"Heard Boone's filly was impressive this morning." Dino's voice was muffled by the thud of his boots as he rushed to catch up.

Mark gave a wry nod, amazed his race assistant could be so upbeat. Nothing ever worried Dino. "That's right," he said slowly. "Horse ran great. Rider said Belle's never felt better."

"Things are picking up now that you're training for Old Man Boone." Dino flashed his irreverent grin. "But somehow I can't see you kissing ass to keep him."

Mark shrugged, unable to banish the image of Lefty's limp body, although Boone was certainly a more optimistic topic. His mood lightened a notch as he considered Boone's two talented horses. The filly, Belle, was good but the second horse, Ambling Assets, was even better, and it seemed Mark finally trained a horse good enough to compete in the Breeders' Cup.

Success was so close he could taste it.

A truck engine roared. He jerked sideways as a blue Ford whipped past, crunching gravel, going too fast. Dust clogged his nose as the vehicle cut along the squat row of barns, leaving a spiraling trail of gray.

"Damn. Doc's truck," Dino said. "Pity the sucker."

*Beep.* Mark stilled then pulled his ringing phone out, his gaze locked in the direction of the speeding vehicle.

"Better come quick, boss," Carlos said. His voice thickened with a heavy accent and barely-concealed panic. "Boone's filly is colicing. I already called the doc."

Mark snapped the phone shut, running even as he jammed it back into his pocket. "Colic, Belle," he said over his shoulder.

His stalls were in barn forty-eight, usually a five-minute walk, but he charged through the cloying dust left by Doc's truck and was there in less than a minute. A knot of people gathered in the shedrow but they stepped back, forming a grim-faced passageway.

Mark groaned when he spotted the beautiful filly thrashing in the straw. The signs of shock were obvious: darkened eyes, increased respiration, trembling muscles.

"Gotta get up, baby," he said, joining Carlos at her head. "Hurry up with the Banamine, Doc!" Sweat streaked Belle's neck, and her eyes rolled with pain as they urged her to her feet.

The vet injected a shot of pain reliever and pushed a tube up her left nostril so oil could be pumped into her stomach. She was too distressed to argue. Her sleek body trembled, wracked with belly pain.

"Carlos, grab a blanket. Dino, hook up the trailer." Mark heard the snap in his words and tried to calm his voice around Belle but could barely control his dismay. Only an hour ago, the filly had radiated health. She'd worked four furlongs and been prancing when her groom led her away to be bathed and cooled.

*Trish.* His eyes narrowed as he scanned the circle of anxious faces. "Where the hell is Belle's groom?" he asked.

"Don't know, boss." Carlos dipped his head, avoiding Mark's gaze as he scuffed his worn boot in the dirt. "Don't think the filly was cooled out after her work."

Mark's mouth clamped. He'd suspected it had been a mistake to hire Trish, despite her impressive credentials. She was too young, too selfish, too concerned with her own agenda. And admittedly, he'd been swayed by a pretty face.

Belle groaned, a helpless visceral sound that ripped at his gut, and he shoved aside his regret. He'd deal with Trish later. Right now the stricken horse needed him.

"She might make it without surgery," Doc said. "Let's get her to the clinic and see if she responds to the laxative. But you'll need to sign some permission forms, just in case."

*Just in case.* Christ. Sometimes a horse came back after colic surgery, but often they were never as good. And sometimes they never made it back.

He swiped his damp forehead as Dino eased the truck and trailer to the entrance and dropped the ramp with a thud. Belle twisted, biting at her stomach, but Mark tugged her forward. She gamely tried to follow, but her trembling legs splayed.

"Push her on, Dino," Mark said, aching from her pain. Some colics were unavoidable but not this one. For some reason Trish had neglected to cool the filly out after her gallop—utter negligence—and his compassion for the filly roiled with his hot anger.

He tied Belle in the trailer and pressed a kiss against her wet neck. "Come back to me, baby," he whispered. But his voice hardened when he turned to Dino. "She might need emergency surgery. I'll meet you at the clinic once I find out when she last ate."

He stalked past several barns, searching for Trish, using the walk to cool his anger. Maybe she had an excuse—maybe she was hurt, or was upset about Lefty. Understandable. Best to stay open-minded. Give her a chance. Ah, there she was, and she looked fine. He blew out a sigh of relief then jerked to such an abrupt stop his heels trenched the dirt.

She posed outside the track kitchen, flashing gay teeth and flirtatious eyes, flanked by three reporters. A white panel van with red WFAN lettering perched on the edge of the rutted grass, and thick snakelike cables coiled around her feet.

"Yes, I knew Lefty well," she said, her melodious voice carrying through the still air. "Last night was my turn for barn watch. He rode his bike across the infield, probably on the way to the liquor store. I was the last one to see him alive." Her voice tapered to a sigh, and she gave her eyes an exaggerated swipe.

Not a bad performance, Mark thought, crossing his arms. Almost as good as when she'd pleaded for a groom's job. Sounded like she and Lefty were the best of friends when in reality Trish considered hot walkers far beneath her. However, the media was hooked.

"So you believe alcohol contributed to his death? That there was no foul play?" A man with a red Yankees cap shoved a gleaming microphone closer to her face.

"Well, drugs and liquor are a huge problem. Some of the trainers ignore it—" she broke off, as though sensing Mark's hard stare. "I have to go cool out a horse, but we can talk later. Just drop by barn forty-eight. Don't forget my last name. C-H-A-N-D-L-E-R."

She sashayed over to Mark while two reporters openly ogled her ass. "Hi, boss," she said, and her satisfied smile made his gut curdle. "I'm going to be on television today. There was even more press earlier. Not the usual *Thoroughbred Times* or *Racing Form* reporters. This is a big New York station."

Mark's jaws clenched so tightly they hurt. Unbelievable. She'd neglected her job, abandoned a poor horse and pumped Lefty's accident—all for a media interview.

"If we hurry, we can watch the news at your place." She trailed a suggestive finger down his arm. "Where your 'no sex' rule doesn't apply. Just make someone cool Belle out for me."

A muscle ticked in his jaw as he fought his self-loathing. Twice he'd taken Trish home. Simple pleasure, no commitment, but Belle had paid a huge price for his weakness.

Trish's voice trilled on, her fingers tightening over his forearm. "This is so exciting. Lefty never had this much attention when he was alive. He's probably digging it." Mark jerked away from her clinging hand, unable to hide his aversion, and her smile turned to a pout. "What's eating you?"

"Lefty's dead. He's not digging it." The words ground out between gritted teeth. "And Belle just coliced. Did you walk her at all? Did she eat anything?"

"All you ever think about are horses." She flicked her hair over her shoulder in a familiar, provocative move. "I'm going now to walk the filly. Maybe later, I'll go home with you."

She still didn't get it. Expected to get by with a wiggle and a smile, but he was finished thinking with his dick. "You're not going anywhere near Belle," he said wearily. "She's fighting for her life because of your neglect. You're fired. I'll give you three months' pay. Dino will have your check ready by the end of the day."

"You're firing me? Me?" She tapped her shapely chest in disbelief. "I can get a job with almost any of the top trainers."

"Good. Go get one." He spun away, disgusted with her, but was even more disgusted with himself. She'd been a mistake, one he wouldn't repeat. Frivolous girls always upset the dynamics of a race stable. They'd certainly messed up his father's. Best to stick to his usual hiring policy. From now on, the only type of female allowed in his shedrow would be fat, forty and flatulent.

Tears blurred Jessica's vision as she absorbed the numbing headline. *Olympic Hopeful Engaged to Team Trainer.* A cry choked in her throat, and the paper slid from her stiff fingers. Anton, her ex-boyfriend, and Cindy, her best friend—engaged! She hadn't even received a courtesy call.

Last year she'd been the team darling. Last year she'd been the woman on Anton's arm. Last year a knee injury had knocked her off the ski team. Her friends and sponsors had dumped her so quickly, her head spun. And now this.

People were pricks.

She leaned forward, automatically rubbing the ridge of swelling that extended along her right knee. The best doctors her grandfather could find hadn't helped. Sure, she could walk, even ski, but never again would she race.

A dog barked an amiable greeting, and Jessica glanced through the window as Casey, the caretaker's black Lab, crossed the manicured lawn to greet a sleek Audi. Finally Gramps was home from one of his countless business trips. Maybe he'd join her when she took Casey for a walk. The dog was eleven, fat and arthritic; she could keep pace with him. Later, if she had enough energy, she'd dust off her ski trophies.

Shit. She gave her head a weary shake. Whiners had always irritated her, and it seemed she was turning into one. She reached down and retrieved the newspaper, hating how she'd let Anton push her into another tailspin.

Minutes later, her grandfather strolled into the library, carrying his briefcase along with the whiff of expensive cologne. "Good evening, Jessica. The office said you didn't come by again today."

The words were mild, but his tone carried a bite. He'd always pushed for her to join the huge Boone enterprise and with her mother no longer alive to run interference, that pressure had escalated. Her grandfather had a ruthless streak that was often daunting. Still, Jessica usually could handle men, and it was time to regain control of her floundering life.

"I've been looking at the employment section," she said. "And apartments." Disapproval darkened his face, but she took a deep breath and forged on. "I appreciate your job offer and letting me live here until I finished my degree, but I wouldn't be happy working at Boone."

Her grandfather raised a palm. "Now be reasonable," he said. "There's no need to leave. But it *is* time to stop playing on a mountain. Time to forget that life, forget those friends, move on."

Her chest twisted at his casual dismissal of years of dedication, but she kept her voice level. "All my so-called friends are training in Europe," she said. "And I *have* moved on."

His briefcase thumped on the floor, and he picked up the newspaper, evading her hasty attempt to snatch it. "So I see," he said as he scanned the black glasses and moustache she'd drawn on Anton and Cindy's beaming faces. He tossed the paper on the table, his face inscrutable. "It's lonely since your mom died, so naturally I prefer you live with me on the estate. And that you work at Boone. But maybe you have another plan? An idea for a business…maybe something that could support you?"

He was a wily negotiator accustomed to control, and his caustic tone filled her with despair. She hardly had enough energy to function, let alone fight Gramps. It seemed over the past year, her customary grit had fizzled. The only time she felt alive was when she was outside with Casey. Dogs were so loving, so non-judgmental, so faithful.

Impulsively she leaped to her feet and faced her grandfather. "But I do have a plan. I intend to start a dog day care." He looked blank, and her words tumbled out. "That's a place where people take their dogs so they're not cooped up all day. I'd brush them, walk them, play with them. I'm happiest when I'm outside. Casey keeps me sane."

Her grandfather's mouth tightened to a thin line. He sank into a dark leather armchair and smoothed a crease from his tailored gray pants. "It's clear you haven't thought one minute about a real career," he said slowly. "I told your mother all that skiing was a mistake. At least she did something useful and helped me entertain." He frowned so deeply his bushy eyebrows touched. "But she was crazy to let you live in Europe. She—"

"Please, Gramps." Jessica hated her grandfather's disparaging tone and rushed to deflect the inevitable criticism of her mother. "I don't want to work for Boone. And if Mom were alive, she'd encourage me to start my own business. Don't you see, the dog idea is perfect. Perfect for me."

He snorted. "I can't see you scooping poop. Or living on a pauper's income."

"Money isn't everything," she said. "And I've never been extravagant. Or lazy."

His piercing gaze made her squirm, and she averted her eyes. Lately, she had been sleeping a lot. Couldn't seem to shake her odd lethargy. "I never used to be lazy," she choked, struggling with her own doubts.

"You don't know anything about looking after a bunch of animals. What makes you think you can run a kennel?"

"Of course I can run a kennel." She grabbed a framed photo off the mantle, waving it with renewed vigor. "I know tons about animals. Remember the ponies at camp? I fed them hay and cleaned their stalls. Every day. And working outside is way better than being cooped up in an office."

She squared her shoulders and tried to look confident, aware her grandfather would pounce at any sign of weakness. "My business courses said no career can be successful unless you love it. I just need a little startup money. And if I can't borrow from you," she gave a deliberately negligent shrug, "I'll go to my friend's bank."

His eyes narrowed, and he studied her face over steepled fingers. For a long moment, neither of them spoke. She slipped a hand behind her back and crossed her fingers, trying to hide her desperation. She didn't have a friend at any bank, didn't have any other options, only knew she had to escape her grandfather's control.

He waited another full minute, but she held his penetrating gaze.

"Here's the deal then," he finally said, his voice thoughtful. "You'll work at Belmont racetrack. No credit cards, no money except what you earn. If you last until the end of the fall meet, I'll finance your dog kennel. If you quit or are fired, you'll live here and work at Boone. Agreed?"

"Agreed." She triumphantly thumped the picture of her and a rather nasty gray pony back on the shelf, scrambling to remember everything she knew about Belmont Park.

The venerable New York track was in Queens, about a two-hour drive. Gramps had started racing ten years ago when she'd been fourteen and immersed in the ski circuit. However, she'd accompanied him once to the track. The dinner had been delicious, the hats elegant and the suited men chatty and helpful. She frowned, trying to remember the horse barns, but their table had been high in the clubhouse, behind a spotless sheet of glass.

Didn't matter. She'd see the animals soon enough, and at least she'd be working outside. The job shouldn't be too difficult. All her old magazines had said horses were much easier to handle than ponies.

She pumped Gramps's hand to cement the deal, ignoring her twinge of unease at his smug smile.

Mark pulled out the desk drawer and flipped through his owner listings. Edward T. Boone. Time to call the man. He hated giving owners bad news, but at least Belle's prognosis was good, and maybe Boone wouldn't want many details. Incompetence was something Mark didn't tolerate, but he couldn't lie. It was a relief Trish was gone and his female staff were now steady women—older, committed women.

Boone's voice, crisp and confident, answered the phone on the second ring. Mark squared his shoulders. Owners paid the bills; they deserved the unvarnished truth.

"Good morning, Edward. Your filly, Belle, had a bout of colic this morning," Mark said. "We sent her to the clinic, but she's okay. Didn't need surgery. We just received the final clear. They'll watch her for a few days." He squeezed his eyes shut, waiting for Boone to ask the cause.

"What's the bottom line?" Boone asked.

"Bottom line?" Mark cracked open his eyelids. "Your horse is fine, but she'll miss the stakes race next week." Regret thickened his words. Belle had been training perfectly, almost as well as Boone's colt, and would have been a key contender.

"But I have the company box reserved." Boone's voice hardened with impatience. "Clients flying in to watch. She has to run."

"Sorry. She can't."

Mark sensed the scowl on Boone's patrician face, could feel the displeasure radiating through his phone, but remained silent. He'd only met Boone eleven months ago, and it was clear the man craved control. However, Belle's health was Mark's first priority, and he refused to run a horse that wasn't ready, no matter how many people Boone had invited for dinner. Unfortunately a trainer also had to please his owners, and Boone's reaction was ominous.

"You don't want clients watching a poor race. Seeing a sub-par result," Mark added, guessing that angle might sway Boone much more than Belle's welfare.

"Definitely not." Boone gave a disgruntled sigh. "Okay. Maybe she shouldn't run. But I do need a favor."

"Sure." Mark tried to ignore the distaste that soured his mouth. The man hadn't even asked the cause of Belle's colic. To Boone, it was always the bottom line, and the hell with the horse. Owners could be strange and ruthless people. Shaking his head, Mark propped his boots on the corner of his desk and tucked the phone against his shoulder, his mind already jumping back to Belle and the best feeding program for colic recovery.

"My granddaughter needs a job," Boone said. "Needs to see what grunt work is all about. She won't last a week on the backstretch but should learn plenty. And the experience will straighten her out. Force her into a real career."

*A real career.* Mark's hand tightened around the phone at the man's blatant condescension, but his voice remained level. "And you want me to do the straightening?"

"Yes," Boone said. "She'll be safe with you, and she's experienced with horses. Had lessons at summer camp."

Mark jerked forward so abruptly his boots slammed the floor. A greenie! Just what his barn needed. "Not a good idea." He forced his fingers to loosen around the phone. "The backside is a different world. Hard, physical...even dangerous."

"Oh, I don't expect her to last longer than a week. Don't want her to." But Boone's chuckle lacked humor, and Mark understood now why the man was reputed to be a cutthroat negotiator. "I just want her eyes opened. Want her to see the opportunities she's passing up. She'll quit and be working for me long before Breeders' Cup rolls around."

The wily bastard. Just the mention of Breeders' Cup made Mark's stomach kick. Finally he trained a horse fast enough to compete—Boone's colt, Ambling Assets, was his big hope. Good enough to run. Good enough to win.

But owners could move their horses to different trainers at any time, and Boone's reference to Breeders' Cup wasn't an accident. It was a threat. A girl for a horse. A no-brainer.

Mark paused but knew what his decision was long before he spoke. "Sure," he said. "Send her by Monday morning."

## ABOUT THE AUTHOR

Bev Pettersen is an award-winning writer and two-time finalist in the Romance Writers of America's Golden Heart® Contest. She competed for five years on the Alberta Thoroughbred race circuit and is an Equine Canada certified coach. Presently, she lives in Nova Scotia with her husband and two teenagers. When she's not writing novels, she's riding. Visit her at www.bevpettersen.com.

Made in the USA
Coppell, TX
04 September 2020